DEMOCRACY'S INFRASTRUCTURE

PRINCETON STUDIES IN CULTURE AND TECHNOLOGY
Tom Boellstorff and Bill Maurer, series editors

This series presents innovative work that extends classic ethnographic methods and questions into areas of pressing interest in technology and economics. It explores the varied ways new technologies combine with older technologies and cultural understandings to shape novel forms of subjectivity, embodiment, knowledge, place, and community. By doing so, the series demonstrates the relevance of anthropological inquiry to emerging forms of digital culture in the broadest sense.

DEMOCRACY'S INFRASTRUCTURE

Techno-Politics and Protest after Apartheid

Antina von Schnitzler

PRINCETON UNIVERSITY PRESS

Princeton and Oxford

Copyright © 2016 by Princeton University Press
Published by Princeton University Press,
    41 William Street, Princeton, New Jersey 08540
In the United Kingdom: Princeton University Press,
    6 Oxford Street, Woodstock, Oxfordshire OX20 1TR

press.princeton.edu

Cover art: *Cartography I* (2009) by Clive van den Berg (reproduced courtesy of the artist)

Library of Congress Cataloging-in-Publication Data

Names: von Schnitzler, Antina, 1975– author.
Title: Democracy's infrastructure : techno-politics and protest after apartheid / Antina von Schnitzler.
Description: Princeton : Princeton University Press, 2016. | Includes bibliographical references and
    index.
Identifiers: LCCN 2015045836| ISBN 9780691170770 (hardcover : alk. paper) |
ISBN 9780691170787 (pbk. : alk. paper)
Subjects: LCSH: Political participation—Technological innovations—South Africa. | Technology—
    Political aspects—South Africa. | Citizenship—South Africa. | Communication in politics—
    Technological innovations—South Africa. | Mass media—Political aspects—South Africa. | South
    Africa—Politics and government—1994–
Classification: LCC JQ1981 .S365 2016 | DDC 323/.0420968—dc23 LC record available at
    http://lccn.loc.gov/2015045836

British Library Cataloging-in-Publication Data is available

This book has been composed in Janson Test LT Std

Printed on acid-free paper. ∞

Printed in the United States of America

10 9 8 7 6 5 4 3 2 1

For my mother, Vera,
and in the memory of my father, Paul

Contents

Acknowledgments

In the writing of this book I have incurred innumerable debts. First and foremost, I would like to thank the members of the Phiri Concerned Residents Forum and the many residents of Phiri who opened their homes and made time for conversations. I am also grateful to the members of what was at the time the Anti-Privatisation Forum's Research Subcommittee whose company both sharpened my questions and forced me to think about their relevance beyond the academy.

This book began its life as a doctoral thesis in anthropology at Columbia University. I would like to thank the members of my committee, Partha Chatterjee, James Ferguson, Mahmood Mamdani, Timothy Mitchell, and David Scott, for their support and their insights. Each of them in their own way taught me how to think differently about writing, scholarship, and politics. I was lucky to be surrounded by a wonderful group of fellow students at Columbia, many of whom gave feedback on my writing. I'm especially grateful to Mireille Abelin, Siva Arumugam, Yogesh Chandrani, Ryan Chaney, Ruchi Chaturvedi, Nadia Guessous, Anush Kapadia, Yukiko Koga, Nadia Loan, Sofian Merabet, Juan Obarrio, Poornima Paidipaty, Suren Pillay, Manuel Schwab, Ravi Sriramachandran, and Arafaat Valiani. Long before I began graduate study, Richard Wilson's seminars on political and legal anthropology at the University of Sussex set me on this road, and I'm thankful to be able to draw on his advice still.

At The New School, I am fortunate to have a supportive and intellectually engaging group of colleagues in the Graduate Program of International Affairs, in the Department of Anthropology, and across several other departments. Rachel Heiman, Erica Kohl-Arenas, Manjari Mahajan, Gustav Peebles, and Janet Roitman each gave excellent feedback on chapter drafts. I am also grateful to Jonathan Bach, Michael Cohen, Sakiko Fukuda-Parr, Sean Jacobs, Nina Khrushcheva, Hugh Raffles, Sanjay Ruparelia, Everita Silina, Nidhi Srinivas, Ann Stoler, and Miriam Ticktin for conversations and advice along the way, and to the staff at GPIA for their support, in particular Christina McElderry and Philip Akre. I am especially grateful to

Stephen Collier who has been an incisive interlocutor from the time I first began thinking about this project, and who read and commented on many chapters of the final product.

Over the years, many friends and colleagues beyond The New School have read chapters or shorter pieces that became part of the book and gave insightful feedback. Amongst them I owe particular thanks to Ujju Aggarwal, Nikhil Anand, Andrew Barry, Geoff Bowker, Dominic Boyer, Bernard Dubbeld, Cassie Fennell, Paul Kockelman, and Peter Redfield. I benefited from discussions with many other friends and colleagues over the years, including Hannah Appel, Andrea Ballestero, Franco Barchiesi, Patrick Bond, Brenda Chalfin, Sharad Chari, Akhil Gupta, Gabrielle Hecht, Kregg Hetherington, Ulrike Kistner, Premesh Lalu, Trevor Pinch, Richard Rottenburg, Melanie Samson, Suman Seth, and Paige West. Brian Larkin has been an inspiring interlocutor on things infrastructural, and I have been grateful for his generous advice throughout.

The semester I spent as a Visiting Fellow at the Kellogg Institute for International Studies at the University of Notre Dame provided me with much needed time and a supportive environment in which to focus on writing. Thanks to Paolo Carozza and the faculty and staff at the Kellogg for making this possible and especially to Paul Ocobock and Catherine Bolten, who provided helpful feedback on one of the chapters. A few months at the Wits Institute for Social and Economic Research (WiSER) at the University of Witwatersrand provided a generative intellectual community as I was revising the manuscript. I would like to thank the faculty and staff at WiSER, and especially Sarah Nuttall, Catherine Burns, and Achille Mbembe, for their comments on a paper that became part of the book. I owe particular thanks to Keith Breckenridge, who generously read and commented on several chapters of the manuscript.

I would also like to thank the many engineers, consultants, City of Johannesburg officials, and staff at Johannesburg Water and Eskom who made time for interviews and conversations, and who let me enter into to the world of infrastructure technology, utility management and municipal politics. I am also grateful to the staff at the Centre for Applied Legal Studies at Wits and to many social movement activists who generously gave advice and provided documentation, in particular Jackie Dugard and Dale McKinley. Archivists at the Department of Historical Papers at the University of the Witwatersrand and at the South African History Archives were immensely helpful in their guidance.

Old and new friends in South Africa made time for feedback and conversations, opened their homes, and provided company, in particular Ruchi Chaturvedi, Ivor Chipkin, Sarah Duff, Pamila Gupta, Julia Hornberger, Bridget Kenny, Caroline Kihato, Jennifer Makoatsane, Jabulani Molobela, Loren Landau, Juan Orrantia, Suren Pillay, Nafisa Essop Sheikh, Stephen

Sparks, Salim Vally, Hylton White, and Eric Worby. I am also grateful to Ahmed Veriava and Prishani Naidoo, who were housemates, friends, and intellectual fellow travelers at the same time. Thanks also to the other members of our reading group at the Brixton house: Andy Clarno, Claire Decoteau, Nicolas Diltiens, Pier Paolo Frassinelli, Molefi Ndlovu, and Caroline Tagny.

At Princeton University Press, I am very grateful to Fred Appel, Debbie Tegarden, and Juliana Fidler for their help and advice along the way, and to Jay Boggis for his careful copy-editing. I would also like to thank the editors of the Princeton Series in Culture and Technology, Tom Boellstorff and Bill Maurer, for their support and their comments, and two anonymous reviewers who provided insightful feedback and suggestions. I am also indebted to Clive van den Berg, who very generously allowed me to use one of his works for the book cover.

My students and research assistants at the New School have helped me in countless ways over the years. Among them I am especially grateful to Randi Irwin who not only prepared the index, but also provided invaluable help and many excellent suggestions as I was revising the manuscript. In South Africa, I am immensely grateful to Molefi Ndlovu and Jabulani Molobela, who assisted me on two separate occasions in this research. I could not have completed this book without the virtual writing group with Nadia Loan, Poornima Paidipaty, and, especially, Nina Sylvanus, friend and primary partner-in-crime in the labyrinthine process that is writing a book.

The research for this project was supported by a Dissertation Fieldwork Grant from the Wenner-Gren Foundation, and by grants from Columbia University and The New School. I completed the writing of this book with help from a Hunt Postdoctoral Fellowship from the Wenner-Gren Foundation and a Visiting Fellowship at the Kellogg Institute for International Studies at the University of Notre Dame. Shorter versions of Chapters 4 and 6 have appeared as "Traveling Technologies: Infrastructure, Ethical Regimes, and the Materiality of Politics in South Africa" in *Cultural Anthropology* (2013) and "Performing Dignity: Human Rights, Citizenship, and the Techno-Politics of Law in South Africa" in *American Ethnologist* (2014). Some of the arguments in this book were first articulated in "Citizenship Prepaid: Water, Calculability, and Techno-Politics in South Africa" in the *Journal of Southern African Studies* (2008).

This book would not have been possible without the support of many close if far-flung friends and family members who provided help, advice and distraction. Thanks especially to Mireille Abelin, Ujju Aggarwal, Gary Campbell, Katharina Gärtner, Claudia Grenzer, Matthias Halabian, Anna Held, and Annie van Vooren-Sebastian. Infinite amounts of thanks are due to my family: to my brother Werner and my sister-in-law, Aiki Mori–von

Schnitzler, and, especially, to my mother Vera, and my late father Paul von Schnitzler. My parent's inspiration, care, and encouragement along the way, even when their hope that I might eventually come home began to fade, has meant more to me than they perhaps realized. I am also grateful to Doris Hewage and my late father-in-law Prema Hewage, my second family, whose warmth sustained me even over a long distance. Lastly, but really first and foremost, without Thushara Hewage's intellectual inspiration, his help in all possible ways, and above all his love, it is difficult to imagine how this book could have been completed.

DEMOCRACY'S INFRASTRUCTURE

Chapter 1

INTRODUCTION

_____

Democracy's Infrastructure, Apartheid's Debris

In July 2004, just over ten years after the inauguration of Nelson Mandela as South Africa's first democratically elected president, a violent protest occurred in Diepsloot, a mostly informal township settlement inhabited by about 150,000 residents north of Johannesburg. Trash cans were overturned, sewage spilled in the streets, two council offices were burned, and the major road leading to the wealthier suburbs was blockaded with burning tires. Cars that dared to drive past were pelted with stones. The police responded with massive force, deploying water cannons, stun grenades and rubber bullets. The entire settlement was blocked off and designated a crime scene, a blanket indictment reminiscent of apartheid policing tactics during the 1980s. For three days, only minibus taxis were allowed in and out of the area, while journalists and other onlookers were barred from entry.

One of the first large-scale violent expressions of discontent in the post-apartheid period, the protest caught government officials, politicians, and the police off guard.[1] It also starkly interrupted the nation-wide celebrations of ten years of democracy that had begun three months earlier. Most immediately, it was unclear how the protest should be handled and by whom. Senior police officers deployed in the area appealed to the provincial government arguing that this was a "political situation" that required the intervention of the ANC-led government. The provincial minister for housing, Nomvula Mokonyane, countered that residents were involved in "criminal

---

1   One month later, in August 2004, a similarly dramatic protest would occur in Harrismith, in the eastern Free State province, during which one teenage protester was shot and killed by police. Further protests in other provinces followed in September and from then on spread rapidly to the rest of the country.

1

acts," which, as such, she maintained, were the responsibility of the police. This initial interpretive quarrel already hinted at the incomprehension and bewilderment the protests had caused amongst government officials and public commentators alike. Although many within the ANC establishment had been quick to dismiss previous, smaller demonstrations as staged by "ultraleftists" or disgruntled former party members, given its scale and intensity, the situation in Diepsloot was left in an interpretive vacuum for days. Who were the protesters, and how could residents be so ready to resort to violence and destroy public infrastructures? Through what interpretive grids could protest in the postapartheid period be rendered intelligible?

Initial media accounts of the protesters as irrational, faceless mobs soon gave way to interpretations translating them into more familiar vocabularies. As a media report by a prominent journalist put it, clearly in an effort to render Diepsloot and its predicament legible to his largely middle-class readership, the township was "not much like a luxury holiday resort" and could only be described as a "sprawling, dusty, rubbish-strewn area."[2] This characterization, of course, described many places in South Africa and could not fully explain the situation. Meanwhile, government and ANC commentators cast the demonstrations in conspiratorial terms, arguing that the protesters had been incited by "outside forces" with criminal or even counterrevolutionary intent. Others suggested that the protesters had yet to learn the proper codes for civic engagement in a liberal democracy. Eventually, President Thabo Mbeki himself publicly deplored the residents' lack of patience and understanding of the functioning of democracy. The protests thus also became an occasion to dispel latent anxieties over postapartheid state legitimacy and the rule of law by forcefully reasserting the state's monopoly on violence; at issue here too was a battle over the intelligibility of state authority (Roitman 2005). Casting the protests as criminal rather than political acts served to transcend such uncertainties and re-established boundaries around the shape of legitimate civic behavior.[3]

The Diepsloot protest, as an event, shook the public imagination, precisely because it posed a challenge to the very project of postapartheid "transition." Indeed, the protest challenged not merely a particular policy or a specific local councilor; more fundamentally, it challenged the dominant imaginary of South Africa's liberal democracy, in which the political domain is clearly delimited, where violence is the prerogative of the state, in which citizens have "channels" of communication, and where a thriving public sphere provides the location for deliberation and debate. Thus,

---

2   Jeremy Gordin, "Diepsloot: Anatomy of an Abusive relationship," *Sunday Independent*, July 11, 2004.

3   See here also Rosalind Morris's discussion of the changing significations of "criminal" and "political" violence and its relation to state power (Morris 2006).

the protest could be seen as not merely a moment of opposition, but as an instance of what Rancière (1999) calls "disagreement," that is, a challenge to the very terms and assumptions of an existing political language game.[4] Perhaps most glaringly, the protests exposed the growing chasm between the ANC-led government and many poor residents of informal settlements and townships, and the declining capacity of the nationalist language of liberation to rein in discontents.

The standoff was eventually brought under control by a mix of police repression and attempts at conciliatory meetings with residents, but Diepsloot was only the spectacular beginning of a series of protests all over the country that would continue in the years to come. Year after year since then, demonstrations, "riots" and public violence have preoccupied state officials and the public imagination. Various initiatives to address them have been unable to stem the tide of discontents.[5] By 2013, police statistics showed a massive incidence of protests while many journalists regularly called South Africa the "protest capital" of the world.[6] Two years later, in 2015, the Gauteng Premier announced that the province was setting up "war rooms" in each municipality to deal with the protests directly.

Over time, the term "service delivery protest" has come into common usage, often entirely independent of the form or content of such protests. "Delivery," the fetishized goal of the immediate postapartheid period, conjures up histories of unfulfilled expectations for transformation, but also narrowly circumscribes the terms through which such protests can be understood. Framed in this way, the protests become simple, if perhaps "unreasonable" and "impatient," claims for material resources from the state, often linked to an assumed, deeply embedded "culture of entitlement" amongst residents of townships and informal settlements.

Less often remarked upon is the striking form many of these protests take and the centrality of infrastructure as both object and medium of making claims on the state: protesters have spilled sewage and rubbish in the streets, destroyed water tanks, blocked roads, and ripped out pipes and meters; indeed, it is often this feature that leads many commentators to see such protests as "irrational" outbursts. Less visibly, the postapartheid

---

4   See here also Agamben's analysis of the protest at Tiananmen Square (Agamben 2000: 85–89) and Barry's related distinction between politics and the political (Barry 2002: 270).

5   "War rooms set up to deal with service delivery protests in Gauteng—Makhura" *News 24*, July 21, 2015. This followed earlier measures, like the five-year plan proposed in 2013 by then Cooperative Governance Minister Sicelo Shiceka to "eliminate delivery protests by 2014." See "Shiceka: No Service Delivery Protests by 2014," *Mail & Guardian (Johannesburg)*, October 21, 2009. For academic analyses of delivery protests, see, e.g., Alexander 2010; Atkinson 2007a; Booysen 2007. For a particularly compelling analysis, see Von Holdt et al. 2011.

6   See here also recent ethnographic work on bureaucracy and material state practices (Das and Poole 2004, Gupta 2012, Hoag 2010, Hull 2012).

period has also been defined by widespread illicit acts involving infrastructures, such as the nonpayment of service charges, the bypassing, tampering, or destruction of water and electricity meters, and illegal connections to services. Such protests and popular illegalities often uncannily resemble the tactics of the antiapartheid struggle. Yet, today, they lack the political languages of liberation that authorized and gave them meaning in the past. In the absence of such larger narratives, nonpayment, illegal reconnections, and violent protests are often framed by officials and the media as irrational, amoral, or criminal acts. Thus, they become the responsibility of the courts and a diverse array of experts, including engineers, utility officials, or local bureaucrats.

If violent protest is often indexical, an effort to "gain visibility" and to render "palpable" questions and concerns for which there is no space in the public sphere (Žižek 2007: 53), this book explores the terrain which these protests periodically catapult into the public imagination. As a political spectacle, the Diepsloot protest and its reception pointed to the gulf that divided the location of formal politics from a seemingly apolitical administrative terrain that makes up the experiential reality of many, especially poor, South Africans. If the normative domain of postliberation politics and civil society is located in spaces such as media and party offices or parliamentary and city council debates, everyday experiences of the state are often primarily shaped by waiting lists for housing, latent threats of evictions or forced removals, leaking pipes, inaccessible infrastructures, illicit electricity connections, intermittent and unreliable incomes, disability grant and indigency applications, and frequently unresponsive councilors and ward committees. This precarious terrain is connected to the state primarily via administrative bodies and is subject to their actions and discretionary powers, ranging from modest care to abject neglect and, at times, capricious intervention. These are places whose primary connections to the state are mediated by police, courts, utility officials, local bureaucrats, and, as I will elaborate in the chapters that follow, by technical-administrative devices such as meters, pipes, wires, and official documents and certifications.[7] Here, as in many poor townships and informal settlements in South Africa, residents come into contact with and are interpellated by the state not only as citizens, but also, and often primarily, as members of "population," entangled in administrative relations and procedures and the objects of governmental care or neglect (Chatterjee 2004).

This book explores how such administrative links to the state became a central political terrain during the antiapartheid struggle and how this

---

7   In May 2013, the Gauteng police commissioner announced that in the 40 days between April 1 and May 10, 2013, there had been 560 protests in Gauteng province alone. See Khadija Patel "Public Protests: Gauteng Pressure Cooker" *Daily Maverick*, May 16, 2013.

terrain persists in the postapartheid present. Infrastructures, fiscal relations, and judicial procedures thus emerge as sites in which the ethical and political questions once central to the antiapartheid struggle continue to be mediated, negotiated, and at times contested. In the paradoxical context of "liberation and liberalization" (Comaroff and Comaroff 2001), in which citizenship has been extended to an unprecedented number of people at the same time as the entitlements conferred by citizenship are often in question, I examine the techno-political forms and registers in which contemporary conflicts unfold and in which claims on the state are expressed. Given that the normative locations of politics are often de facto inaccessible to many poorer township residents and shack dwellers, this book attends to a politics that takes shape in less visible locations and in often unfamiliar technical forms. I explore this techno-political terrain conceptually, historically, and ethnographically, not only in order to understand the rise of protest in South Africa in more open-ended terms, but also because this terrain provides a productive vantage point onto a number of broader questions concerning formations of postapartheid citizenship, modes of narrating historical transformation, and conceptions of the political.

Below, I map the larger concerns that animate this book and the critical historical and conceptual problem-space in which my narrative unfolds. The next section introduces the small piece of infrastructure that became the lens of my ethnographic and historical research. I then provide a theoretical discussion of the concept of techno-politics developed in this book. The second half of this chapter sketches the paradoxical historical moment of the "transition" and its aftermath, which is the intellectual and political horizon against which the questions I ask throughout have taken shape and become intelligible.

THE SOCIAL LIFE OF A PREPAID METER

The chapters that follow explore a range of larger questions—about citizenship, social obligation, and the political—by historically and ethnographically following the life of a small device: a prepaid water meter. A prepaid meter is a device, which, apart from measuring networked services such as electricity, gas, or water, automatically disconnects users in cases of nonpayment. In order to access services, users have to purchase and load up credit tokens in advance, either by entering a numerical code or by using a magnetic key or card. Failure to do so results in immediate "self-disconnection." While the meter is one of many increasingly sophisticated infrastructure technologies that mediate access to flows of goods, information, and money in many places of the world today, it is also a distinctly

South African thing.[8] First deployed during the 1980s to help combat the antiapartheid rent boycotts, in the past two decades, and in a context of ongoing mass nonpayment and neoliberal reforms prescribing "cost recovery," prepaid meters have become ubiquitous, making South Africa the place with the largest number of installed prepaid meters in the world. Although prepaid meters are increasingly also being installed in middle-class homes, where they are often preferred to untrustworthy municipal bills, for now the meters are primarily deployed in poorer, historically black townships and informal settlements. Beyond the by now standard prepaid cell phones, most residents in places like Phiri, Soweto, where I carried out much of my research, are now connected to electricity and often water via prepayment devices. "Living prepaid," with often only temporary access to services and flows of water or electricity punctuated periodically by cutoffs, has thus become an increasingly normal condition for many poorer residents of informal settlements and townships.

Living prepaid mirrors life in a moment in which income has become precarious, where reliance on a regular monthly wage is the exception rather than the norm.[9] Here, payment for basic services is no longer shaped by the cyclical temporality of regularly recurring monthly salaries and bills; instead, income as well as payment is often incremental and ad hoc. The increasing deployment of prepaid meters—and the end of monthly utility bills this entails—thus reflects larger temporal and experiential shifts in which access to services is unstable and where the threat of automatic disconnection due to nonpayment is always present.

Beyond structuring life temporally, the meters are also semiotic instruments aimed at shaping behavior, enforcing metrological scrutiny, and curtailing consumption. While the threat of cutoff is what makes many residents object to prepaid meters, it is paradoxically also this ability to prevent debts from accumulating that often makes them attractive. Prepaid meters, in this sense, are technologies of precarity that reflect the multiple dilemmas and vicissitudes of life after the "end of the salary" (Mbembe and Roitman 1996). Thus, they provide a window onto larger shifts in experiences of time, consumption, and life after formal employment.

Today, prepaid meters have become the normal state of affairs for many and are most often an unremarkable aspect of daily life. And yet, as

---

8 Such mediating devices include, for example, payment technologies (Maurer 2012), biometric technologies (Breckenridge 2014; Fassin 2011), logistics (Chalfin 2010; Cowen 2014), media technologies (Larkin 2008), but also less visible ones like sieves or spam filters (Kockelman 2013).

9 Conservative estimates put South Africa's unemployment rate at about 25 percent, but in poor areas like Phiri this statistic often jumps to over 50 percent. Many people in places like Phiri, where I carried out much of my research, are reliant on government grants and informal and often intermittent forms of income. Franco Barchiesi (2011) has explored the increasing precarity of work and its consequences in South Africa.

I elaborate in this book, the meters continue to be unruly, periodically becoming the subject of public debate, protest, and legal action. They are also often bypassed or "bridged" by residents, making the meters useless and giving residents free access to services. Here, a technical politics develops involving engineers and residents in a battle over securing and bypassing the devices.

My focus on the prepaid meter as both an ethnographic object and an analytic vantage point is in part due to this ubiquity and political salience in South Africa. When I arrived in Johannesburg to begin my fieldwork, prepaid water meters were what most preoccupied social movement activists, affected Soweto residents, and what drew the attention of the media. However, beyond their ubiquity and political visibility, I focus on the meters also because of their peculiar techno-political history. As I explore in Chapter 4, the prepaid meter was first invented in nineteenth-century Britain to extend gas to the working classes. Then called "penny-in-the-slot-meter," it became integrated within the larger Victorian project of moral reform and working class "improvement." In the 1980s, the prepaid meter was appropriated and redeveloped in South Africa by apartheid-era engineers as a technical tool to counter the antiapartheid "rent boycotts." Renamed the "Budget Energy Controller," and used primarily for electricity, it was deployed, in the words of one apartheid-era bureaucrat I spoke to, as a "political technology" that was specifically designed to break the boycotts. It is this techno-political history of the meter in the late-apartheid period that has ironically turned South Africa into a global industry leader in the development of prepayment technology and one of its primary exporters in the aftermath of apartheid.

Following the travels of a small technical device, and the social worlds it is shaped by and that it in turn helps shape, reveals the continuities between the late and postapartheid formations and the manner in which this administrative-technical history continues to shape the present. Indeed, I suggest that this focus on infrastructure and, more specifically, on a seemingly ordinary technical device, provides an epistemological vantage point onto the disjunctures of democracy after apartheid and a different way of thinking about the periodization and multiple temporalities and experiential realities of "transition."

The chapters that follow explore this domain of the administrative not primarily as a site of economic deprivation, nor as one defined solely by sovereign violence or abandonment, which is how residential spaces of the poor have often been analyzed, but as a techno-political terrain on which central questions of the antiapartheid struggle are continually reformulated, negotiated, and at times—and often via series of protracted detours—resolved; a terrain where the distinction between the political and the administrative is often blurred. This terrain is at once a pedagogical ground to make and unmake political subjectivities in the aftermath of apartheid and a site of disagreement at which questions of needs, belonging, and citizenship are negotiated and sometimes contested. Thus, in the many instances I analyze in this book, the administrative is a location in which the *work of making liberal democracy* occurs and where its fault lines and failures become apparent in ways ranging from the spectacular to the mundane.

This politics in the register of the administrative is not deliberative, detached, or unencumbered, as in the idealized public sphere proposed by political theorists, most centrally by Jürgen Habermas (1989); nor is it by definition a "counterpublic" that would define itself directly and self-consciously against a more dominant public, as described, for example, by Nancy Fraser (1990). Indeed, as I elaborate below, in many instances, this is a politics defined precisely by the absence of a public or by its fundamental redefinition, often through material, sensory, and affective forms. This book explores how this terrain is constituted historically from the late-apartheid period to the present and how, against the backdrop of an increasing obsolescence of older modernist political idioms, a particular, often technical or nonpublic form of politics emerges from it.

"Democracy's infrastructure," then, is at once a metaphor for the diverse ways in which democracy is grounded in and stabilized by seemingly apolitical technical means and an ethnographic object of investigation—socio-technical assemblages made up of pipes, wires, and meters; the ethical regimes and techno-political calculations through which they operate; and the modes of politics they enable and afford.[10] Exploring democracy from the perspective of its infrastructures thus also reframes the conventional story and periodization of South Africa's "transition."[11] In turn, this infrastructural perspective opens up conceptual space for a more expansive theory and vision of what it means to act politically in the postcolony and beyond (Mbembe 2001).

TECHNO-POLITICS: INFRASTRUCTURE AND THE MATERIALITY OF POLITICAL CLAIMS

The story I tell in this book is at one level a distinctly South African story, one that is located conjuncturally in between the late and postapartheid periods. And yet, South Africa, as in so many other instances, also emerges here as a productive epistemological location—that is, a location that

---

10   My use of the term "socio-technical assemblage" is inspired by actor-network theory (cf. Callon 1986; Latour 2005) and by anthropological extensions of this concept (Collier and Ong 2005).

11   See recent scholarship that has called for a rethinking of the historiography of the antiapartheid struggle (see, e.g., Lalu 2007, 2009; Pillay 2009).

enables us to think differently about contemporary analytic problems, that provides critical purchase on questions with a longer historical arc and that, in turn, holds broader significance in relation to the conceptual and imaginative horizons of how we study and conceive of the political.[12] In particular, by focusing on the infrastructural and the technical as modalities of political action, this story unsettles conventional and normative accounts of the political as existing in a separate domain, marked by "free" circulation, rules and norms of "civil" engagement and attendant behaviors.

My analysis is inspired by recent scholarship that has urged a rethinking of liberal-secular accounts of the political, by exploring affective, embodied forms of political subjectivity and focusing on new locations of ethical and political formations that are often below the threshold of visibility for normative conceptions of political action (Connolly 2002; Hirschkind 2001; Mahmood 2005; Valiani 2011). Here, the political is not delimited in a sphere beyond the private concerns of daily life, nor does it necessarily take the form of public deliberation or demonstration. If, as much scholarship has suggested, infrastructures are not simply neutral conduits but instead central to the constitution of modernity in a diversity of ways—fashioning socialities, subjectivities, and affective capacities (Edwards 2003; Larkin 2008)—an ethnographic approach to this politics of infrastructure, I suggest, similarly opens up conceptual and methodological space for an exploration of forms of the political that take shape outside its conventional locations and mediations.[13]

Such a rethinking of normative liberal accounts of the political is particularly important in postcolonial contexts, in which the formal political sphere, itself in part a legacy of colonial modes of government, is often inaccessible to large sections of the population—from the residents of informal settlements to the informally employed or those subject to "traditional" authorities or clientelist relations. As Partha Chatterjee (2004) contends in his account of "political society," here, central political questions are often contested via administrative connections to the state, such as the provision of housing or basic services. In such contexts, the political emerges not in what is normatively assumed as the political sphere; rather,

---

12   For larger arguments on the global south as an epistemological location of innovation, see Comaroff and Comaroff 2012, Ferguson 2006, and Mbembe 2014.

13   As many accounts suggest, infrastructure is precisely that which remains invisible and only becomes visible when it breaks down (cf. Graham and Marvin 2001; Star 1999). And yet, such breakdowns too are often a "normal" part of infrastructure, in particular in the global south (Larkin 2008). It can also, as I suggest here, be purposefully rendered visible and turned into a "matter of concern" (Latour 2004) through protest. For recent ethnographic work on infrastructure, see Anand 2012; Appel 2012; Bjorkman 2015; Carse 2014; Chalfin 2014; Collier 2011; Elyachar 2010, 2012; Fennell 2015; Fredericks 2014; Harvey and Knox 2015; Hetherington 2014; Heiman 2015; Kockelman 2010; Larkin 2008; Schwenkel 2015; von Schnitzler 2008, 2013. For an overview, see Larkin 2013.

it is at *the level of administration* where political questions are often de facto engaged and negotiated.

While Chatterjee urges us to recalibrate our understanding of the locations of postcolonial democracy, here, I focus on the material terrain and technical forms of engagement that define this administrative register. My account builds on and extends theorizations of techno-politics by Gabrielle Hecht (2009, 2012) and Timothy Mitchell (2002, 2011) that have productively analyzed the imbrication of the political and the technical. In Hecht's and Mitchell's theorizations, the concept of "techno-politics" refers to the ways in which political actions are embedded within technical forms and, conversely, the ways in which the technical shapes political questions. Thus, techno-politics may denote the ways in which large-scale engineering or infrastructure projects function as vehicles or expressions of larger political goals and forms of power, but it also and more broadly foregrounds the materiality of politics and political expression (Barry 2001, 2013; Bennett 2009; Braun and Whatmore 2010; Winner 1980).

In the chapters that follow, I explore a more micro-political and mundane form of techno-politics. At once less grandiose and more embedded within life's everyday fabric, this techno-politics unfolds in smaller and more intimate domains and involves the shaping of subjectivities, practices, and dispositions.[14] Focusing on a small mediating device like the prepaid meter not only opens a vista on the transformations such devices may produce in households and subjectivities, but also on a number of larger questions concerning citizenship and belonging. Embedded within technologies like the prepaid meter are ethical and political visions and expectations; they are scripted with anticipations of users' behavior (Akrich 1992; De Laet and Mol 2000; Latour 1992). And yet, such technologies are also "unstable" objects (Larkin 2008); once they leave their makers, they can be retooled for other ethical and political projects and reimagined to do work within a multiplicity of formations.

From its beginnings in the nineteenth century as a moralizing device to its apartheid reinvention as a technology of counterinsurgency, the meter has more recently become part of new ethical imperatives in the context of neoliberal reforms and demands for environmental sustainability. Thus, it participates in a larger shift toward the increasing investment and trust in small technical devices to effect dramatic change. The last thirty years have witnessed the growing popularity of smaller-scale and temporary techno-political solutions to questions previously considered structural. Small devices appear technical and neutral, rather than substantive. They are less ambitious, less permanent, and often remain agnostic about long-term goals,

---

14   I am here inspired by ethnographic studies that have explored how technology mediates subjectivity, ethics, and new forms of social life; see, e.g., Boellstorff 2008; Coleman 2012; Dow Schull 2012; Kelty 2008.

frequently giving up on the sorts of knowledge claims and future horizons that defined modernist development projects. In this way, they are part of a wider shift from large state projects to more micro-logical forms of intervention that define both neoliberal and humanitarian projects.[15] Indeed, such small-device heuristics bear more than a family resemblance to neoliberal epistemologies that give up on the ability of collective knowledge and radical social transformation. Such neoliberal forms of reasoning often recode prior political techniques rather than inventing new ones from scratch. They work on existing realities rather than aiming to build them from the ground up, as was the *telos* of most modernist varieties of development, and they "reprogram" rather than change the whole hardware or system (Collier 2011).

Following the travels of the meter genealogically, I explore the assemblages of ethics, politics, and technics through which such moments are constituted. I trace how infrastructure is "inscribed" with and comes to mediate a diversity of competing ethical projects, political disagreements, and subterranean conflicts that often concern central questions of civic virtue, social obligation, and the rights and duties of citizenship.[16] Thus, rather than simply or solely a conduit for power, in the politics of meters, pipes, or wires—and the fiscal, judicial and socio-technical practices that subtend them—infrastructure itself becomes a political terrain on which such questions are negotiated and, at times, contested. Here, the political is mediated and becomes manifest in different material forms. It is these diverse forms and modalities of politics that this book explores.

APARTHEID TECHNO-POLITICS

The rise of modernity is often associated with the increasing centrality of technics and the forms of thought, habits, and sociality produced by them.[17] From the nineteenth century onward, large technical systems were both tools and symbols of modernizing state projects that became increasingly

---

15   Peter Redfield (2012), for example, analyzes humanitarian "life technologies," whose minimalist design aids a correspondingly "minimal biopolitics" that is no longer tethered to state infrastructures or long-term visions. Stephen Collier (2011) associates neoliberalism with "microeconomic devices" that enable the "re-programming" of older infrastructures, rather than their complete overhaul or rebuilding, while Michel Callon et al. (Callon et al. 2007) focus on "market devices" as key instruments for the constitution of market relationships.

16   See Madeleine Akrich's and Bruno Latour's work on this semiotic-material conception of inscription (Akrich 1992; Latour 1992).

17   Indeed, much of the philosophical critique of modernity from Heidegger (1977) to the Frankfurt School has precisely focused on the increasing importance of technics and the instrumental rationality associated with it (Horkheimer and Adorno 2002; Habermas 1971; Marcuse 1964).

linked to ideals of national progress and the integrated, networked city (Graham and Marvin 2001; Hecht 2009; Hughes 1999). At the same time, networked municipal services—centralized water, gas, and electricity provision in particular—and the relationship between state and citizen they construct were bound up with the rise of "population" as an administrative category of government distinct from, yet mapping onto, the juridical subject of sovereignty. In a context of industrialization and rising labour mobilization, "the social" became both a way of making such conflict intelligible and a distinctive terrain open to intervention through a multiplicity of programs, mechanisms, and techniques (Donzelot 1988; Hacking 1990). In this context, municipal infrastructure materially mediated a biopolitical relation between state and population through which the latter was rendered both measurable and subject to regulation (see also Joyce 2003; Otter 2007). Pipes, wires, roads, and rails increasingly linked up all citizens in what Graham and Marvin (2001) have called the "networked metropolis."

Colonial modernity was similarly materialized and instantiated via infrastructures and technics. Unlike in Europe, where infrastructure was often tied to the rise of a regime of modern citizenship, infrastructure in the colonies was primarily linked to processes of extraction and a biopolitics closely bound up with the project of colonial domination. The biopolitical connection between the state and its subjects preceded the connection of political representation—"population" preceded "the people" as a juridical subject (Chatterjee 2004). Colonial infrastructures became a means to extract resources while also constituting colonial territories as unified, governable spaces. Indeed, the "operation of the colonial state became deeply enmeshed in a network of technological apparatuses, institutions, and practices" (Prakash 1999: 161).[18]

In several ways, apartheid as a political project similarly depended upon and was conjured into being by specific infrastructural modalities of power. This was particularly so in the urban areas, in which, following the ideology of grand apartheid, black residents were stripped of citizenship and designated "temporary sojourners" whose permanent home and political representation were envisaged to ultimately be in the rural Bantustans. Infrastructures became both symbols and conduits of apartheid state power, but they also shaped habits and the senses. Such infrastructural modalities of power thus operated at a number of distinct registers that ranged from the symbolic, to the biopolitical and the sensory. Together, they produced a very specific political terrain, one whose remains shape the contemporary politics of infrastructure.

---

18   For a range of literature on colonial infrastructures, see Adas 1990; Bear 2007; Goswami 2004; Larkin 2008; Prakash 1999; Redfield 2002.

This imbrication of the technical and the political took a number of forms. First, and most visibly, apartheid was infamously symbolized via its infrastructures. Think of the segregated public transport and amenities, the jarring images of race-specific entrances or "whites only" benches that came to metonymically represent the injustices of apartheid. Here, infrastructure and access to them became subject to juridical regulation by the battery of racial legislation that defined the early apartheid period, most symbolically charged, in the Reservation of Separate Amenities Act of 1953. Beyond the symbolic, however, apartheid was also, and more basically, made functional via its infrastructures insofar as apartheid rested on a grand scheme to channel and police mobility. Indeed, it could be argued that apartheid was precisely *about* infrastructures. "Separate development" meant the use segregated infrastructures—from schools, to transport or public spaces. It also entailed the production of a racial economy, which depended on the infrastructure of the pass law system by which millions of people were channeled via labor bureaus, rail tracks, and passes to factories, mines, and farms, to scientifically manage labor supply. This system, in turn, was predicated on innumerable technologies, large and small.

Apartheid, as a racist state project built on what Stephen Gelb (1991) called "racial Fordism," aspired to create a thoroughly engineered society, founded on a trust in numbers and techno-scientific expertise.[19] Indeed, apartheid was unthinkable without the administrative power of large parastatals, the technical forms of accounting, measurement, and identification that defined the labour bureau system, and the techno-science of race and identity on the basis of which groups were often created and managed.[20] In a great variety of ways, apartheid infrastructures thus worked not merely to enable circulation—which is what we often think infrastructures are primarily designed to do—but as much to impede, prescribe, and prompt movement.

As Ivan Evans (1997) has argued, apartheid's form of rule was distinguished from its segregationist predecessor by its focus on the administrative powers of the local state. In the urban areas more specifically, Evans pointed to the centrality of infrastructure in containing black opposition. After the appointment of Hendrik Verwoerd as Minister of Native Affairs,

19   Gelb's term "racial Fordism" describes the distinct organizational form of the apartheid economy, that followed the Fordist model organizationally, but without being based on mass consumption, as the consumer goods market was initially largely limited to the white population. On the question of measurement and number, see Theodore Porter's discussion of "trust in numbers" and Posel's analysis of the "mania of measurement" that defined apartheid (Porter 1996; Posel 2000). See Breckenridge (2014) for an analysis that complicates previous arguments in relation to the capacity and effects of such state knowledge practices.

20   On large parastatals see Clark 1994 and Sparks 2013. For an account of the technologies of the pass law system, see Breckenridge 2014; Hindson 1987a; Posel 1991. On apartheid techno-science, see Bowker and Star 2000; Dubow 1995; Edwards and Hecht 2010.

"native administrators became deeply enmeshed in providing cheap, mass-produced housing, public utilities, and mass transport to the African working class," which in turn was central to "disorganizing African opposition" (Evans 1997: 7). In this way, infrastructure and urban planning also became central to the production and maintenance of race and racial categories.[21]

With the multiple ways in which this apartheid techno-politics produced and sustained this system, there also came particular ways of being in the world. In the absence of political rights, township residents experienced the state primarily via administrative connections. The state was made manifest in the most spectacular fashion via its repressive policing powers and the racist necropolitics on which it relied throughout (Mbembe 2003). But in its various local guises, the state was also the provider and landlord of plots and houses, infrastructures and basic services, and collector of payments and rents. Thus, apartheid was not only an ideological and repressive project, it also helped bring into being much more mundane modalities of power and modes of existence that produced a set of habits, sensory environments, and forms of sociality.[22]

As Jacob Dlamini (2009: 129) suggests, being in the urban areas was also a "felt experience" that in turn produced "embodied memories." This was particularly true for the early African migrants to the city who "spoke of [the urban experience] as a series of new sounds, smells, textures, tastes and sights" (ibid.). But it continued to shape the urban experience throughout the apartheid period, as infrastructures and associated bureaucratic procedures played an ever-increasing role in shaping these more sensory and embodied experiences of state power.

If apartheid infrastructures were often primarily designed to prevent the emergence of a (counter)public, this was most obvious in the mass building of townships from the 1950s as spaces intentionally without important city features. Conceived as mere dormitories for laborers and built far away from the white city centers, the townships had no plazas or public squares, and business operations, if they existed at all, were heavily restricted. Instead of building and supporting a public, infrastructures often followed a security or military logic (Robinson 1996). The grids of streets were planned such that they could be easily surveilled and closed off. Within the townships, radial roads led to spaces built specifically to be used as potential weapon arsenals in case of protests. Similarly, electricity cables were

21   For further literature on this link between race, infrastructure, and urban planning during the period of segregation and early apartheid, see Parnell and Mabin (1995); Robinson (1996); and Swanson (1977).

22   See here in particular recent fictional and autobiographical accounts, e.g., Jacob Dlamini's *Native Nostalgia* and Ivan Vladislavić's *Portrait with Keys: Joburg & What-What*, but also the large body of South African urban social history (Bonner and Segal 1998; Mabin 1992; Gaule and Nieftagodien 2012) and architecture (Judin and Vladislavić 1998).

first extended to the townships to service tall flood-light poles to facilitate surveillance at night. Only much later, and in a shift toward more biopolitical and commercial concerns, did residents of townships receive electricity in their homes.

During the successive states of emergency in the 1980s, this link between infrastructure and security intensified, as emergency provisions gave the military powers to "assume jurisdiction" over basic services, such as water and electricity (Murray 1987: 249), and evictions were increasingly carried out in the presence of the military and security forces. Here again infrastructures were used not to produce or to maintain a public, let alone a postapartheid nation; on the contrary, apartheid infrastructures were deployed to prevent a public from coming into being.[23]

To some extent, if in a very different way, this absence of a public also came to define the wealthier white suburbs which were also, if of course much less severely, marked by the absence of certain public infrastructures. The apartheid state invested heavily in the white areas. And yet, in terms of their use, infrastructures were often *de facto* privatized. For example, given the reliance on cars, there were often few street lights or full pavements. Parks and other public spaces were relatively unimportant, because most whites had access to and preferred the safety of backyards or indeed large gardens or private country clubs. And yet, even in the absence of pavements, the streets became locations for domestic workers to congregate and socialize during break times, and this is how they are used in many areas to this day. Indeed, many of these separations introduced in the apartheid era continue, in part because of the intransigence of infrastructure (Collier 2011).

Given these multiple ways in which infrastructure symbolized, produced, and secured apartheid, and given the absence of a legitimate formal political sphere, it is unsurprising that the antiapartheid struggle unfolded on a similarly infrastructural terrain. Although the liberation movement became known internationally for its nationalist demands for political rights, it was often organized through localized struggles, many of which took infrastructure as both object and terrain of struggle in a wide variety of ways. Through actions by the armed wing of the ANC, such as the spectacular bombings of rail tracks, power plants, or, infamously, the Sasol oil refinery and the Koeberg nuclear power station, infrastructures became part of a symbolic form of guerilla warfare. On a less spectacular scale, but often more effectively, the burning of passbooks, perhaps the most iconic instantiation of grand apartheid, similarly operated on this symbolic plain.

23 And yet, as later chapters elaborate, such spaces often provided the grounds for the development of counterpublics, in particular in the context of the antiapartheid struggle (cf. Ashforth 2005; Dlamini 2009). Moreover, in the absence of certain key infrastructures informal forms of infrastructures proliferated (cf. Simone 2004).

But infrastructure also became a political terrain in much more mundane and less symbolically evident ways, from bus and rent boycotts to the non-payment of service charges and multiple small acts of sabotage. Such "popular illegalities" often remained on a murkier administrative terrain.[24]

If bus and rent boycotts, the nonpayment of service charges, the burning of passbooks, and small acts of sabotage were central in politicizing seemingly neutral, technical-administrative links to the state, they were also sites for the cultivation of political subjectivities, not merely or even primarily in the form of ideology, but also in the production of oppositional habits, affective attachments, and embodied stances of defiance against the state. Such protests and small acts of sabotage were often highly localized affairs, triggered by specific events or mundane complaints, such as a rate hike or the threat of an eviction; frequently they were direct responses to the everyday violence of apartheid.

Over time, the liberation movement often subsumed such localized protests, boycotts and popular illegalities within the larger progressivist *telos* of liberation, re-articulating them in a modernist nationalist language and ascribing to them an intentionality and historicity that at times differed from the residents' own experiential realities and multiple forms of reasoning for engaging in them. Partly because of its rationalist-modernist conception of politics, the liberation movement expected that such illegalities and protests would end or could simply be switched off after the first election. Given that all South Africans now had full citizenship rights, so the reasoning went, they would now also refrain from such "criminal" activities.

And yet, such acts and protests continued or re-emerged in a multiplicity of ways. In the absence of the authorizing language of liberation, protests and acts of evasion are today often coded by officials and the media as criminal, irrational, or simply self-interested acts. Thus, nonpayers today are no longer "rent boycotters," but "free riders" or "economic saboteurs." They no longer negotiate with government over payment, but are adjudicated in courts of law. The insurgent politics of the struggle is here reframed within a liberal-secular politics; that is, a politics in which the political and the administrative spheres are clearly distinguishable, where violence is the prerogative of the state, and where the foundations of law are no longer in question.

This moment in the 1990s was often framed in the grammar of a globally circulating post–Cold War discourse of "transition"; and yet, this way of emplotting liberation could not quite capture the intransigence of apartheid that hovered just below talk of "reconciliation" or the "rainbow

---

24   The term "popular illegalities" is used by Foucault (1977) in *Discipline & Punish* and usefully taken up by Greg Ruiters (2007) in relation to South Africa. Jeremy Seekings (1988a) refers to the "hidden forms" of resistance during the antiapartheid struggle, as I elaborate in Chapter 3.

nation." Indeed, it could not apprehend the administrative-infrastructural terrain, the affective registers and embodied stances toward the state that lived on after the end of apartheid, what one might, borrowing from Ann Stoler (2013), call "apartheid's debris." [25] It is for this reason that infrastructures provide a productive vantage point to foreground these registers and to make apparent the *work* of *making* liberal democracy, work that is often incomplete and defined by failures as much as successes.

MAKING CITIZENS: "TRANSITION" AND THE WORK OF MAKING LIBERAL DEMOCRACY

For much of the twentieth century, equal citizenship was the central demand and aspirational horizon that animated a diversity of movements. Such demands were articulated as claims to national self-determination in the colonies and, especially in former settler colonies, as demands for recognition and full inclusion within a larger political community. Citizenship held out an emancipatory hope, one often closely linked with the successive achievements of rights as mapped out by T. H. Marshall (1992) or, in the case of the South African liberation movement, in socialist-inspired terms.[26] Viewed from this longer historical arc, the moment of liberation in South Africa was symbolic for the end of an era of juridical distinction between citizens on the basis of race.

And yet this conjuncture was paradoxical. It was a moment when the imagined future came to pass at the same time as any imagination of a future outside of liberal democracy came to be viewed as an anachronistic oddity (Scott 2014). By the time South Africans attained full citizenship in 1994, liberal democracy had not only become a globally normalized and normative condition, it had also been firmly anchored to and signified within a larger neoliberal project that became hegemonic in the aftermath of the Cold War. The triumphalist rise of liberal democracy to global hegemony provided the dominant idiom through which transitional projects

---

25 For Stoler, "imperial debris" references "the longevity of structures of dominance, and the uneven pace with which people can extricate themselves from the colonial order of things" (Stoler 2008: 193). For a close exploration and theorization of apartheid's remainders, see Chari (2013, 2014). For other recent ethnographies that focus on (post-)colonial remainders, see Hansen (2012) and Obarrio (2014).

26 T. H. Marshall's account is relevant in particular for the ways in which it narrativized citizenship in teleological terms, as a story of an increasing addition of rights, from civil to political and, finally, social rights. It is this story that also has often shaped the activist imagination.

could be authorized, in the process often foreclosing other ways of conceiving of political community.

In the immediate aftermath of liberation, a mass of scholarly and technical writing appeared that narrated this moment as one of "transition." This was a globally mobile literature peculiar to the post–Cold War moment, which rendered commensurable political change in places as diverse as Russia, Latin America, and South Africa. In framing the widespread emergence of liberal democracy in terms of transition, this literature—at its most polemic with Fukuyama's "end of history" and Huntington's "third wave of democratization"—suggested an inevitable *telos*, a modular notion of change that rendered the obstacles in its way primarily as procedural and technical. In this triumphalist moment, it divided the world into successful liberal democracies and countries on their way there.

Much justified criticism has been launched against this literature, its teleological hubris and glaring omissions (see, e.g., Burawoy and Verdery 1999). And yet, "transitology," as the academic subfield came to be known, did not merely gloss over more complex realities in its specific account of the end of apartheid. As a concept mobilized in this fraught moment, "transition" had a performative dimension with practical consequences. Much as Michel Callon (2007) has argued for economics, political science did not merely describe reality but, via its various subfields, actively helped make it. "Transition" as a concept entailed the mobilization of a whole field of academic-technical knowledge that shaped new ways of apprehending the social and new forms of intervention. From conflict resolution and trauma experts, to legal and constitutional reform initiatives, transitional justice mechanisms and numerous consultants working out the reform and restructuring of governmental institutions, "transition" enabled and produced reality, rather than merely describing it. In South Africa, a whole array of NGOs and development consultancies sprung up while older organizations of the liberation movement were retooled toward new goals (for example, creating a "culture of human rights" instead of the previously ubiquitous "advancing people power"). This was a transnational field flush with donor monies, deploying a globally mobile expertise that could be made operational in any context deemed "emerging from authoritarian rule." Transition expertise shaped not just the discourses of the futures available for the new South Africa, but also its political and legal institutions and the organization of "civil society."[27]

27   One might think here of the diverse ways in which survivors of apartheid-era violence became "trauma patients," or the ways in which institutions like the Truth and Reconciliation Commission adjudicated the distinction between criminal and political behavior, in the process producing particular postapartheid subjects (e.g., "survivors") and a larger normative vision; see Buur (2001), Kistner (2003), Ross (2003), and Wilson (2001). See also Heinz Klug's (2000) discussion of the "global constitutionalism" and its impact on South Africa and Julia Hornberger's work on human rights and policing (Hornberger 2011).

And yet, the capacity of such expertise was always limited. If "transitology" was central in shaping the larger institutional and discursive terrain within which South Africa entered the end of apartheid, the *work* of making democracy went far beyond such broad-stroke activities and the grafting of liberal institutions and terminology onto the fraught postapartheid terrain. Indeed, it is precisely the speed with which South Africa became, in Neville Alexander's (2002) felicitous term, an "ordinary country" that belied the extent of transformative labor required to make liberal democracy including, crucially, liberal citizens.[28]

Most importantly, as I elaborate in Chapter 3, this project ultimately came to focus on the reform of existing political subjectivities and of the stances, affective investments, and embodied memories of relating to the state. These kinds of labors could not be performed by global experts, in part because in the rationalist-instrumentalist matrix through which such experts viewed the world, historically constituted political subjectivities were difficult to discern as "problems." They could not, for example, apprehend the often sharp disjuncture between experiences of national and urban citizenship—what Ivor Chipkin has called the "non-identity between the national and the local state" (Chipkin 1995:38)—that is a legacy of both apartheid modes of governing the townships and of the specific manner in which the antiapartheid struggle unfolded. In this book, I trace the more piecemeal, micro-political and often subterranean strategies required to "make" citizens. I explore the techno-political *work* of producing and maintaining liberal democracy, and the simultaneous failures and transformations of this project in a context of neoliberal reforms, on the one hand, and the legacies of apartheid, on the other.

In the liberal political imagination, the achievement of citizenship is often understood as the conferral of political rights upon an unmarked individual. Neglected in this story is the extent to which citizens are not "a priori moral subjects," but actively formed and shaped (Burchell 1995:549). As David Burchell argues in his study of the formation of early modern citizenship, "citizenly self-cultivation" had to be carefully manufactured, including an emphasis on secularization, self-discipline, and the overlaying of the concept of virtue with an idea of "manners" (Burchell 1995: 449; see also Hirschkind 2001; Pocock 1985). Citizenship, Burchell shows, entailed more than simply a juridical category or a set of procedural practices, but comprised a certain number of historically contingent assumptions about the kinds of behaviors, dispositions, habits and virtues that define relationships to the state in a context of modernity (see also Isin 2002). In much of Europe and North America, this fashioning of the modern citizen took

---

28   As Chipkin (2013) suggests, the ANC relied on its own nonliberal understanding of democracy, the state, and politics, which in the aftermath of apartheid increasingly clashed with liberal conceptions.

shape in various ways over centuries, via a diverse range of disciplinary and governmental forms, and is indeed an ongoing, iterative project.[29] Similarly, in the postcolonies, producing the nation and its citizens has been an aspiration and ongoing process, rather than an achievement, one often defined by continuities with the colonial forms of governing and the violence that preceded it.[30] Indeed, liberalism, in both its metropolitan and its colonial iterations, *required* a diversity of (often decidedly illiberal) mechanisms, techniques, and pedagogical interventions that would enable particular citizen-subjects to emerge (Mehta 1999; Scott 1999).

In postapartheid South Africa, having come "late to the table of the comity of nations" (Alexander 2002: 1), this process of constructing liberal democracy—and of "making citizens"—involved a dramatic transformation of the relationship between society and state, at least formally. Most important, the establishment of a new political regime, and the shift from antiapartheid movement to governmental authority this entailed, necessitated the institution of new forms of conceiving of and practicing the political (Adler and Steinberg 2000; Chipkin 2003). As Timothy Mitchell (1999) has suggested, the "state effect" is achieved via the performance of an internal boundary between society and the state; in postapartheid South Africa, much work was required to redraw this boundary so that the new political regime could be differentiated from the old, and the liberation movement could be turned into a governmental body. By extension, an important aspect of reform involved the resignification of particular behaviors and stances, and their reclassification within a new grid of intelligibility that would clearly separate the political from other domains.

Behaviors previously sanctioned as legitimate tools of the antiapartheid struggle (from nonpayment to petty sabotage or evasion and various types of violence) were now viewed as apolitical acts (such as crimes, misdemeanors, or behavioral pathologies) to be rectified by administrative action (the police, courts, and the health and education systems). Achieving such transformations required more than institutional reforms, and included much more subtle modalities of change, such as public rituals of resignification, obvious examples being the symbolic work of the Truth and Reconciliation Commission, the popular distribution of the new constitution in small booklets, or publicity campaigns urging township residents to join

29   These projects have been analyzed in a multiplicity of ways, including most prominently, Althusser's analyses of ideological state apparatus (Althusser 1971), Foucault's studies of the disciplines and governmentality (Foucault 1977, 2008), and more recent elaborations of ongoing projects to make citizens (e.g., Cruikshank 1999; Donzelot 1988; Hacking 1990; Rose 1999). See also Norbert Elias's analysis of the "civilizing process" (1982).

30   The precise nature of postcolonial continuity and disjuncture is the subject of much debate (cf. Chatterjee 1993; Cooper 2002; Mamdani 1996; Mbembe 2001; Roitman 2005; Scott 1999).

the reconstruction effort (Comaroff and Comaroff 2006a). Less visibly, it required the establishment of new political ontologies and metrologies, that is, a new ordering of political concepts, meanings, and norms.[31] An important aspect of such reforms was the resignification of concepts that were central to the liberation struggle. Freedom, democracy, rights, violence, and, indeed the concept of politics itself were—often ambivalently— transformed from the insurgent significance of the struggle against apartheid and reformulated within a liberal democratic frame.

But these reframings were not merely symbolic or discursive, nor were they purely institutional or procedural. They also required countless piecemeal interventions that involved technics, matter, and bodily transformations. Perhaps the most important task in the postapartheid period was to reform ethical and political habits, attitudes, and stances.[32] This entailed stripping the political content from certain dispositions and behaviors, which had been politically significant during the antiapartheid struggle. Thus, in the moment when black South Africans were officially recognized as political beings, many of the domains and modalities through which they had often asserted and claimed this status during the antiapartheid struggle were now deemed apolitical. This discursive-material reframing happened at a variety of registers and in a diversity of arenas, most centrally in the conception of violence and its legitimacy (cf. Von Holdt 2013). Given their centrality to both apartheid modalities of governing urban areas and to the multiple forms of resistance with which they were met, this book examines payment, basic services, and infrastructures as key sites of this form of techno-politics. Infrastructure—conceived here broadly as socio-technical assemblages of materiality, discursive, fiscal, and organizational forms and relations—thus becomes both a site and a vantage point to track this techno-political work of making democracy.

MAKING CITIZENS IN NEOLIBERAL TIMES

Projects of resignification and reform have been common in most postindependence or postrevolutionary moments; however, in a context of widespread neoliberal reforms, such modernist projects of nation building

---

31   The concept "political metrology" is inspired by Andrew Barry's theorization of "metrology" and "metrological regimes" (Barry 2006; 2002) on the one hand, and, on the other, by Annemarie Mol's notion of "ontological politics" as a politics "to do with the way problems are framed" (Mol 2002: viii).

32   Such projects to produce "moral citizens" in South Africa have been insightfully explored by Ivor Chipkin (2003) in relation to housing and by Kelly Gillespie (2008) in relation to prisons and the post-apartheid moralization of security.

became both problematized and significantly transformed. For much of the twentieth century, state-centric paradigms of social citizenship dominated not just state techniques and political rationalities, but also often animated and inspired the imagination of social movements and activists making claims on the state. This interventionist mode of social government had as its *telos* the horizontal integration of the nation and as its object "the economy" (Mitchell 2002, 2011). It was also defined by an allied set of techniques that included solidaristic mechanisms such as insurance, cross-subsidization, and social security. In Europe, and to a lesser extent in the United States, welfare, Keynesianism and the New Deal produced particular regulative environments, while in much of the global south, the developmental state was seen to fulfill a similar function, albeit one often linked to modernization projects or more socialist-inspired forms of state-led development. Such projects of nation building were tied to and relied on large-scale infrastructures and associated governmental techniques. In South Africa, this paradigm inspired the liberation movement in a variety of ways, perhaps most iconically in the 1955 Freedom Charter that laid out a nonracial, democratic future when South Africa would be governed by "the people" and a public program of services and redistribution via nationalization would end inequality.

Yet, beginning in the 1970s and intensifying in the aftermath of the Cold War, this understanding of the state as a central agent in development waned rapidly. While in Europe and the United States welfare was increasingly seen as overly bureaucratic and productive of dependent citizens, in the global south the growing dominance of neoliberal reform initiatives—often enforced by structural adjustment programs—led to the designation of the state as the primary obstacle to development. By the end of the Cold War, many of the postcolonial projects of emancipation were in disarray, while the futures that animated them increasingly appeared far removed from the reality that came to pass (Ferguson 1999; Piot 2010; Scott 1999).

Viewed against the backdrop of this history, the moment of liberation in South Africa took shape at an ambivalent juncture. It was simultaneously the last nationalist project to succeed a minority government on the African continent and the first to do so under dramatically transformed conditions in which the modernist dreams of anticolonial nationalism had been shattered in many places. Most South Africans thus gained full citizenship in a moment in which there were increasing doubts globally about what exactly this status conferred beyond the right to vote. In the chapters that follow, I explore how both the task of making citizens and the grounds for making claims on the state have been transformed at this paradoxical juncture.

A large ethnographic literature has productively explored the post-apartheid neoliberal reforms in South Africa and their cultural and political effects; my account connects these contemporary reforms with a longer genealogy of neoliberal ideas in South Africa.[33] In Chapter 2, I explore an earlier moment in which neoliberal texts circulated and became productive in South Africa. In the late 1970s, neoliberal ideas were explicitly taken up by apartheid-era economists and officials in a search for solutions to the multiple crises that confronted the apartheid state from the early 1970s onwards.[34] Thus, conceptually translated and repurposed for South Africa, these ideas came to influence proposals for urban reform, both via official apartheid-era programs and more haphazardly via interventions by private organizations and foundations linked to the mining sector during the 1970s and 1980s. Crucially, such reforms were often aimed at shifting some of the most contentious political questions raised by the antiapartheid movement (regarding citizenship, political rights, and urban belonging) to an administrative, technical terrain. The power and impact of such reforms were always limited, but they helped bring into being the infrastructural terrain that in the 1980s emerged as one of the most important arenas of the antiapartheid struggle.

While critical analyses of neoliberalism in South Africa have at times relied on narratives of betrayal with clear global and local agents, along with ascriptions of causality and responsibility,[35] from the perspective of this more local, "infrastructural" historical perspective, the emergence and effects of neoliberalism appear at once more haphazard and in many respects more vexing and durable. This history of the circulation of neoliberal ideas also destabilizes conventional ways of thinking about neoliberalism and enables a tracing of such continuities and discontinuities across several registers and multiple terrains. Thus, rather than being merely an effect of the external influence of international financial institutions in the aftermath of liberation in 1994, by the late 1970s, neoliberal thought had already emerged as a conceptual resource that could be pragmatically drawn on by reformers and linked to a larger project of urban reform and counterinsurgency.

Against this backdrop, the "transition" emerges not as a clear-cut shift from an authoritarian regime to liberal democracy, but as an ongoing and

33 For ethnographic work that has productively explored the multiplicity of effects of this contradictory moment of "liberation and liberalization" in South Africa, see Comaroff and Comaroff 2001, 2006a; Decoteau 2013; Dubbeld 2013; Hart 2002; Makhulu 2010; Morris 2008; Robins 2010; White 2012.

34 Throughout, I analyze neoliberal thought as a "political rationality"; that is, as a form of conceptual-practical knowledge (cf. Collier 2011; Foucault 2008; see also Gordon 1991; Lemke 2001; Rose 1999).

35 Most prominently, Patrick Bond (2000) argued that the negotiations that ended apartheid were an "elite transition." This paradoxical context of the transition has been analyzed in a wide variety of ways by critical scholars; see Habib and Padayachee (2000), Marais (2001), McKinley (1997), and Saul (2001).

often protracted project of reform that not only has a longer history, but also takes shape in a host of different and often less evident locations.

OPERATION GCIN'AMANZI ("SAVE WATER!")

When the Diepsloot protest occurred, I had just begun my research in Johannesburg and Soweto. Initially, my intention was to study the new social movements that had emerged in response to the neoliberal 1996 Growth, Employment and Redistribution (GEAR) strategy and to Igoli 2002, a local restructuring program that had corporatized most of Johannesburg's services. Since the late 1990s, many social movements and community groups had begun targeted organizing around infrastructure and basic services, including housing, electricity, and water.[36] Throughout my fieldwork, I worked with the Research Subcommittee of one such movement, the Anti-Privatisation Forum (APF), then an umbrella group for a range of residents' groups sprinkled throughout the townships and informal settlements in Gauteng, South Africa's wealthiest province, which encompasses several major urban centers, including Pretoria and Johannesburg. In the weekly meetings of the committee in the APF offices in Braamfontein, just north of downtown Johannesburg, delegates from residents' groups reported back about ongoing concerns and protests; activists trained each other in writing and research methods so that they could conduct their own studies; and community meetings were held to disseminate their findings.[37] The committee also produced research reports and pamphlets and reported to the larger organization with substantive feedback. When I joined, most of our research was concerned with the widespread installation of prepaid meters for both electricity and water, since this was the most pressing concern in many communities.

The most vocal opposition emerged against Operation Gcin'amanzi (Zulu for "Save Water"), a large, multiyear infrastructure project initiated by the Johannesburg Water company, to upgrade Soweto's ailing infrastructure and to install prepaid water meters in all of its households. The utility, though still publicly owned, had been recently corporatized and was managed by subsidiaries of the multinational Suez Group, whose staff had

36   For work on post-apartheid social movements, see Ballard et al. (2006); Dawson (2010); Dawson and Sinwell (2012); Desai (2002); Naidoo and Veriava (2005, 2009); Pithouse (2008); van Heusden and Pointer (2006); Wafer (2008).

37   Two large reports were produced on prepaid water meters in Orange Farm and Phiri (Coalition against Water Privatisation 2004, 2005).

been central in planning Operation Gcin'amanzi.[38] The project, the largest water prepayment metering installation in the world, ended the apartheid-era unmetered water connections, which were now seen as inefficient and environmentally unsustainable, given large water losses in Soweto. Instead of the flat-rate connections that had provided most Sowetans with unlimited water until then, now each "stand" (plot) in Soweto was being fitted with a prepaid water meter that automatically dispensed the small nationally mandated free basic amount of water every month.[39] Once the basic lifeline ran out, residents had to purchase water credits from the local utility offices, in order to avoid the automatic cutoff of water supply.

If "saving water" was a central goal of the project and at the heart of its PR campaigns, another, less emphasized reason for embarking on it—and one that this book will focus on—was the widespread nonpayment for services in Soweto. Prepaid metering, utility officials hoped, could be a technical solution to the problem, enforcing payment by "self-disconnecting" any account without credit. As a measure to administratively manage mass-based nonpayment, the project was thus also a technical modality for addressing the forms of fiscal disobedience that had continued from the anti-apartheid rent boycotts of the 1980s into the present.[40]

Operation Gcin'amanzi began in 2003 with a "prototype" project in Phiri, a poorer area of Soweto in which the utility had identified particularly high water losses. Phiri became the project's laboratory for testing and experimenting with the technology and for gauging what other measures would be needed to roll out the project to the rest of Soweto. From the beginning, Operation Gcin'amanzi was engulfed by protests, resistance, and controversy, which would continue as the years went on, ranging from the illicit bypassing of meters, to large marches, local protests, and, eventually, a constitutional court case against the city and the utility on the basis of the right to water. Objections to the project were multiple, ranging from health concerns about water cutoffs, especially when many residents were suffering from AIDS, to complaints about a lack of consultation and persistently malfunctioning meters. Given that both the project, and prepaid water meters more generally, were only implemented in historically black

38   "Corporatization" is a technical term that describes the process of turning utilities into companies with the City as shareholder. Once corporatized, utilities are thus private companies that are publicly owned. As I elaborate in Chapter 5, this organizational form is different from both privatization and conventional public ownership.

39   South Africa's "free basic water" policy, in part a result of the right to water recognized in the constitution, mandates municipalities to grant "indigent" residents a "lifeline" provision of water. In Johannesburg, this initially meant 6000 liters of water per month per household. This amount is calculated on the basis of an 8-person household, with each person receiving 25 liters per day. I elaborate on this policy and its calculation in Chapters 5 and 6.

40   The term "fiscal disobedience" is Janet Roitman's (Roitman 2005).

townships and that Soweto residents were not, as in the historically white areas, given the option of a regular credit meter, activists and lawyers argued that the project was also racially discriminatory. It is primarily due to these various forms of opposition that the project remains unfinished today. Indeed, by 2015, the utility conceded that most of Soweto's over 130,000 prepaid water meters had been bypassed by residents and that they were forced to install new and more secure types of meters.

In this book, I take Operation Gcin'amanzi—its planning, contentious implementation, and the surrounding debates, protests, and legal action—as an ethnographic site from which to explore the constitution of a larger techno-political terrain that straddles the late and postapartheid periods. Operation Gcin'amanzi is both an anchoring point for my narrative and a lens through which to explore apartheid's less apparent histories and their contemporary resonances and remainders. Drawing on ethnographic research with residents and activists in Soweto, with city officials, engineers, and meter manufacturers in Johannesburg, with apartheid-era bureaucrats and antiapartheid activists, and on research in engineering and local government libraries and the archives of the antiapartheid struggles, I explore how payment for basic services became a site for the articulation of long-standing questions about the promise of citizenship in the postapartheid period.

In focusing closely on Operation Gcin'amanzi, then, I analyze how, in the aftermath of apartheid and in a context of neoliberal reforms, many of the central questions of the antiapartheid struggle—concerning the rights and duties of citizenship and the shape of democracy in the "new South Africa"—were reframed as technical-managerial and procedural questions. If, as many suggest, in a context of neoliberal reform citizenship becomes "thin," I suggest it does so in part, because many previously political or civic operations and concerns are now "framed" outside of the domain of the political (Callon 1998). In the aftermath of apartheid, the politics of infrastructure, basic needs, and life itself—forms of politics that were often articulated via and subsumed within the political languages of the nationalist movement during the antiapartheid struggle—have become sites for the negotiation of key questions of postapartheid citizenship concerning local democracy, belonging, and the bounds of civic obligation and social rights.

By examining the debates, protests, legal battles, and changes in everyday life elicited by an infrastructure project and, indeed, by a seemingly mundane technical object, I track the ways in which such ethical and political questions are delegated and transduced to technical spheres.[41] As I argue throughout this book, such delegations and transductions do not

41   I am here drawing on Stefan Helmreich's (2007) use of Silverstein's original formulation of transduction (2003). Latour's concepts of "delegation" and "translation" focus our

necessarily mean that the political disappears, but rather that it is mediated in new and at times less apparent forms. Tracing these multiple, less
visible transformations at an infrastructural register, this book explores the
shape of postcolonial democracy, new forms and locations of postapartheid
politics and the less apparent ways in which apartheid inhabits the present.

DEMOCRACY'S INFRASTRUCTURE

This book is guided by two linked lines of inquiry that run through each
of the chapters. First, my account conceptually, historically, and ethnographically traces how in the late-apartheid period infrastructure emerged
as a techno-political site of administrative and governmental intervention
where successive crises of apartheid were played out and negotiated. I also
explore its continuities in the present, as this terrain becomes the location where citizenship is fashioned through a variety of measures ranging
from repressive policing practices, to civic pedagogies and technical interventions. Second, the following chapters examine the politics and forms
of disagreement spawned by this terrain, from the rent boycotts during
the antiapartheid struggle to the contemporary protests, social movement
activism, and continuing popular illegalities. I trace the technical politics
that emerges as township residents and activists mobilize expertise and the
infrastructures themselves to make claims on the state, and I examine how
this often invisible terrain at times becomes a site of public disagreement, in
particular during spectacular protests, but also through media debates, election campaigns, or high-profile legal action in the Constitutional Court. In
disputes over payment for service charges, water cutoffs or evictions; in the
spectacular destruction of infrastructure during protests, the more silent
bypassing of water or electricity meters, and the mobilization of numbers
and expertise, I suggest, a different political terrain comes into view.[42]

While the chapters that follow are organized chronologically, they also
each focus on specific forms of techno-politics and the shifting assemblages
of ethics, technics, and politics through which they emerge. In the next
two chapters, I draw on the histories of the 1970s and 1980s to examine
how infrastructure became central to apartheid's forms of power and, in

---

attention on semiotic-material forms of translations which "inscribe . . . words into *another
matter*" (Latour 1992: 249, emphasis in original).

42   By "political terrain," I mean on the one hand the discursive problem-space within
which certain political languages resonate whereas others cannot (cf. Scott 1999). On the
other hand, I use the term to reference the importance of forms of making political claims—
the techniques, idioms, and materialities of acting politically.

turn, to trace the often less visible, "technical" histories of the antiapartheid struggle. As histories of the present, these chapters seek to unsettle the periodization of the transition and to provide the grounds to think anew about questions that have become seemingly commonsensical. In turn, the ethnographic chapters closely follow the life of the meter, from its design by engineers and "guerrilla technicians," to its working in Soweto residents' yards, its deployment at protests, and, finally, its appearance in court.

Chapter 2 locates the beginnings of a specifically neoliberal techno-politics in South Africa in the conceptual and practical responses to the 1976 Soweto Uprising. Drawing on archival research and interviews with apartheid-era economists and functionaries, the chapter provides a close reading of the political styles of reasoning that emerged as neoliberal thought was appropriated by the state and private organizations in response to the systemic crises of the 1970s. I trace the move away from the macro-techniques of grand apartheid and toward more micro-political techniques at the level of the administrative and the technical. This late-apartheid techno-politics, and the neoliberal archive that often inspired it, enabled a form of counterinsurgency mediated by infrastructure and administrative techniques.

In Chapter 3, I focus on the particular infrastructural political terrain these late-apartheid reforms helped bring into being. In order to account for the intensity of resistance with which Operation Gcin'amanzi was met, I return to the "rent boycotts" of the 1980s when township residents used mass nonpayment for service charges as a powerful weapon against the apartheid state. The chapter draws on archival records and interviews with apartheid-era local bureaucrats and former antiapartheid activists to explore how nonpayment became politicized during the antiapartheid struggle beginning in the 1980s and how, from the 1990s onwards, it was "reframed" as a technical, rather than a political problem. Thus, against the backdrop of this history, Operation Gcin'amanzi and the meter itself emerge as attempts to sever the historic link between nonpayment, infrastructure, and claims to citizenship and belonging.

Chapter 4 explores the micro-political battle between residents tinkering with the technology and engineers trying to secure it. Technology itself thus becomes a political terrain for the negotiation of ethical and political questions of civic virtue and citizenship. I also trace the meter's techno-political history from its invention in Victorian Britain to the late-apartheid period and into the present. At each moment, I suggest, the meter was harnessed to distinct ethical regimes and political projects. Drawing on my ethnographic fieldwork at industry meetings and offices, I explore how engineers make the device functional in the postapartheid moment. In following the travels of a small technical device and the ethical and political worlds it is shaped by and that it, in turn, helps shape, this chapter also conceptually reconsiders the relationship between ethics, politics, and technics.

Chapter 5 ethnographically follows the planning and contentious implementation of Operation Gcin'amanzi from city offices, local utility staff workshops, and consultation forums to the meetings of activist groups and local protests against the project by a local residents' group. I examine how the installation of prepaid water meters, and the curtailment of water services they entailed, transformed relationships within and between households. Specifically, the chapter focuses on the multiple forms of intervention attending the corporatization of water provision and the semiotic-material work of making water calculable. In turn, I examine the "countermeasures" produced by Phiri activists, as they took up numerical practices to make claims on the state.

In the aftermath of waves of ultimately unsuccessful protests against the project, five residents from Phiri took the City of Johannesburg to court on the basis of their constitutionally enshrined right to water. Chapter 6 ethnographically tracks the case from its beginnings to its dismissal by the constitutional court. Moving between ethnographic encounters and interviews with the residents and lawyers involved, this chapter explores the ways in which the residents, in order to articulate their claims in the register of rights, had to rely on the calculative languages they sought to oppose. Within the judicial logic of the case, suffering and "basic needs" became measurable variables to be weighed against competing calculations authorized by expert knowledges. This legal techno-politics involving experts, residents and legal officials became central to the adjudication of key ethical and political questions in the postapartheid period.

———————————

Looking at political change from the perspective of this administrative-political terrain enables a different story of the transition to be told, one in which time proceeds less linearly, where change is less dramatic, more piecemeal and often murky, and where apartheid's material intransigence continues to shape daily life in a multiplicity of ways. It is in this sense that I am interested here in apartheid's "debris" and its contemporary remainders. While the first general election in 1994 marks the beginning of democracy in South Africa, the continuities and discontinuities with the late-apartheid era unfold at different speeds, at diverse registers, and at an uneven pace. If during the liberation struggle, protests against administrative interventions by the apartheid state were both articulated via and appropriated by nationalist languages of self-determination, in the immediate postapartheid period, such languages were no longer as easily available as idioms of opposition.[43] Protest has thus often become spectral; dispersed,

———————————

43   While social movement activism in the postapartheid period has consistently drawn on earlier liberation idioms, repertoires, and tactics, so-called delivery protests have taken wide variety of forms and modes of expression (cf. Von Holdt et al. 2011).

and splintered into a diversity of locations that may unfold on a more micro-political terrain and that may range from violent and spectacular expressions of disagreement to the silent bypassing of a meter. Rather than senseless, mute acts of violence and uncivic behavior, such acts need to be read against the backdrop of a historically constituted terrain that usually remains invisible and below the radar of normative domains of political engagement.

In South Africa, there is today a wide disjuncture between the globally circulating miracle narrative of liberal democracy with its free and fair elections, rights discourses, and civil society, and local experiences of democracy that are oftentimes shaped by apartheid and its infrastructural legacies. While the waves of contemporary protests are clearly often bound up with material demands on the state, they are *also* in many instances a reflection of the ways in which apartheid's intransigence is materialized in roads, pipes, bureaucratic forms, administrative fiat, and indeed in embodied forms of ethical and political knowledge. This intransigence is reinforced in the present democratic moment in which a new set of reforms and state projects are built on the ruins of the old, and in which the relation between the administrative and the political has been reconceived in a liberal frame. Retelling this history of apartheid from the perspective of its infrastructure thus also brings into view the ways in which the liberal order of free circulation often rests on illiberal foundations. It is in this sense, that this is also decidedly *democracy's* infrastructure.

Chapter 2

THE "DISCIPLINE OF FREEDOM"

*Neoliberalism, Translation, and Techno-Politics
after the 1976 Soweto Uprising*

Freedom is an artifact of civilization [that] was made possible
by the gradual evolution of the discipline of civilization
which is at the same time the discipline of freedom. . . .
We owe our freedom to the restraints of freedom.

F. A. HAYEK 1978A: 163

By the standards of students of the liberal principles, the
southern African plural urban society is in need of a great deal
of reform before it could be expected to function well.

J. A. LOMBARD 1978: 72

In 2003, the recently corporatized utility company Johannesburg Water
announced Operation Gcin'amanzi (Zulu for "Save Water!"), a new infrastructure project for Soweto. The project would repair leaky pipes and
upgrade water mains, and thus reduce the large-scale water losses the utility had identified in Soweto. Most important, if less emphasized in publicity materials, it would also install prepaid water meters in all Soweto
households. With a name that invoked both the militant language of the
liberation struggle and older tropes of self-reliance often associated with
post-Independence developmentalism, the project appeared, from afar, to
be just one amongst many ongoing efforts to remedy apartheid-era inequalities and to reverse decades of neglect. And yet, in the aftermath of the
project's announcement, and long before the first prepaid water meter had
been installed, a media storm erupted. In the public debates that ensued, it

31

soon became apparent that what was at stake was always more than just the project itself. Throughout the heated arguments involving social movements, union activists and left-leaning academics on the one hand, and the utility, the City and at times the Minister for Water Affairs and Forestry himself on the other, larger lines of battle emerged around the postapartheid present.

For its proponents in the city government and the water company, Operation Gcin'amanzi would make water provision more efficient in a context of large water losses in Soweto; the meters, they argued, were simply a more effective and sustainable method to distribute and manage a scarce resource. The corporatization of water provision and the management contract awarded to the team from Suez had brought private-sector expertise that could "build capacity," which in turn would permit the state to do its job better and, ultimately, enable overall improvements in quality of life for the majority. As such, they argued, Operation Gcin'amanzi was simply a form of technical improvement that was ultimately in the service of the larger goals of liberation and, as ANC posters throughout the country put it, "a better life for all."

For the activists who organized protests and wrote op-eds in the papers, however, the metering project was a direct outcome of the corporatization of water services prescribed by Johannesburg's local restructuring program *Igoli 2002*, and thus one step in a broader move toward the commodification of essential services. Operation Gcin'amanzi, they argued, was the brainchild of Suez, the French water multinational whose subsidiaries had been hired to manage Johannesburg Water shortly before the project was announced. Rather than a mere technical transformation, to the activists Operation Gcin'amanzi was emblematic of much wider political and economic transformations precipitated by the neoliberal Growth, Employment and Redistribution (GEAR) reform program embarked upon in 1996 by the ANC-led government. In this way, Operation Gcin'amanzi was also summoned as proof for larger arguments about the ANC's "sellout" of the liberation struggle and its giving up on the promise of the Freedom Charter and the more social democratic 1994 Reconstruction and Development Program (RDP).

Such narratives of postapartheid betrayal resonated strongly in the 1990s and early 2000s.[1] They offered a language with which to understand not only the slow pace of transformation, but also the sometimes peculiar policy choices of the new government and the increasing centrality of commercialization and privatization in reform proposals. Such narratives often attributed postapartheid failures and disappointments to a mix of individual self-interest, a lack of ideological steadfastness, and an external

1   For critical literature on the transition, see Bond 2000; Habib and Padayachee 2000; Marais 2001; Murray 1994; Saul 2001; Terreblanche 2002.

bulldozer of neoliberal policy advice administered by globalized capitalist forces and their proxies. As part of this larger story involving powerful global actors, local moral failings, and betrayals of political principles, Operation Gcin'amanzi became a staging ground for the much larger question of postapartheid futures and aspirations.

Whether implicitly or explicitly, for many critics and social movement activists at the time neoliberalism—conceived as a specific set of economic policy prescriptions, including liberalization, deregulation, and privatization—became a referent for a larger complex of complaints. As a performative term, neoliberalism enabled a productive problematization of the postapartheid present that constituted a diverse array of grievances as distinct problems with clear lines of causality and proposals for redress.[2] In their resonance with globally circulating critiques of neoliberalism by activists and protest movements elsewhere, such narratives also drew on shared oppositional idioms, helped build larger alliances and mobilized action in a moment otherwise saturated by the now-hegemonic languages of liberation.[3]

Although this way of framing the problem was strategically effective insofar as it provided the means both to critique the increasing global dominance of neoliberal policy paradigms and to demand accountability from the ANC-led government, it also risked narrowing the terms through which postapartheid transformation and its discontents could be understood. In their focus on the global and on the economic, such critiques risked eliding the longer political history of the townships since the 1970s, a history that has shaped the present in a multiplicity of ways.

In this chapter, and in different ways in the next, my goal is to conceptually recalibrate the understanding of neoliberalism, the technical and the political that has often been mobilized in debates in South Africa and elsewhere. Before returning to Operation Gcin'amanzi in later chapters, here I explore an earlier moment of neoliberal theorizing and the historical dynamics through which neoliberal ideas first circulated and became effective in South Africa. In the context of the systemic crises of the late 1970s, neoliberal ideas were translated and appropriated by economists, state officials, and urban reformers as a conceptual resource to rethink apartheid modalities of governing urban black populations.

---

2 I use the term problematization in Foucault's sense as the "transformation of a group of obstacles and difficulties into problems to which the diverse solutions will attempt to produce a response" (Foucault 1998: 118).

3 Some of the most vocal objections to Operation Gcin'amanzi were shaped by larger and more principled objections to the neoliberal reforms of 1996 by more radical, now often excluded parts of the liberation movement, disappointed ANC members, and an internationally circulating activist discourse against neoliberalism or what was then widely referred to as the Washington Consensus.

This chapter traces the transformations in political styles of reasoning and governmental techniques that such reforms often haphazardly introduced. Specifically, I examine the shift away from the blunter techniques and imaginaries of "grand apartheid" toward more oblique micro-political techniques at the level of the administrative and the technical in the aftermath of the 1976 Soweto Uprising. This period produced a series of piecemeal urban interventions, often inspired by neoliberal principles, in which housing as well as urban services and infrastructures became central. Crucially, the reforms proposed in this period sought to shift some of the most contentious political questions—regarding citizenship, political rights, and belonging—to an administrative and increasingly deracialized terrain. As they embarked on the dual task of reforming the apartheid state whilst defending its basic premise of minority rule, reformers pragmatically drew on neoliberal ideas and associated forms of technical expertise in an effort to depoliticize the resurgent antiapartheid movement. In the next chapter, I then explore the failures and unintended effects of this shift as it was opposed by the liberation organizations and ordinary residents during the 1980s. It is this techno-political terrain that would emerge in the 1980s as one of the most important arenas of the antiapartheid struggle.

NEOLIBERALISM, TRANSLATION, TECHNO-POLITICS

One task of this chapter is to tell this less apparent history of administrative transformation in South Africa's urban areas—and Soweto more specifically—but this history also enables us to think anew about neoliberalism in the global south more generally. Neoliberalism has often been analyzed as a globally uniform economic policy paradigm imposed without regard for context on a diversity of places, and much anthropological writing has focused on exploring its often messy and unintended social and cultural effects.[4] Here, I suggest that we should take places in the global south seriously not merely as recipients of neoliberal policies, but as epistemic locations in which neoliberal thought is adapted, reformulated, and produced. In turn, such extensions and translations in the "periphery" have shaped the neoliberal tradition as a whole.[5] In the late-apartheid

4   Many critiques have suggested that studies of neoliberalism fail to take into account the unintended outcomes and failures of neoliberal reforms in practice (see, e.g., Hart 2008; Kipnis 2008). While studies of the practical effects of neoliberal reforms have been immensely illuminating, here, I suggest that attention to the conceptual edifice and translation of neoliberal thought is similarly crucial.

5   As Premesh Lalu (2013) has shown, South African and South Africa–based economists like William Hutt were in fact central to shaping the neoliberal project in its early inception in the Mont Pelerin Society. See also Plehwe et al. (2006).

moment, neoliberalism emerges not as a homogeneous program imposed from the outside, but rather as a conceptual resource for critical reflection on apartheid and as a form of practical reason and a technical set of tools that animated the small-scale reforms introduced in the townships after the Soweto Uprising.[6]

Elizabeth Povinelli has coined the term "liberal diasporas" to refer to the ways in which the liberal doctrine was "translated" and "dilated" as it moved toward settler colonies, in the process transforming not just the societies in which it was elaborated, but liberalism itself (Povinelli 2002: 14). If Povinelli is primarily concerned with the "material mediation" and effects of liberalism, here, I join her insights with Stephen Collier's insistence that we take seriously (neo-)liberal *thought* as "a form of critical reflection on governmental practice" (2011: 2). My focus will be on the travel and *local translations* of neoliberal thought, that is, on the ways in which neoliberal ideas were appropriated and adapted conceptually by South African economists and bureaucrats and made operational in the fraught context of the late-apartheid period.

Examining the travel of neoliberal ideas requires taking seriously the epistemic modalities and ontological premises through which such ideas unfold and take effect in historically distinct ways.[7] This chapter provides a close reading of a series of texts in order to trace these conceptual translations. This particular "fieldwork in philosophy" is inspired by Talal Asad's claim that what has historically distinguished anthropology from other disciplines is less the ethnographic method and rather "the comparison of embedded concepts . . . between societies differently located in time or space" (Asad 2003: 17).[8] Conceived as an effort of conceptual comparison, then, this chapter explores the process of translation through which particular intellectual traditions come to inhabit new contexts and the concepts that become salient in such processes of translation.

The next section outlines the ambivalent historical relationship between liberalism and apartheid, which in important respects shaped the reception of neoliberal ideas in the late-apartheid period. In order to attend to the

6 Neoliberalism, as a set of policy advice, traveled in many ways: via the compulsions associated with structural adjustment programs, but also in looser discursive formations, such as advice by global institutions or the training of local experts in the North. While I am here interested in the conceptual question of translation, the more sociological question of the dissemination of expertise has been usefully addressed by Plehwe et al. 2006; Mirowski and Plehwe 2009; and Walpen 2004.

7 If neoliberalism "makes its world," as Timothy Mitchell (2009) suggests, it thus does so in historically specific ways. Similarly, if as Michel Callon (2007: 331) suggests, expertise—that is, statements, utterances, and programs for action—"spreads its world with it," such expertise does not begin its work on a tabula rasa, but always in conjunction with prior programs of action.

8 On "fieldwork in philosophy," see Bourdieu (1990) and Rabinow (2007).

specific ways in which neoliberal thought became effective in South Africa, I then provide a close reading of two neoliberal thinkers: Friedrich Hayek, a key figure in the neoliberal movement and co-founder of the Mont Pelerin Society,[9] and Jan Lombard, an influential South African economist who took up Hayek's thought—and in particular its emphasis on "order" and "tradition"—in his search for ways to reform the apartheid state project. The latter part of this chapter focuses on how these ideas were in turn mobilized conceptually and adapted practically by late-apartheid-era urban reformers as part of a larger project of counterinsurgency in the 1970s. Attending to the more piecemeal urban transformations that often took a technical form elucidates how infrastructure, payment, and the administrative domain became sites of contention whose legacies continue to shape the present. Thus, as a history of the present, this chapter explores this late-apartheid techno-political terrain both in order to render intelligible its contemporary remainders and to refashion the conceptual grounds for thinking about neoliberalism, infrastructure, and politics in the postapartheid moment.[10]

THE AMBIVALENCES OF APARTHEID LIBERALISM

> "Liberty" must always be understood as "liberties"; . . . the two
> questions viz. (a) what liberties to strive for; and (b) who is to
> enjoy them, have always been answered in concrete historical
> contexts . . . in such a way that an absolute claim, in other words,
> for absolute liberties for "all" men has, in practice, turned out to
> be a limited claim for specific "liberties" for a determinate class, or
> group of human beings. [T]he concrete historical setting in which
> the classical doctrine of liberalism was evolved, did not include
> the setting of a multi-racial society, such as we have here in South
> Africa, in which, moreover, one racial group, and this one a minority
> group, is, and is determined to remain, the dominant group. Of

9   The Mont Pelerin Society was an influential neoliberal "thought collective" founded by Hayek in order to provide a space in which to rethink liberalism that had been thrown into crisis in a context of the increasing hegemony of Keynesianism and other more statist models of regulating the economy. Its members included the most influential neoliberal thinkers from Milton Friedman to James Buchanan and Ordoliberals like Wilhelm Röpke (Plehwe et al. 2006; Mirowski and Plehwe 2009; Walpen 2004).

10   While this chapter draws on archival research and on interviews I conducted with apartheid-era bureaucrats, economists, and antiapartheid activists, it is primarily a reading of key texts and a reconsideration of the extensive scholarship of this period to fashion a new perspective on the present.

> such a setting, the classical thinkers of liberalism had no first-hand experience. Hence, I hold that liberal ideals have to be re-examined and rethought in their application to a society of this type.
>
> —ALFRED HOERNLÉ, *SOUTH AFRICAN NATIVE POLICY AND THE LIBERAL SPIRIT* (1939: IX).

> Freedom can only be associated with economic growth and material welfare if the sense of responsibility in the society is of a highly economic kind, i.e. if people are able and willing to read the signs of the market, to make the necessary calculations and to act upon their findings. . . . "But in fact it is probable that not one tenth of the present populations of the world have the mental and moral faculties, the intelligence and the self-control that are required for it."
>
> —SOUTH AFRICAN ECONOMIST JAN LOMBARD QUOTING ALFRED MARSHALL (LOMBARD 1978: 69)

Liberalism in the colonies often tended to forget its central ethical and political principles when faced with the exigencies of imperial domination, but in the context of colonial and apartheid South Africa liberal conceptual coherence was stretched to its limits in particularly dramatic ways. Apartheid, as a racist state project reliant on a strongly regulated economy,[11] was an illiberal project par excellence; and yet, its origins and initial forms of reasoning were in fact a solution proposed by liberals to the problem of groups outlined by Hoernlé in the quote above. Throughout South Africa's colonial history two liberal traditions competed with each other, as they did within the British colonial project as a whole.[12] The first, which one might term Millian, was based on a progressivist-assimilationist project that envisioned that the "civilizing mission" would eventually "uplift natives" toward full membership in colonial society. In South Africa, this strand came to be known as Cape liberalism and was practically materialized in limited franchise for "civilized natives" and a concomitant rationale for segregation on the basis of civilization (Dubow 1989). The second tradition, in part a response to the failure of the first, gave up the project of assimilationism in favor of institutional separation, what came to be known, in colonial administrator Frederick Lugard's elaboration, as

---

11 See here in particular Dan O'Meara's work on *volkskapitalisme* (O'Meara 1983) and Gelb's analysis of apartheid's "racial Fordism" (Gelb 1991).

12 On liberalism and empire, see Mamdani (1996), Mantena (2010), Mehta (1999), and Stokes (1959). Brian Larkin observes this tension between different strategies of colonial rule within colonial administrations and even individual officials (Larkin 2008: 24).

"indirect rule." This tradition was elaborated in the early Natal colony and involved a more conservative focus on the maintenance of groups on the basis of ethnicity and race (Chanock 2001, Mamdani 1996).

Although South African liberal historiography tended to depict apartheid as the outcome of the crude racism of the Boer republics, many scholars have argued that its initial conceptual formulation should be seen within the context of the latter liberal tradition in which assimilationism was replaced with a focus on the maintenance of group differentiation (Dubow 1989; Rich 1984).[13] As indicated in the quote above, the leading liberal intellectual and reformer Alfred Hoernlé saw the "multiracial" nature of South Africa as a problem that could ultimately not be solved through assimilationist strategies (cf. Legassick 1976).[14] In South Africa, unlike what he depicted as the more "homogenous" European context, assimilationism and colorblindness would inevitably lead to the domination of one group by the other. It was in response to this liberal problematic, that Hoernlé proposed the idea of "total separation," which he believed, unlike its predecessor segregation, could be made consistent with liberal principles, in that it gave each population group political rights within its "own" society, thus avoiding the inevitable inequalities associated with assimilationism. In the 1940s, Hoernlé's suggestions were taken up by more moderate Afrikaner nationalists in an effort to render Afrikaner nationalism compatible with liberal principles. It is in these writings that the term "separate development" first appears with direct reference to Hoernlé. Only much later are the notions of separate development and later "separate freedoms" taken on by the more hardline, antiliberal nationalists, such as Hendrik Verwoerd. As Hermann Giliomee put it, "the terminology of the 'progressive' or 'liberal' Nationalists had conquered the National Party, or rather the party had conquered the terminology" (Giliomee 1987: 371). What

---

13   Liberal historians presented apartheid as the outcome of a battle between the Cape liberal tradition of the nineteenth century and the "frontier tradition" of the Boer republics. In the 1970s, this liberal narrative was challenged by Marxist scholars, who not only sought to show that the origins of apartheid lay in the segregationist policies advocated by liberals in the interwar years, but also that the apartheid project was in the service of *both* farming and mining interests, most centrally in the form of "cheap labor" (Wolpe 1972; see also Johnstone 1970; Legassick 1974), but also as a mode of social control (Dubow 1990). In ascribing apartheid to Afrikaner prejudice, Wolpe et al. argued, liberal historians not only misrepresented history, but also actively provided a smokescreen for the beneficiaries of apartheid (cf. Posel 1991: 8–18; Dubow 1989).

14   Reading interwar liberals such as Jan Smuts or Alfred Hoernlé, it is clear that the introduction of "groups" posed a conceptual problem for South African liberal thinkers, which was solved by superimposing the question of security, often with reference to the threat of "Bolshevism." In this sense, the liberal debates within South Africa between the 1920s and the 1940s, while preoccupied with the particular predicament of South Africa, were also reflective of a global crisis of liberalism during that period.

made apartheid unfathomable for liberals then, was initially less the *concept* of "separate development," but rather the ways in which it practically unfolded; that is, on the one hand its association with race and, on the other, the centrality of the state and state intervention, including the epistemology and associated techniques on which it came to rest.

The global move toward statism began in the interwar years, in particular with the rise of fascist and socialist state projects. In South Africa, this translated into a racist state project split into a democratic, welfarist sphere for whites, and Afrikaners in particular (O'Meara 1983; Terreblanche 2002), and a project that envisaged granting "sovereignty" via despotic, "traditional" authorities to the black majority. Social provisioning was thus segregated with most state support for housing, services, and employment going to the white population, while the black population was ruled through a bureaucratized state apparatus designed primarily for purposes of control rather than guided by a biopolitical imperative of care (Dubow 1989). This bifurcated state project, and the peculiar racial economy it produced— *Volkskapitalisme* (O'Meara 1983) or what Stephen Gelb (1991) termed "racial Fordism"—was based on bureaucratic infrastructures that channeled black laborers via labor bureaus to the farms and mines.

While apartheid rested throughout on race-based exclusionary practices, the political rationalities that authorized it and the governmental techniques through which it was secured changed throughout in large part as a response to the crises produced by various forms of resistance (Ashforth 1990; Posel 1991). Important for my purposes here is the way in which racial separation and white supremacy came to be rationalized in the context of "grand apartheid."[15] The ideological defense of "separate development" was in large part based on a cultural relativism that argued for the need to "protect" African cultures from the influences of modernity, in particular "the market" and industrial society. This motif encompassed all areas of life, including, centrally, the economy.

Separate development was rationalized by positing that the black man lacked the capacity to interact productively in "market society" and, thus, should be allowed to develop along "his own" path without interference from the white capitalist economy. As Hendrik Verwoerd, then still Minister of Native Affairs, put it in defense of the policy of prohibiting private investment in the homelands, "we will not let the wolves in, those people

15 "Grand apartheid" designates the larger ideological project of "separate development" that was hegemonic in the 1960s and 1970s. It sought to remove the black population from the urban, now "white" areas, to relocate them to and grant them "political representation" in the black "homelands" or Bantustans, in the process denying them South African citizenship. By contrast, "petty apartheid" references the more intricate and often symbolically charged racial segregation of public space, amenities and restrictions on interracial sex and marriages.

who simply seek where they can make money in order to fill their own pockets" (Verwoerd, as cited in Hutt 1965: 59). In a speech entitled "Separate Development" Verwoerd more explicitly suggested that "the white man took years to learn how to be a good trader and many Bantu traders are still deficient as regards capital and knowledge and commercial morality" (Verwoerd 1958: 12). This suggestion, as many pointed out at the time, was of course ludicrous—most black workers had been working in industrial conditions for a long time—but it enabled a framing of South Africa's economy as limited to the "white" areas, while migrant labor was externalized on the basis of "national" boundaries, a matter of "international cooperation" rather than a part of one economy.[16]

In the urban, now "white" areas, this economic rationale for separate development translated into stringent legislation and regulations instituted throughout the 1950s. Black business ownership was severely restricted, and the informal economy was heavily policed. Black urban residents, then, were not only political nonsubjects, they were also prevented from becoming economic subjects, except as wage laborers. As I elaborate in later chapters, consistent with such policy prescriptions, infrastructures, if they existed at all, were basic and usually oriented toward security concerns. Housing was public and rented from the state. In the townships, infrastructure and housing was over time managed by diverse administrative constellations, including an array of local institutions and parastatals, all ultimately controlled by the central government.

A small number of liberals had throughout the 1950s and 1960s protested apartheid and in particular the economics on which it was based. Several economists, such as W. H. Hutt, a founding member of the Mont Pelerin Society who lived and worked in South Africa, wrote influential, explicitly neoliberal treatises against apartheid, based in large part on economic arguments positing that "the market is color-blind" and should be deregulated (Hutt 1964: 173).[17] And yet, this vocal liberal criticism was always limited and diminished in the first decades of apartheid, not least because the economy was growing rapidly in the 1950s and 1960s. This changed in the 1970s and

---

16   The absurdity of the grand-apartheid ideology becomes particularly apparent when one looks at an Urban Foundation survey carried out in the early 1980s in which 77 percent of Soweto residents stated they regarded themselves as "permanent residents with no ties with the independent and non-independent homelands" (South African Institute of Race Relations 1982: 310). See here also James Ferguson's (1990) analysis of the ways in which Lesotho's "national economy" was constituted in development discourse.

17   Elsewhere, Hutt more explicitly suggested that "South Africa's salvation" would be found in "classical liberalism" (Hutt 1965). Though Hutt was aware of Becker's *The Economics of Discrimination* (1957), which advanced a similar argument, he does not mention it in his account. See Lalu (2013) for an extended exploration of Hutt's work. For another liberal economist's account, see Horwitz (1967). Horwitz, like Hutt, was a life-long member of the Mont Pelerin Society. The liberal critique of apartheid became more influential in the 1980s (see, e.g., Lipton 1986).

1980s when the system of racialized Keynesianism began to crumble and South Africa became locked into what Saul and Gelb (1981) at the time diagnosed in Gramscian terms as an "organic crisis." The crisis was in part global: just as other state projects began to falter in a context of stagflation, the downturn of the economy put severe strains on the viability of state bureaucracy. However, in South Africa, the crisis was also precipitated by the reinvigoration of the liberation movements that had gathered steam since the early 1970s, the decline of the Portuguese Empire, the coming into power of liberation movements of its northern neighbors, and, perhaps most importantly, by the series of protests and mobilizations that began with the Durban Strikes in 1973 and the Soweto Uprising in 1976.

It was at this moment of crisis that apartheid reformers began to look to ideas from elsewhere, and to neoliberal thought in particular, for solutions. As they did so, they grappled with the question of how neoliberalism could be made relevant to South Africa. Before exploring this South African translation of neoliberal thought in more detail, it is necessary to elaborate the specific neoliberal ideas on which they drew in some more detail, examining in particular their premises, logics, and prescriptions. My focus will be on Friedrich Hayek, because it was often specifically his thought that was attractive to and taken up by apartheid-era reformers. As I elaborate below, it was Hayek's attachment to "culture" and "tradition," and the limits and "discipline of freedom" this by extension entailed, that rendered his thought particularly compelling, as it offered a language with which to articulate the reform of the apartheid state, whilst retaining its basic premise—minority rule.

THE HABITS OF ECONOMIC MAN

> Though it sounds paradoxical to say that in order to make ourselves act rationally we often find it necessary to be guided by habit rather than reflection, or to say that to prevent ourselves from making the wrong decision we must deliberately reduce the range of choice before us, we all know that this is often necessary in practice if we are to achieve our long-range aims.
>
> F. A. HAYEK 1960: 66

Much scholarly and popular critique of neoliberalism has revolved around its anemic conception of human nature defined by self-interested, utility-maximizing behavior. And yet, many of the most influential thinkers in the neoliberal tradition explicitly rejected this account of human nature. For

Hayek, *homo economicus* was no more than "a celebrated figment," which he associated with the "rationalist tradition." According to the Scottish Enlightenment tradition to which he traced his thought, on the contrary, "man was by nature lazy and indolent, improvident and wasteful, and it was only through the force of circumstance that he would be made to behave economically or would learn to carefully adjust his means to his ends" (Hayek 1960: 61). This sentiment is shared by many thinkers within the neoliberal tradition; here, humans are not imagined as cold-blooded utility-maximizers, but rather as deeply enmeshed in cultural ties, guided by embodied habits and as responsive to environmental conditions and constraints.[18] Similarly, while neoliberalism is often depicted as a narrow economic doctrine promoting the withdrawal of the state to "free" the market, one of the key innovations of neoliberal thought—what made it *neo*liberalism—was the understanding that "markets" do not simply emerge, but have to be actively enabled and carefully maintained, and that mechanisms of "order" and *particular kinds* of intervention would be central to the emergence and stability of the "free society."[19]

While neoliberal thought is defined by great internal diversity, there is a recognizable set of stakes and concerns—a set of "moves" to follow James Ferguson (2007)—that unite it in what one might define as a "tradition" in Alasdair MacIntyre's formulation. Rather than a monolithic doctrine, a tradition in this sense is a dynamic space of discourse and practice that coheres in its common stakes and shared terms of debate (MacIntyre 1981). This tradition, as I elaborate below in a brief reading of neoliberal texts, is defined by two countervailing liberal impulses. On the one hand, it is linked to the modern liberal tradition with its emphases on progressively and universally realizable "civilization," the sovereign individual subject, and a vision of negative freedom. On the other hand, however, the problem of "order" is explicitly recognized and often resolved with reference to an antirationalist epistemology centered on "tradition," the centrality of embodied rules and "tacit knowledge."[20] It is this combination of Kantian and

18   This is particularly true for the Austrian School, which was heavily influenced by the Scottish Enlightenment, and also for the Ordoliberals who explicitly drew on Christian ethics (Walpen 2004). But even Chicago School neoliberals emphasized, for example, the importance of the family (Becker 1981).

19   On this interventionism, see the work inspired by the regulationist school (Brenner and Theodore 2002; Jessop 2002; Peck, Theodore, and Brenner 2009) and studies of governmentality (Gordon 1991; Lemke 2001; Rose 1999).

20   Many of these surprising features of neoliberal thought can be traced to its emergence in the interwar years in a moment of economic crisis and the rise of totalitarianism when classical liberalism appeared under siege from multiple directions. It is this specific political and intellectual conjuncture that led early neoliberal thinkers—from the Austrian school to the Ordoliberals—to focus on how liberalism could be joined with a focus on order and stability.

Humean impulses within the neoliberal tradition—and in particular their respective stances on the possibilities and techniques of intervention and "reform"—that becomes important as it is translated into new contexts, and to the late-apartheid moment in particular.

It is this tension that is also at the heart of Foucault's analysis of the figure of homo economicus in his 1978–1979 lectures on the Chicago School and the Ordoliberals. If classical liberalism was premised on a *naturally* self-interested human nature, neoliberal thinkers now view humans as malleable creatures located within specific environments. By extension, as Foucault suggests, while in classical liberalism, *homo economicus* was "intangible" from the point of view of governmental reason, he now appears as "someone who responds systematically to systematic modifications artificially introduced into the environment. . . . From being the intangible partner of laissez-faire, *homo economicus* now becomes the correlate of a governmentality, which will act on the environment and systematically modify its variables" (Foucault 2008: 270f.).

This de-naturalization of *homo economicus* had far-reaching conceptual and, ultimately, practical consequences. It required an account of how humans became utility-maximizing and how they could be made to become so. Given that human nature is now conceived of as dependent on environment and context, it also necessitated an account of the *particular* environment in which *homo economicus* could develop and operate. This, in turn, produces a particular reason of state, requiring the state to intervene in order to construct and secure the premises for the market to take shape. It is this focus on the continued centrality of state intervention that was particularly attractive to apartheid-era reformers. Much like during the colonial context, however, this conception of *homo economicus* as an aspirational figure licensed a pedagogical imperative that would ultimately reinforce key pillars of apartheid's edifice, while rationalizing them in liberal terms.

THE "DISCIPLINE OF FREEDOM"

One of the central foundations of the neoliberal turn is a critique of rationalism and the promotion of an epistemology based on individual tacit knowledge.[21] I want to elaborate this turn here briefly by looking specifi-

---

21 Much of the neoliberal conceptual edifice was built in the context of the famous "socialist calculation debate" during the 1920s. Hayek's larger social and economic theory is derived from his often overlooked work in psychology, *The Sensory Order* (1952), in which he developed a philosophy of mind that showed the human capacity for knowledge, and thus reason, to be limited.

cally at how it emerges in Friedrich Hayek's thought. Hayek was not only one of the most influential neoliberal thinkers, his writings—and his focus on epistemology in particular—were also explicitly taken up by South African reformers in a quest to find a solution to the multiple crises of the apartheid state in the 1970s.

Hayek grounds the neoliberal project conceptually in a critique of rationalism and the Enlightenment. For him, the primary flaw of statist projects is not moral or political, but epistemological; at the heart of the rise of socialism and Keynesianism, he argues, is the rationalist belief in the human capacity for total knowledge, and hence for state intervention to effect radical change. Human beings, argues Hayek, are not innately rational, rather, what connects the "natural" field of instinct and the development of reason is culture (in earlier work referred to as "tradition" or "habit").[22] As Hayek put it in *Law, Legislation and Liberty*, "culture is neither natural nor artificial, neither genetically transmitted nor rationally designed. It is a tradition of learnt rules of conduct which have never been 'invented' and whose functions the acting individual does not understand" (Hayek 1978a: 155). Culture, conceived as a slowly, evolving set of embodied rules enabled the discipline of instincts and thus facilitated and governed the emergence of a "spontaneous order" and the development of the free society.[23] Hence, "what has made men good is neither nature nor reason but tradition" (Hayek 1978a: 160). For Hayek, then, as the quote opening this chapter suggests, freedom was a slowly evolved "artifact of civilization" and always dependent on specific forms of discipline. Freedom could only emerge through "the restraints of freedom."

In Hayek's mobilization of the concept, "culture" thus becomes central to a particular political ontology and, by extension, a resource for a specific governmental reason.[24] This conception of culture as an "ordering principle" neatly solves the central neoliberal dilemma of the

---

22   Elsewhere, Hayek more explicitly points to the usefulness of anthropology in his critique of rationalism: "If the ethnologist or social anthropologist attempts to understand other cultures, he has no doubt that the members frequently have no idea as to the reason for following particular rules, or what depends on it. Yet most modern social theorists are rarely willing to admit that the same thing applies also to our own civilisation" (Hayek 1978b: 4).

23   Knowledge of society for Hayek cannot be centralized in any institution or individual mind. The belief that social institutions can be shaped by human reason and intention—what Hayek (1978a) calls the "constructivist fallacy"—misconstrues the ways in which such institutions come into being. It is not through intentional human design, but through a slow, unconscious process of evolution defined by "tacit knowledge" and "sensory" modes of perception that most social institutions are formed (Hayek 1945, 1952; Polanyi 1966).

24   I use the term "political ontology" in Stephen Collier's (2011) sense as "propositions about what government is, about the objects on which government works, and about the ends toward which it is directed" (Collier 2011: 18; Gordon 1991).

inherent limits to knowledge and the need for "order."[25] Given culture is both what makes us reasonable and fundamentally unknowable, Hayek argues that the rationalist faith in state intervention is detrimental. Due to their hubris—believing that the social can be known—rationalists interfere with social institutions that have a logic of their own, developed over generations through an evolutionary process of selection. At the apex of cultural evolution, Hayek positions the free market society, in which a "spontaneous order" will ensure the maintenance of the "free society." For Hayek "culture" (or "tradition") thus acts as a conceptual resource to critique the rationalist state projects–fascism, socialism, and later Keynesianism—that are the political and historical horizon against which his thought develops.

Hayek's framework is based on a number of contradictions that he never resolves. Most obvious is his paradoxical attachment to both a conservative account of tradition and to liberal principles of progress and universality articulated in Kantian terms.[26] As the philosopher John Gray has suggested, this leads Hayek into a fundamental dilemma:

> When Hayek writes of markets as devices for the preservation and transmission of tacit knowledge, he views them as complex cultural institutions that are embedded in customs and traditions. It does not occur to him that this view cannot be combined with the universal claims that economic liberals . . . make for free markets. If markets are complex, deeply embedded social institutions they will vary with the cultures in which they operate (Gray 1998: 155).

While Gray thus dismisses Hayek's entire framework as conceptually and practically moribund, his identification of this tension in Hayek's work provides important clues to similar contradictions that would periodically surface, in particular as neoliberal reforms were taking shape outside Europe and the United States. For if in his formulation, neoliberal ontology assumes pre-existing, slowly evolved social institutions with an inevitable bend toward "freedom" and the "market society," how can neoliberalism be relevant to contexts where such institutions take a different form, shaped, for example, by colonial or socialist legacies? Moreover, if, as Timothy Mitchell (2009: 389) suggests, these contexts "were already formatted with

---

25 In *Law, Legislation and Liberty*, Hayek draws on Geertz in support of this argument. As Hayek, citing Geertz, puts it "Man is precisely the animal most desperately dependent on much extra-genetic, outside-the-skin control mechanisms, such cultural programs, for organizing behavior" (Geertz as cited in Hayek 1978a: 199n; Geertz 1973: 44).

26 Philip Mirowski traces Hayek's thought to a "reactionary modernism" associated with Jünger, Schmitt, Sombart, and Spengler, whose key characteristic included the attempt at reconciling "strains of German romanticism with modernist technological means-ends rationalism" (Mirowski 2011: 213).

the help of economic expertise," what modalities of translation are required in order to make neoliberal thought relevant to contexts not formatted on the model of European social modernity?

Specific and more indirect forms of intervention thus often became central to such reforms—an emphasis on gradualism rather than radical transformation, and on recoding and incorporating existing contexts in order to redirect them toward a new trajectory. As Dieter Plehwe (2009: 249) has shown in his account of the Mont Pelerin Society's debates on the Third World and colonialism in the 1950s, this reasoning was central to the neoliberal critique of modernization theory and development economics. Prominent Ordoliberal Wilhelm Röpke, for example, accused development economics of a "narrow economism/technicism" and "a lack of consideration of a wide range of spiritual and moral as well as sociological questions" (ibid.). This was of particular concern in the context of the Cold War, when many feared the destruction of "traditional cultures" would make them easy targets for socialist expansion.[27] At the same time, Röpke argued that industrialization was bound to fail, due to "the lack of a liberal tradition required to succeed in manufacturing (. . . punctuality, reliability, inclination to save and create, etc.)." A successful approach would require "endless patience," "deep human understanding," "flexible adaptation" and "*smart connections to the existing*" (Röpke as cited in Plehwe, 2009: 249; my emphasis). In other words, here the conceptual contradiction in neoliberal thought is pragmatically resolved by the possibility of *gradual* transformation and the incorporation of prior traditions, even illiberal ones. Indeed, Röpke himself infamously defended apartheid on these grounds (Röpke 1964; Slobodian 2014).[28]

In contradistinction then to modernization theory, which according to Rostow's stage model required an interventionist "push" to bring "stagnant" traditional societies to "take off" (Rostow 1960), in the 1950s, neoliberal

---

27   Neoliberal thinkers were not united on the question of the Third World. Most, however, treated the postcolonial world as an "exception" where other means would be applicable and necessary. Dieter Plehwe's research in the archives of the Mont Pelerin Society provides a fascinating account of how the MPS dealt with the questions of colonialism and postcolonial development in 1950s (Plehwe 2009).

28   Throughout the early Mont Pelerin Society meetings, the question of apartheid is a central concern. In its beginnings, the only non-Northern MPS members were South African or South Africa–based economists, including William Hutt, Ludwig Lachmann, S. Herbert Frankel, and Ralph Horwitz, who wrote and spoke frequently on apartheid South Africa at MPS meetings. Apartheid also became central to the ways in which neoliberal thinkers would later theorize development, race, and the global south. As Quinn Slobodian (2014) shows, neoliberal thought was often founded on deeply racialized world views of a "white Atlantic." Much like the colonial context elucidated the limits of liberal principles, apartheid thus could be seen as a limit case for neoliberal reform.

reformers argued for more gradual and indirect forms of intervention that would take into consideration and harness the "noneconomic." "Flexible adaptation" and "smart connections to the existing" thus bridged the contradiction between the conservative emphasis on evolved traditions and the progressivist *telos* of the "free market society." Crucially, the target of reform is not the subject itself, but the environment in which it can flourish. Here, *homo economicus* emerges as a normative and aspirational rather than ontological concept.

If, as Povinelli (2006: 13) has argued, liberalism is "phantom-like" in that it is "located nowhere but in its continual citation as the motivating logic and aspiration of dispersed and competing social and cultural experiments," neoliberalism, perhaps even more so than the classical and modern liberal traditions that preceded it, is defined not only by a pragmatic flexibility, but, in its emphasis on tradition, by a conceptual dependence on the contexts within which it is elaborated. As such, neoliberalism is indeed a "motivating logic and aspiration" rather than a fixed blueprint to be more or less perfectly realized. This reliance on the contexts in which it unfolds should not be seen as a failure of the neoliberal project "in practice," but rather as deeply inscribed in its conceptual foundations. Thus, in this sense, while liberalism *appears* to be located nowhere, it can only exist as a strategic response to an existing problem. This strategic, situated quality of neoliberal thought is observable both in neoliberal reformers like Hayek, for whom that backdrop was the rise of statist projects in Europe and, in a very different way, in apartheid-era neoliberals whose thought was shaped by the crisis of the apartheid state and the racial Fordism on which it was based.

As in so many other instances, studying the reception of neoliberal thought in the extreme context of apartheid South Africa clarifies dynamics that might in other contexts appear more opaque. Here, sections of South Africa's liberal intelligentsia believed themselves to be confronted with not one, but several illiberal obstacles: the Verwoerdian apartheid state, the Afrikaner constituency relying on and supported by the system of racial Fordism, the (then largely socialist inspired) liberation movement, and what reformers at the time deemed the "traditional socialism" of the African population. As I elaborate below, at the height of the crisis of the 1970s and 1980s, neoliberalism became both a language and an archive for a critique of apartheid, and it inspired a set of techniques that could be selectively harnessed to a particular techno-political form of counterinsurgency. Much as liberalism turned pedagogical in the colonial context (Mehta 1999), in the crisis-ridden moment of late apartheid, neoliberal reformers often opted for selective and frequently illiberal forms of interventionism in the name of safeguarding the "road to freedom."

AFTER SOWETO: RETHINKING THE URBAN

In June 1976, hundreds of students were killed during what came to be known as the Soweto Uprising. The event of 1976 catapulted South Africa back into international consciousness. The black-and-white image of the dying thirteen-year-old student, Hector Pieterson, being carried by a teenage boy and accompanied by his anguished sister, circulated globally and became iconic for the repressive violence of apartheid. And yet, less spectacularly, 1976 also marked a turning point in apartheid modalities of urban rule. While workers had become increasingly militant, with the 1973 Durban strikes as the most visible, forceful sign, the students who rose up in Soweto—many inspired by the Black Consciousness Movement—were a political subject that appeared new to the apartheid state. The immediate response was violent repression, leading to the killing of nearly 500 students. And although repression continued to be the main response to any sign of overt resistance, the Soweto Uprising had hit the core of grand-apartheid strategies of rule. Indeed, the very excess of violence with which the protesters were met was a sign of the state's inability to predict or understand the intensity of urban revolt.

The Soweto Uprising was an "event" that could not be readily apprehended within the existing logic of apartheid.[29] Parliamentary debates taking place as the uprising was ongoing, provide insights into the radically divergent attributions of causality and suggestions for remedial action. While many *verkrampte* (conservative) politicians saw in the "riots" the dangers of "urban terrorism" and "communist infiltration," liberal representatives often primarily focused on the abysmal living conditions in the townships and locations.[30] Most striking here is how little political elites of all stripes in fact appeared to know about the townships. It is not surprising, then, that the aftermath of 1976 witnessed the emergence of a myriad of research efforts, conferences, books, and commissions of inquiry that sought to comprehend the subject in revolt.

While immediate responses to the protests—articulated most clearly in the Cillié Commission set up to investigate "the riots"—variously suggested that the school children had fallen victim to "outside agitators" or, ironically, to their radical parents who, it was claimed, had sent them into the front lines, the larger response over the next few years made it clear that the Soweto Uprising became the trigger for a more fundamental rethinking of grand-apartheid forms of rule. Motivated by both security and

---

29   In this sense, 1976 was an event in Janet Roitman's terms (2005: 22) a "productive moment in which the concepts and suppositions that serve to establish the most appropriate means and ends of power are challenged and rethought."

30   See, e.g., "Riots in Soweto and Elsewhere" (Hansard, June 17–21 1976), col. 9632 ff.

economic concerns, over the ten years following the uprising, the apartheid government contemplated and partially introduced a number of reforms that, either by design or in effect, moved away from the grand-apartheid ideologies that had shaped both economic and urban policies up until this point. Importantly, such "reforms" did not ultimately shake the basis of minority rule; indeed, they primarily provided new forms of rationalizing apartheid and new proposals for governmental interventions to prop up minority rule. What I want to focus on in discussing these reforms here is the centrality of neoliberal ideas, on the one hand, and the increasing importance of the administrative sphere—infrastructure and housing in particular—on the other.

In response to the organic crisis of the 1970s, the South African government embarked on "total strategy." First announced by then–Defense Minister P. W. Botha in the 1977 White Paper on Defense, total strategy was a multipronged initiative that included military, economic, social, and political interventions to protect the white regime against what it claimed was a "total onslaught" from internal and external enemies alike. In order to counter these perceived challenges, Botha argued it was necessary to take "interdependent and co-ordinated action in all fields—military, psychological, economic, political, sociological, technological, diplomatic, ideological, cultural, etc. [W]e are today involved in a war" (as cited in Mann 1988: 54).

Total strategy was, at one level, a program of counterinsurgency that sought to bring security concerns to bear on all aspects of life and entailed the heavy militarization of ever-increasing spheres of society and state. However, it was also inspired by neoliberal reforms taking place elsewhere. As Michael Mann (1988: 56) observed, total strategy was "part of the global anti-statist crusade that has, in the era of Reagan and Thatcher, been described as 'monetarism.'" To counteract economic decline, the South African government followed the trends it saw developing in the United States and the UK, seeking to adopt monetarist measures and to reduce spending. And yet, Mann continued, this application in South Africa was "contradictory" since it was "applied in the context of a reformist initiative" in which selective state spending to deal with the political crisis would ultimately be central (ibid.). Thus, in South Africa, monetarist attempts at restructuring the economy ran into the countervailing need for *more* state intervention in order to address the political crisis. What Gelb and Innes (1985) called the "double-bind of monetarism" in South Africa thus ultimately effected a transformation not a reduction in state intervention and spending (cf. Fine 1995).

Many of the reforms proposed at the time were influenced by free market or monetarist principles, including, for example a move toward liberalization first advocated by the De Kock Commission on monetary policy in 1978 and later by the Kleu Commission on industrial strategy in 1983.[31] Most attention, however, was given to the question of urbanization, and, specifically, to the question of "urban blacks." In the late 1970s, two commissions of inquiry—known as the Riekert and Wiehahn Commissions—were set up in order to make sense of and to devise policies to deal with the question of labor and the related one of the urban black population. Both commissions arrayed the diverse set of dynamics that confronted the apartheid state during the 1970s—the rising labor protests, the inability to police influx control, the economic crisis, the impact of the liberations taking place in bordering countries—into coherent "problems" that could then be responded to with solutions (cf. Ashforth 1990; Hindson 1987a). Indeed, as specific problematizations of late-apartheid crises, these commissions provided perhaps the most literal elaboration of a new political ontology, which brought new realities into being and rendered the urban intelligible as a field of intervention.

As Adam Ashforth (1990) has argued, the Riekert Commission, which had been set up to investigate "manpower utilization," envisioned the decentralization, deracialization, and depoliticization of separate development by dissolving the state's bifurcation and instead turning influx control into an administrative matter of the lower tiers of government. Apart from novel dividing strategies and new discourses of security, Riekert also, and for the first time, introduced "a commitment to 'free enterprise'" for urban township residents that was "seen as a means of deflating the communist 'onslaught'" (Posel 1984: 3–4). Similarly, the Wiehahn Commission suggested,

> [F]ull involvement, participation and sharing in the system of free enterprise by all population groups with as little government intervention as possible would not only give all groups a stake in the system but would ensure a common loyalty to both the system and the country (RSA 1979).

In practice, this meant that while migrant labor and persons without Section 10 (urban residence) rights were to be cast out and policed more forcefully, urban residents were promised training and more job security and mobility within the urban areas in the hope they would develop into "labor aristocrats" (Ajulu 1981: 22) who would act as a buffer against the rising tides of resistance.[32] Thus, selective deracialization was to be achieved

---

31   Similarly, it was in the 1970s that many projects of privatization were first contemplated. See, for example, Stephen Sparks' work on the privatization of SASOL begun in the late 1970s (Sparks 2013).

32   Section 10 rights, that is the right to remain in urban areas, were indicated in the passbooks or "dompas" that each black person had to carry at all times.

by separating urban from rural populations—"insiders" from "outsiders." It is in the form of urban incorporation that we can see the first steps not only toward an explicit break with the project of *Volkskapitalisme*, but also the construction of a new regime of control that relied on, yet also considerably diverged from, earlier forms of governing the townships.

Crucially, the commission also envisaged the increasing decentralization of township control from the Bantu Affairs Administration Boards (BAABs) to the establishment of black local authorities, which would in turn pave the way for the withdrawal of subsidies from and privatization of housing and infrastructure services.[33] Thus, "the full costs of reproduction were to be imposed directly through rates and taxes levied on consumers, home owners and African businessmen in the townships" (Hindson 1987a: 84). Rather than attaching separate development primarily to persons (ethnic and racial identification via passes, labor bureaus, and so forth), which had turned it into a political question of rights, influx control would be shifted "to the nonpolitical sphere of the administration of 'things'— houses and jobs—into which people fit. Control and justification could then be achieved by simple recourse to the 'economic rationality' established and validated through the production and distributions of material things" (Ashforth 1990: 212).

Given up in such a scheme, then—at least in theory—was the earlier apartheid state project with its emphasis on direct planning of population movements and its faith in centralized state knowledge and intervention. Instead, what emerged in the late 1970s was an ideal of a decentralized, technocratic administration, which would "structure compliance with authority into the basic conditions of social life, rather than make it a direct result of a more 'political' exercise of power with manifold implicit questions of 'justice'" (ibid.). In other words, apartheid was here envisaged as moving toward a more oblique, molecular mode of exerting control. In the process, it was hoped that central political questions could be turned into administrative, technical, and, indeed, often infrastructural problems. While Riekert's core strategy—the insider-outsider division—failed, in part because it ultimately held on to the apartheid fiction of independent Bantustans, this thrust toward a decentralized techno-politics would define South Africa in the years to come.[34]

33   Though *de facto*, Soweto often continued to receive subsidies, with the aim of tempering risks of further revolts (cf. Seekings 1990: 13).

34   As Hindson (1987b) noted, in assuming a clear separation between urban workers and rural migrant workers, Riekert disavowed the existence of a large and increasing commuter workforce that straddled the two spheres. The envisaged reforms foundered in the face of numerous challenges from trade unions, squatter struggles, sabotage from local administration board bureaucracies, and, crucially for my purposes here, urban resistance to the institution of black local authorities.

Before returning to the centrality of infrastructure and the administrative in such reforms, it is helpful to elaborate on how the political rationality of apartheid was transformed in the face of the crises of the 1970s and in conversation with projects of neoliberal reform happening elsewhere. The post-1976 problematization of apartheid took a variety of forms, many of which reflected the increasing ideological struggles within the apartheid state. Discourses of free enterprise, as Deborah Posel (1984) noted, entered total strategy in the form of a technocratic rationality whereby government actions were to be judged on grounds of efficiency rather than in ideological terms. Central to these were the increasing popularity of (neo)liberal ideas amongst sections of the Afrikaner elite. As Posel (1984: 4) suggested, policy debates during the late 1970s increasingly relied on a "new language" that not only became an "instrument of control itself," but also for the first time since the establishment of apartheid relied on liberal parameters.

The ambiguity and contradictoriness of this break with previous apartheid rationalities is most apparent in the discussions between *verkrampte* (conservative) and *verligte* (moderate, literally: enlightened) Afrikaners in government circles (Charney 1984). In her discussion of these debates, Posel noted that from the 1970s two discourses came to co-exist: the Verwoerdian idea of apartheid that re-affirmed a moral defense of separate development, and a more pragmatic one emphasizing adaptability and "purposive reforms" (ibid.: 11). An important aspect of the latter reasoning was the need for an urban black middle class whose values would protect against "total onslaught," and it is here that neoliberal theories that had risen to prominence in Europe and the United States could be productively drawn on. Indeed, "free enterprise" and "economic liberalism" became key words in the larger effort to reform apartheid. While much literature at the time was preoccupied with showing the multiple ways in which the reforms fell short, with many suggesting that they were no more than a sham (Hindson 1983; Wages Commission 1979), here, I want to explore and take seriously the modes of reasoning they relied upon, attending in particular to the ways in which neoliberal ideas—and Hayek's more specifically—were received and repurposed by late-apartheid reformers. Thus, my focus is on the political rationalities that animated these reforms and on the ways in which infrastructure was mobilized as a solution to a diverse set of problems.

FREEDOM, WELFARE AND ORDER (1978)

In 1978, two years after the Soweto Uprising, Jan Lombard, one of the most influential South African economists writing at the time and later deputy governor of the South African Reserve Bank, sought to assess the relevance of the Hayekian framework for South Africa. Lombard's account is of interest not only because he was a frequent economic advisor of the National Party (NP) government, but also because he spoke from within an established Afrikaner hegemony, rather than as part of a more established liberal circle that had often critiqued government on liberal grounds.[35] As part of a larger *verligte* critique, Lombard's was a pragmatic search for a way out of the crises of apartheid, rather than a utopian liberal blueprint or a radical critique of the apartheid state.

The central question he addressed in two publications—*Freedom, Welfare and Order* (1978) and *On Economic Liberalism in South Africa* (1979)— was the problem of the applicability of "economic liberalism" to South Africa. Arguing that separate development was a "sinking philosophy" whose emphasis on centralized economic control and continual attachment to "race" was responsible for South Africa's "peculiar political problem" (Lombard 1979), Lombard proceeded to outline how "economic liberalism" could provide solutions to South Africa's multiple dilemmas. Structuring his account is the problem of "urbanization" that animated many of the debates in the aftermath of the Soweto Uprising. For Lombard, it was the increasing breakdown of the central apartheid strategy of influx control and the failure of the grand-apartheid plan of instituting Bantustans that necessitated a rethinking of received ideas of governance. The neoliberal framework was attractive to Lombard, precisely because neoliberalism (unlike classical liberalism) included a focus on "order" and a gradualist approach to reform, for Lombard did not want to entirely abandon "separate development," but to re-invent its foundations to make it compatible with liberal norms. This proposal for a neoliberal reform of separate development in order to facilitate what Lombard described in explicitly Hayekian fashion as the "evolutionary progress towards the free society" (ibid.: 27) had several key points, all of which converged on the question of the level of preparation of the South African population for a liberal society.

Drawing on neoliberal theorists, and most centrally on Hayek, Lombard argued that "individual freedom and individual responsibility are two sides of the same coin" and that, hence, liberal society could only function in a context where the "sense of responsibility in the society is of a highly economic kind, i.e. if people are able and are willing to read the signs of the market, to make the necessary calculations and to act upon their findings" (Lombard 1978: 69). Crucially, Lombard argued that South Africa was unlike "common societies" due to "differences in the economic rationality

35   For more radical "free market" proposals inspired by Hayek et al. which circulated during the 1980s, see Wassenaar 1977 and Louw 1986, both affiliated with South Africa's Free Market Foundation. Both viewed the "free market" as the panacea for apartheid's political and economic crisis (cf. Innes 1987).

and productivity" (ibid.: 26). Later in the book, he elaborated: "the majority of Black and Coloured workers in the urban areas of South Africa
lack the ability to use skills and knowledge with the functional competence
needed for meeting the requirements of adult living as *responsible* and *free*
citizens of a *democratic* society" (Lombard 1978: 72, emphasis in original).
Interesting here, and defining for the reception of neoliberal ideas in South
Africa, is the elision performed by the term "free society": the absence of
"economic rationality" entails the absence of "political rationality," that is,
in one stroke economic and democratic reform are conflated. In *On Economic Liberalism*, Lombard more explicitly elaborated the paradox often at
the heart of neoliberal reforms:

> Development economists talk about "the human factor" in this connection. For
> a liberal minded person such expression, which makes human beings the input
> of some total material concept, is almost anathema. In a sense, however, it is true
> that the liberal order depends for its success upon such human qualities as the
> will and the ability of the individual members of society to make their own deci-
> sions, to calculate the costs and benefits to themselves of alternative behaviour
> (Lombard 1979: 38–39).

Lombard here implicitly articulates the argument more explicitly spelled
out by Gray: the "spontaneous order" advocated by Hayek and others in
fact required specific forms of pedagogy and intervention that would make
individuals take on the roles envisaged for them. Indeed, Lombard's solution to this dilemma was that neoliberalism would need to be preceded by
substantial reforms in order to succeed in South Africa. For these reasons,
Lombard suggested, a period of "benevolent paternalism" "in preparation for freedom" must necessarily precede the liberal society. In South
Africa—"a culturally underdeveloped country"—such paternalism would
include a "programme of fundamental cultural reforms" (1979: 35). During such reforms—regrettably—"the principle of democracy cannot yet
come fully into play" for those "people who are being prepared culturally
for their future responsibilities as mature and free men" (ibid.: 39). He
concluded: "Since a liberal order depends wholly upon the consistency and
rationality of individual behaviour, the transition from paternalism to liberalism must be determined by circumstances" (ibid.: 51). In other words,
the key obstacles to the applicability of neoliberalism—culture, behavioral
dispositions—would require reform.[36] Neoliberalism emerges here not
only as a critique of apartheid (and the racialized Keynesianism it upheld),

---

36   Lombard's pronouncements on the lack of economic rationality are not isolated instances, but were widely used to justify ongoing apartheid. Stanley Greenberg's fascinating
study of the rationality of apartheid-era bureaucrats in the 1980s revealed similar ideas, with

but also as a new matrix to rationalize group differentiation as an exceptional, but necessary precursor to economic liberalism.

Importantly, the *logic* of exception has been transformed. While grand-apartheid ideologues viewed "urban blacks" as nonpersons, that is, as persons who in the future would be accommodated in the "traditional homelands"; now, "urban blacks" were believed to be in the midst of a transition period, a pedagogical stage toward becoming "free persons." While the ultimate effect remained the same—the black urban population would continue to be denied political rights, now on the basis of indefinite deferral—the rationality that authorized apartheid had shifted. Simultaneously, the continued denial of political rights could be rationalized as a necessary aspect of the "economic road to democracy," as Lombard put it. Reforms, Lombard suggested, would include the separation of groups based on economic rather than racial distinctions while maintaining a territorially based system of differentiation. Thus he proposed to move from racial "group areas" to (ostensibly) nonracial "depressed areas" along with a simultaneous effort toward the decentralization of the state with the aim of depoliticizing local government. Decentralization would "limit the area of politics in social affairs as much as possible" (ibid.: 16) and remove the question of citizenship rights that were at the heart of political struggles.

Lombard's writings enable us to trace the contours of a neoliberal techno-politics by which increasing issues and domains would become subject to administrative-technical and often indirect or private forms of government. Thus, it was hoped they could be removed from the public domain and, by extension, from the terrain of nationalist claims by the liberation movement. It is important to note that neoliberal thought was not received as a blueprint. Rather, reformulated and adapted by practical thinkers like Lombard, neoliberal ideas were operationalized as a part of a larger program of countering the antiapartheid movement. Beyond decentralization, this focus on depoliticization could also be observed in other "classically" neoliberal reforms into the 1980s. Thus, for example, while South African proponents of privatization rehearsed many of the arguments then current elsewhere in the world that often focused on increased efficiency and fiscal austerity, they also motivated privatization as an intervention that could depoliticize central areas of persistent struggle, in particular housing and infrastructure. Throughout such reforms, the focus was on the "diminution of the political" (Greenberg 1987: 146), usually by reframing political questions as administrative ones. Despite (or perhaps because of) the ultimate failures of many such reforms, we can here locate some of the conceptual underpinnings for the techno-political terrain on

---

bureaucrats often explaining in culturalist terms the impossibility of a "free market" system in the black areas (Greenberg 1987).

which the antiapartheid struggle unfolded during the 1980s, a terrain that continues to mediate contemporary struggles and protests in the present.

REFORMING THE URBAN

Although Lombard's reflections on the possibilities of "free enterprise" to solve the systemic crisis remained on a largely abstract terrain and were never implemented in the exact way he had suggested, such ideas would soon wield influence in *verligte* policy circles.[37] At around the same time, throughout the late 1970s, there was an increasingly multidisciplinary effort at understanding what was widely referred to as the problem of "the urban black." Beginning with the Cillié Commission set up to investigate the reasons for the Soweto Uprising, there was a sudden interest in the *subjectivity* of the black urban resident, including his (and sometimes her) attitudes, interests, and values. An edited collection published in 1978 by the School of Business Leadership at the University of South Africa (UNISA), Pretoria, entitled *South Africa's Urban Blacks: Prospects and Challenges*, provides a good sense of the explosion of interest in this new subject. Notably, the volume begins with an epigraph from Lombard's *Freedom, Welfare and Order* that encapsulates the motivation for the larger project: "by the standards of students of the liberal principles, the southern African plural urban society is in need of a great deal of reform before it could be expected to function well" (Lombard 1978, as cited in Marais and van der Kooy 1978: 9).

"Political needs," the editors write, make it imperative that urban blacks be studied "at the level of the human being in its entirety" (ibid.: 16). Studying the "problem" would be a prerequisite for reform aimed at enabling "the black man to become a city-dweller able to cope with the challenges of the modern city" (ibid.). Although the apartheid state throughout the 1950s and 1960s had regarded and treated urban residents as "temporary sojourners" who would eventually find their political homes in the Bantustans, the Soweto Uprising had made clear the "permanence of urban blacks" (ibid.). In the book, over a dozen chapters by social scientists, economists, and psychologists examine every aspect of urban black life— from religious beliefs to basic provisioning, work, education, and political behavior. In many of the essays, the "urban black" emerges as a mysterious creature about whom little is known. And while the theory of urban

---

37   Indeed, Lombard himself would play a role in a variety of such reforms (see, for examples, his report for ASSOCOM, Lombard and Pisanie 1985). However, I am here primarily concerned with the general conceptual framework of his thought and the logic of reform that his writings articulated, which became influential and resonated in a diversity of spheres.

adaptation, so prominent since the colonial period, still runs through the collection, with problems of "tribal acculturation" looming latently in the background, the striking feature of the book is the increasing realization that the "urban black" is not only part of South Africa's modernity, but in fact central to solving apartheid's crises.

Lombard's abstract identification of the problem of economic rationality is here backed up by research and data. Most of the contributions are defined by clear racist assumptions and premises, but their starting points— and the *specific logic* of racist reasoning on which they draw—differ from previous understandings in several respects. "Urban blacks," while savvy in many ways, are shown to have a tendency to misread market signals, to irrational consumption and money spending, and to "misunderstand" commercial advertising. In the collection, this lack of economic rationality is emphasized in particular in psychological studies pointing to the need for reforms that "emphasize the development of an individual system of values which will motivate each individual to work for the improvement of the community as well as for economic progress" (Marais and van der Kooy 1978: 95). Counteracting the "natural system of African socialism," reforms must "cultivate a desire to advance themselves" (ibid.). One of the most important tasks would be the introduction of a discipline attentive to long-term goals rather than the satisfaction of "immediate needs": "Instead of his behaviour being regulated by custom, his own choice must determine his behavior, a mechanism which has not yet been formed" (ibid.: 90). Another contributor similarly emphasized the need for an "internalisation of business values that will ensure an effective black contribution to the economy of South Africa" (ibid.: 237). In other words, in studies such as these, the black urban population emerges as deficient, but *potential* economic subjects whose values need to be transformed to enable them to participate fully in the market.[38]

Such studies often had immediate policy implications—indeed, a year later the collection would be cited approvingly by Prime Minister P. W. Botha, and his government increasingly drew on such academic expertise in the formulation of new policy measures, particularly in Soweto

---

38   This collection was just one of many research projects under way in the late 1970s and early 1980s to establish the conditions for the "free market" in South Africa. Another one entitled "Project Free Enterprise" produced studies dealing with similar problematics, such as "An Analysis of the Comprehension of Business and Free Enterprise Concepts among Corporate Employees in South Africa" (University of South Africa 1984). Businesses also came to view the townships as a new market, and advertising campaigns were increasingly produced with the black consumer in mind. As one advertising executive put it, "Needs are the same, but motivations are different and these spring from our social environment [and] tend to shape our aspirations." See "Getting to Know Mrs. Mokete: Why do black people choose one product over another?" *Financial Mail*, June 16, 1978, 888.

(cf. Seekings 1988b: 13). Lombard himself would, throughout the 1980s and early 1990s, be a central advisor to government, often overseeing commissions or the writing of policy documents. While this sudden interest in the subjectivity of the black population was strongest in the urban areas, it was also extended to "development" efforts in the Bantustans. In 1980, the Department of Co-operation and Development (previously the Department of Bantu Administration and Development) established a "Committee on Motivating Studies" staffed by members from the Human Science Research Council (HSRC), the Council for Scientific and Industrial Research (CSIR), and the School of Business at the University of South Africa (UNISA), which had produced the collection on "urban blacks" cited above. The Committee was set up with the primary aim "to look intensively and in a co-ordinated way in a national or ethnic context at the psychological make-up of the Black man, his vulnerabilities and susceptibilities, his likes and dislikes and his own particular view of reality" and to "evaluate the place and part of the Black man in the Western capitalist system and the demands it makes on the individual, community and nation." The "exceptional challenge," the report suggested, was to establish "techniques to motivate members of the Black nations or ethnic groups to achieve more in regard to the accelerated economic growth and development" (RSA 1981). For, the report continued,

> The Westerner's reaction to change is virtually objective because changes are not in conflict with the Westerner's way of life, thinking, values and behaviour patterns. . . . Because he knows the mechanics of his own culture, he is capable of approaching and solving in a scientific way problems that economic change and prosperity may bring about. Ethnologists, sociologists and other professionals, however, are in agreement that the Black man does not react objectively to facts. He is more likely to react to images of facts which are based on his own specific non-material vision of the reality, which is largely mystical. If it is added that the Black man is still strongly linked to the rhythm of his own culture and that innovations and changes are often seen as a threat to the existing . . . order, intensive research is warranted (ibid.).

A 1984 Government Report entitled "Measures which Restrict the Functioning of a Free Market Orientated System in South Africa" similarly noted "less sophisticated consumers" as one set of obstacles to the free market:

> Coming from a culture of poverty and underdevelopment, they are often unaware of the elementary principles of personal or domestic budgeting and consequently buy injudiciously. . . . [T]heir predilection for immediate usage is strong and . . . they are often inclined to build up too much debt. . . . They often

react irrationally to advertisements and allow themselves to be easily misled into ignoring their real needs (RSA 1984: 149–150).

The report, while focused throughout on the vulnerability of the "less sophisticated consumer," moved away from the Verwoerdian idea of "total protection," suggesting that "overprotection of the consumer limits experience which will enable him ultimately to look after his own interest in the market" (ibid.: 153). Similarly, the focus was no longer explicitly on race, but on culture and, more specifically, on a "culture of poverty" and associated behavioral traits. While this still authorized the state's continued racist paternalism, there was increasing agreement that black residents could and should be exposed to "free market forces" in the hope that such forces would have a pedagogical effect. The market, previously thought of as a destructive force against which the "traditional homelands" would have to be protected, was now increasingly invested with ordering, pedagogical capacities.

Particularly striking in such documents is the extent to which research into the subjectivity of the urban black population was perceived as a radically new approach that would provide a key to the multiple problems faced by the apartheid state. While the black population had always been a concern for government and many commissions and research efforts had inquired into "its" behavior and movements, what was indeed new was the focused attention on the subjectivity of individual black residents. The black laborer, previously conceived as an object ("manpower") to be moved around and disposed via labor bureaus, always replaceable by the next laborer to be channeled to the mines, industries, and farms, was suddenly transformed into a subject with differential needs, aspirations, and values.[39] Similarly, urban black residents, previously viewed as a homogenous mass in perennial transition toward relocation to their "traditional home" in the Bantustans, were now viewed as potential market participants (consumers, entrepreneurs, and property owners) whose values, disposition and internal differentiations mattered. Indeed, black subjectivity here emerged as the key—both obstacle and promise—for the success of wider "liberal" reforms.[40]

---

39   See here also Deborah Posel's discussion of the intricate historical connection between consumption and race in South Africa (Posel 2010).

40   Although reformers often cited "African traditions" as primary obstacles, it was often in fact white local bureaucrats who were uneasy with or, indeed, positively hostile to such liberalizing reforms. As Stanley Greenberg's study of apartheid officials in the 1970s and 1980s showed, "labor officials who have been tutored in an administered system find it very difficult to comprehend the market." Indeed, one labor bureau official interviewed by Greenberg asked, in apparent bewilderment, "Isn't supply and demand the same as influx control?" Others were actively opposed or even sabotaged such reforms, suggesting, for example, that if labor was no longer channeled via labor bureaus "the employer would have to get his own labor; he would not end up with the best type of employee" (as cited in Greenberg 1987: 156).

This interest in subjectivity was matched by a new set of techniques that increasingly sought to move away from direct racial discrimination and toward a focus instead on accommodating black demands in a limited fashion and on the creation of an environment in which black residents would be exposed to "market forces." One of the most crucial decisions taken in the aftermath of the Soweto Uprising was the Community Councils Act of 1977. The act replaced the advisory Urban Bantu Councils, which had become known as "Useless Boys' Clubs" due to their powerlessness, with elected Community Councils that held an enlarged set of responsibilities in the day-to-day management of township affairs, including housing allocation.[41] They were introduced in part to act as a more effective buffer between the central state and township residents. In particular, as Murray (1987: 121) noted, it was hoped they would "control the means of collective consumption in the township more efficiently." While these councils were presented as sovereign institutions of local self-government, most decision-making power in fact remained with the Administration Boards, and they remained illegitimate in the eyes of most township residents. The Administration Boards, though officially designated as simply neutral executors of the councils' directives, de facto retained control over all key decisions, from the allocation of housing to infrastructure provision. Thus, here again, the administrative and the political were blurred and often became indistinguishably intertwined. As I elaborate in the next chapter, such processes of rendering the sources of local state power illegible by turning them into technical operations—a specific late-apartheid form of technopolitics—became a key modality of apartheid rule in the 1970s and 80s.

Following the Wiehahn and Riekert commissions' recommendations, many township reforms were directed at improving the living conditions of the urban black population. This would introduce what Morris and Padayachee (1988) termed a "selective Fordism" both to stimulate demand and to ensure security by creating an urban black middle class that could act as a buffer against the inhabitants of the Bantustans, in particular against migrant labor. As part of this effort of dividing urban insiders from rural outsiders, urban areas were also promised upgrades, selective forms of liberalization, and fewer restrictions on mobility. Urban residence, previously tied to passbooks indicating belonging and articulated in racial and ethnic terms, now became intricately tied to officially nonracial material and administrative categories: to housing and infrastructure, on the one hand, and to employment, on the other. Here we see the beginning of a

41 Local franchise was limited to residents who were registered occupants of council houses, and without a criminal record. These provisions de facto excluded large numbers of township residents and were intended to drive a wedge between "insiders" and "outsiders," similar to those advocated by the Riekert Commission.

conception and deployment of infrastructure and the administrative domain as a field of intervention through which society and its environment
could be shaped in a less direct fashion. In this context, neoliberal ideas
emphasizing decentralization, privatization, and the removal of overt intervention by the central state could be selectively drawn on to rationalize
and operationalize a set of reforms through which modalities of apartheid
rule could be shifted whilst holding on to its basic premise of minority rule.

This increasing attention to infrastructure by both government and private actors can be seen in the diversity of projects embarked upon at the
time. In Soweto, the immediate aftermath of the 1976 Uprising witnessed
a mass of programs and expertise designed to practically address the "problems" of urban black life. Importantly, particularly in light of the concerns
of this book, many central aspects of such reforms were technical, with
upgrades in housing and infrastructure given particular prominence. Thus,
the multiple crises of the apartheid state were increasingly displaced onto
an ostensibly apolitical administrative terrain.

As the center of black political life, and perceived as the "mirror of the
South African soul," Soweto was often prioritized in such reforms (Bonner
and Segal 1998: 106). While a variety of large-scale infrastructure schemes
in Soweto were planned in this period, many never saw the light of day as
resistance continued in the townships.[42] One project was the electrification
of Soweto embarked on by the Soweto Council in 1979 and developed
by a private consortium, Engineering Management Services. Importantly,
the capital costs for this project were displaced onto residents in the form
of a levy, which would later provide a central trigger for the Soweto rent
boycott. Meanwhile, the private sector was actively engaged in lobbying
for a new housing policy that would give ninety-nine-year leasehold rights
to township residents. Similarly, the "informal sector," much maligned and
heavily policed by the apartheid state, was now held up as a solution to
rising unemployment and as "an important training ground for Black entrepreneurs" (Sutcliffe, n.d.: 30).

While the state wavered in its support for reform initiatives in the townships, most such projects were undertaken by the private sector, and in particular by the Urban Foundation, an organization with a clear neoliberal
bent. The Foundation had been launched in the immediate aftermath of
the Soweto Uprising, after a business conference entitled "Quality of Life
in Urban Communities" organized by Harry Oppenheimer and Anton Ru-
pert. Funded by a conglomerate of large South African companies—by far
the largest donors being Anglo-American and other Oppenheimer Group

---

42 Such initiatives included, for example, the Development Guidance System drawn
up by the Ecoplan Consortium, a group of engineers, planners, architects, and economists
contracted by the Soweto council (see Ecoplan 1979; Mandy 1984: 206).

mining companies—the Urban Foundation sought to involve the private sector in the improvement of living conditions in the townships "on a non-political non-racial basis" (as cited in Lea 1982: 207). The establishment of the Urban Foundation was perhaps the most apparent sign of the extent to which business and government interests had diverged, with the former holding on to a reformed version of "separate development" and the latter increasingly becoming aware that a "free enterprise system" would ulti-mately be incompatible with it.[43]

The Urban Foundation's activities in the townships were designed, as one report put it, to create a system "in which the advantages of the free enterprise system are accessible to all" (ibid.). Importantly, the Founda-tion viewed its infrastructural work in Soweto as apolitical. Initially, as one member put it in retrospect, its projects were based on a "distinction be-tween essentially political problems (which were not within the compe-tence of private enterprise to change) and 'those problems which it is their legitimate concern to take note of and, if possible, help solve'" (Robbins 1997: 6). Given this distinction, at first the Foundation's work was primar-ily aimed at improving urban living standards (mostly through upgrades in infrastructures) and the creation of a Black middle class including efforts to "encourag[e] the adoption of free enterprise values within the urban Black communities as a counter to the growth of socialism" (Lea 1982: 207). Very soon though, the Foundation began lobbying the government to remove discriminatory legislation. The increasing power and influence wielded by the Urban Foundation is evidenced by the fact that its staff "virtually wrote" the 1986 White Paper on Urbanization (Robbins 1997: 12).

A crucial aspect of these reforms in the 1970s was housing. Most impor-tantly, the Urban Foundation successfully lobbied for security of tenure, which in 1978 led to the introduction of ninety-nine-year leaseholds for township residents "so that private sector involvement could begin" (ibid.: 8). Housing, the Foundation argued, was "being used as a socio-political tool by the government" (ibid.). The liberalization of the housing market would thus not only open it up to private sector involvement, but also de-politicize it by removing it from direct control by the central state. Giving urban residents ninety-nine-year leases, could, it was hoped, turn township residents into de facto property owners, who could, for example, use their tenure to register mortgage loans.[44] Although "site and service" schemes had been important throughout the administration of townships and lo-cations in South Africa, they increased in importance during the 1980s

43   For examinations of this gradual divergence of capital and government and the ideo-logical disagreements within both government and Afrikaner elites, see, e.g., Charney 1984; Giliomee 1982; Greenberg 1987.

44   Title deeds were not granted, as they would have entitled residents to full citizenship rights.

and early 1990s.[45] The Urban Foundation supported and promoted such projects throughout and often linked them to the concept of "self-help," drawing on the ideas of John F. C. Turner, a central figure within the informal housing debates who preceded contemporary neoliberal thinkers on housing such as Hernando De Soto. As a former member of the Urban Foundation explained to me during an interview:

> [Self-help] was a housing approach that said that to the extent that people make their own decisions and are involved in the delivery, it was a developmental process that actually developed the people and made those people more able to deal with life in some way. It was empowering, this is the word we'd use today. It was never used then. . . . And it grew out of the fact that a lot of people were housed in government rental stock and that they had all the dependency stuff that just keeps the cycle of poverty going. You know, the hinge on my door is squeaking, so I call up the housing office to fix my door.

It is here that we can see the link between the increasing focus on urban infrastructures and the rising concern with the subjectivity of the urban black population. In the late 1970s, the private sector viewed housing and basic services as one of the crucial ways to achieve "orderly" reform toward liberalization and "free enterprise." Importantly, in the years to come, this strategic mobilization of infrastructure as a terrain on which to achieve political goals would intensify. If one of the aims of the reforms that began in the late 1970s was the depoliticization of infrastructure and basic services, it in fact achieved the opposite, as the increasingly militant township-based struggles of the following decade showed. In the 1980s infrastructure became increasingly bound up with security concerns and central to the state's efforts of counterinsurgency.

CONCLUSIONS

Many of the "reforms" envisaged by Lombard and others and begun by organizations like the Urban Foundation were never fully implemented or otherwise failed in their ultimate objectives, as they could not and would not address the question of political rights. Partly as a result, mass-based resistance to apartheid surged in the 1980s. And yet, the political rationalities developed here continued to be of influence in the decades to come.

45   Bond et al. track the history of housing policy and the increasing importance of site and service schemes, in particular with the 1991 Independent Development Trust, which was nicknamed "I do Toilets," because they only provided for the most basic of infrastructures (Bond, Dor, and Ruiters 1999: 5).

At the same time, their practical, if haphazard and often unintended effects produced the political terrain upon which apartheid was contested during the 1980s. What emerges in the late 1970s, then, is a particular, neoliberal mode of rethinking apartheid. Neoliberal thought provided the conceptual resources both for a pragmatic critique of grand-apartheid forms of rule and for an alternative set of techniques to *gradually* reform apartheid while holding on to minority rule. Here, neoliberalism emerges not as a ready-made project imposed from the outside, but rather as a series of adaptable concepts and techniques that built upon and often worked through pre-existing contexts. In post-1976 South Africa, this conceptual tool kit could be flexibly drawn on, upholding certain aspects of "separate development" while transforming others, recoding apartheid modalities of rule rather than rejecting them outright.

Illuminated here then also was the neoliberal dilemma between a conservative attachment to "tradition" and the normative *telos* of a "free society" that in the late-apartheid period was solved by a project of reform aimed at the habits and subjectivity of black urban residents. It is this conceptual dilemma—of both removing state influence and shaping the state in a "liberal" direction—that became exceptionally visible as it was translated to the fraught late-apartheid moment. More than elucidating neoliberalism's internal paradoxes, however, these contradictions were explicitly articulated by reformers and, indeed, became an integral aspect of reforms, often authorizing illiberal means to achieve liberal goals.

Finally, in the late-apartheid period, neoliberal thought offered an account of "reform" centered not on the state, but on aspects of daily life, including most centrally a particular kind of techno-politics that aimed at promoting adaptation to the market and at mobilizing state intervention in a seemingly apolitical "administrative" way. In the process, it was hoped, vital political questions could be decentralized, deracialized, and depoliticized. Such reforms increasingly drew on smaller-scale techno-political strategies aimed at the construction of an environment in which the market and its participants could emerge. It is here, too, that the seeds were sown for the emergence of the many localized struggles during the 1980s that took infrastructures as their terrain and object of struggle.

Read from this perspective, the contemporary politics of infrastructure, including the powerful opposition to Operation Gcin'amanzi, can be located not merely as a response to commodification or novel forms of accumulation, but also, and equally importantly, as an ongoing concern with long-standing and often more vexed questions regarding belonging, citizenship, and political community. As later chapters will show, the neoliberal reforms in the postapartheid period were not only built on the remnants of these earlier projects of reform, they often also bear more than a family resemblance to them.

Chapter 3

AFTER THE RENT BOYCOTTS

Infrastructure and the Politics of Payment

> To refuse to give, to fail to invite, just as to refuse
> to accept, is tantamount to declaring war; it is to
> reject the bond of alliance and commonality.
>
> MARCEL MAUSS (2002: 13).

SOWETO'S WATER WAR

The heated public debates in the aftermath of the announcement of Operation Gcin'amanzi were followed by large protests when the first contractors arrived in Phiri to start digging trenches for the project. Unlike the relative politeness of the debates in the media, the opposition Operation Gcin'amanzi encountered in Soweto was intense. Shortly after the first trenches for the new pipes were dug, a group of residents formed the Phiri Concerned Residents Forum and together with activists from the Anti-Privatisation Forum (APF) organized large marches. During such marches protesters often brought prepaid meters with them, carrying them in their hands and on their heads, dropping them outside local government buildings and *toyi-toying* around them.[1] At night, they also dug out the pipes laid for the project in a countercampaign that activists named "Operation Vul'amanzi" (Zulu for "Let the Water Flow"). In the course of the ongoing protests, the prototype project in Phiri became a veritable battleground, what one utility official described to me as a "state

---

1 The toyi-toyi is a militant protest dance that was an essential feature of the antiapartheid struggle.

of war." Some of the protests turned violent, including a burnt-down local utility office and the shooting of a utility contractor working on the site. Soon, both local and international activists spoke of "Soweto's water war."[2] Within a few months, work on the project stopped entirely. As the daily *Sowetan* put it, Operation Gcin'amanzi had been "halted by the people,"[3] at least temporarily.

In the following months, as work on the project began again, protests and demonstrations were increasingly countered by repressive police action, and arrests multiplied. In time, an interdict prohibited residents from approaching utility workers and from protesting close to installation sites, and a permanent private security presence was established to police central locations of the project. Meanwhile, the weekly meeting of the APF's Research Subcommittee, which I attended throughout my fieldwork, became increasingly concerned with strategic questions of how to handle arrests, how to come up with bail money, how to help out residents being cut off from water when they refused the meter, and with tactical questions about how one might oppose the project in the next target area.

An air of war strategizing also infused the utility's daily operations. Classified progress reports on the project had a standing section entitled "Opposition from Adverse Pressure Groups," which detailed how many protesters had been arrested, trial outcomes, and strategies adopted by the utility to counter what it referred to as "sabotage." Utility training sessions held in Soweto for local short-term contract employees that I attended usually involved detailed descriptions of "outside agitators" involved in the protests, ominous warnings of "wolves in sheep's clothing," and tactical instructions about how to deal with the opposition they would encounter along the way. Less visibly, information on the project was tightly policed, with South African researchers often struggling to get access to officials for interviews. Indeed, my own requests for interviews with utility officials were often explicitly granted only because, as a foreigner, I appeared to be an outsider uninvolved with activist groups. During such interviews, many of the senior Johannesburg Water officials I met presented themselves as under siege from unsympathetic researchers and "vandalizing" residents alike. And although the utility was throughout at pains to present the project's successes, one of the architects of Operation Gcin'amanzi, a French engineer from the Suez Group team, conceded in the course of a conversation that for a moment during the protests, he thought the entire project would be derailed by the waves of opposition.

2 Many pamphlets that were produced and circulated at the time used similar language. See, for example, Anti-Privatisation Forum "Johannesburg Has Declared War on the Poor," September 7, 2003.

3 *Sowetan*, August 29, 2003, as cited in Harvey (2005).

How did an infrastructure upgrading project become the subject of such passionate protests? How might one account for the intensity of opposition and the warlike forms it took? These questions were both ones for which I wanted to find answers, and they were intensely debated by government and utility officials, activists and the media. In the search for explanations, much hinged on how the actions of Phiri residents were interpreted; at stake was an interpretive politics of how one might "frame" the nature of the problem at hand.[4]

In a formulation eerily reminiscent of the apartheid-era "agitator thesis," the utility and the City throughout maintained that such resistance was spurred by "outside forces" who had either incited ordinary Phiri residents to action or were themselves responsible for such "sabotage." By contrast, many of the leading activists spoke of the protests as signs of principled popular opposition to the corporatization of the city's water services, and, thus, more broadly to the City's neoliberal restructuring program begun in the late 1990s.[5] If the former presented Phiri residents as law-abiding but gullible township residents seduced and misled by malicious activists from elsewhere, many of the activists saw them as principled political actors following larger ideological goals, which, if not socialist in nature, were at least, they argued, a clear and direct expression of opposition to the ANC's neoliberal policies.[6] In the Manichean world thus created, it appeared that Phiri residents were either entirely unconcerned with political demands or completely and singularly driven by them.

Over months of attending protests and meetings and talking to residents as well as activists, I realized that neither interpretation was entirely wrong. "Outside" activists, that is, activists from other areas in Soweto or from Johannesburg, often did play a role in organizing and representing Phiri residents' diverse discontents—providing "transport money" to help residents travel to meetings, assisting them in the writing of memoranda, running writing workshops, or collectively producing research reports and "popular booklets" for distribution in Phiri. Similarly, there *were* Phiri

---

4   I draw here on Callon's notion of "framing" as a performative act that brings phenomena into being (Callon 1998). If, in Callon's account, processes of framing appear relatively friction-free, here I focus on how framing itself becomes a political terrain.

5   As I pointed out in the last chapter, while activists often referred to "water privatisation," corporatization in fact does not involve the sale of state assets; rather, corporatization is a process whereby a utility or integrated municipal department is "ring-fenced" and turned into a private company with all shares remaining with the City. Thus, it is a reorganization of public services modeled on private sector principles. I explore this organizational form in Chapter 5.

6   The ethical and political questions raised by the representation of social movements is the subject of much debate in South Africa; see, e.g., Naidoo (2010), Pointer (2004), and Walsh et al. (2008).

residents for whom the fight against the prepaid water meters was symbolic of a larger rejection of the ANC and what activists frequently described as its "sellout" after the first election. But these two categories of protesters—the "outside agitators" and the local protesters driven solely by ideological goals—appeared to be in the minority. Most Phiri residents protested for a wide variety of reasons, many of which were to do with very local and localizable concerns—Phiri Councilor Kunene's lack of responsiveness and his arrogance, Johannesburg Water's mercurial interventions and its often patronizing treatment of residents, the latent threats of administrative fiat, and the more general mysteriousness of the local government's operations.[7] They also often had other more mundane complaints, which over the years had become cumulative burdens—from high and often untrustworthy bills and longstanding arguments with the electricity utility Eskom to the bureaucratic vicissitudes of indigency and grant applications, uncertainty about the fate of waiting lists for housing, and suspicions about the makeup of the membership of local ward committees.

Although both leading activists and city officials often located the politics of the protests at the national, or at least the municipal level (for or against neoliberal policies, for or against the ANC), such ascriptions of intentionality missed what was perhaps most striking about the protests that engulfed Operation Gcin'amanzi—that they often took extremely localized and seemingly mundane forms. Indeed, in Phiri protesting residents themselves often drew a clear distinction between the national government, which for many was still identified with the liberation movement, and the local relations and uncertainties with which they were confronted on a daily basis. Many, perhaps most, of the protesting residents in Phiri had voted for the ANC, some were card-carrying members, and there was, as many residents frequently pointed out to me, no necessary contradiction between voting for the ANC in the national elections, while at the same time being in fundamental opposition to the local councilor or the utility—or being discontented with a myriad other problems.

Below, I explore these seeming contradictions by locating them within the larger history of the antiapartheid struggle and the infrastructural modalities through which it unfolded. The previous chapter focused on the shift in styles of political reasoning and the concomitant emergence of a specifically neoliberal techno-politics in the late 1970s; this chapter traces some of the intended and unintended consequences of these transformations. I examine how fiscal relations and the administrative, socio-technical forms that mediate them became a political terrain during the 1980s and how this terrain persists in the postapartheid present. The dramatic manner

7   See here also Bernard Dubbeld's insightful essay on how perceptions of the local state are shaped by the paradoxes of postapartheid citizenship (Dubbeld 2013).

in which Operation Gcin'amanzi became an object of large-scale protest is graspable only by exploring how infrastructure, the provision of basic services and payments to the state have historically been tied to larger questions about citizenship and forms of political expression that developed in the context of the late-apartheid period.

To outline the contours of this political terrain, it is necessary to attend to apartheid's less apparent legacies and to the less visible ways in which the antiapartheid struggle unfolded. Drawing on archival research and historical interviews with antiapartheid activists and apartheid-era bureaucrats, as well as the large literature on township struggles, in this chapter, I reread the turbulent history of the townships—and Soweto more specifically—in the 1980s in order to make sense of the material remainders and the "embodied histories" of this period and their work in the present (cf. Dlamini 2009; Fassin 2007). Indeed, it is only against the backdrop of these less visible late-apartheid legacies—which continue to haunt the present in a multiplicity of ways—that we can render the intensity of contemporary protest intelligible.[8]

Rather than providing an exhaustive historical account of this period, my goal is to draw out two aspects in particular: First, I focus on the techno-political forms that became central to the late-apartheid state's governing of the townships, and that in turn became a crucial ground for the antiapartheid struggle. If the antiapartheid struggle is today often told as a story of a people's linearly progressive steps toward freedom, such narratives often obscure the less clearly progressivist histories of the struggle, its heterogeneity and internal fissures. In focusing on how infrastructure and payment became a crucial ground for the struggle, one that was at times less defined by clearly articulated demands for political rights, and instead often operated on a more murky administrative-political terrain, my goal is to bring into focus the ways in which the late-apartheid formation came to be defined by a specific infrastructural form of power that combined the administrative, the technical, and the fiscal to produce a distinct terrain of struggle.

Second, I track the politics of "framing" township residents' actions, a legacy whose remains are apparent in the present in multiple, often uncanny, ways. Indeed, crucial to the constitution of this techno-political terrain throughout has been an attendant interpretive politics of "framing" the actions of township residents, that is, a struggle over how to define and delimit what "counts" as political, to attribute intentionality, and to delineate the contours and valences of operative terms (cf. Beall et al. 2000;

8 In thus mobilizing the archives of the antiapartheid struggle as histories of the present, I also contribute to recent efforts to reread the dominant histories of the antiapartheid struggle in more contingent ways (see, e.g., Chipkin 2007; Dlamini 2009; Lalu 2007, 2009; Pillay 2009).

Meintjes and White 1997).[9] Whether nonpayment is interpreted as a criminal or as a political act, or as an opportunistic, self-interested and amoral one, is central to how the "problem" is constituted and to how solutions to it are devised. Moreover, modalities of framing produce the conditions of intelligibility in which certain claims can be "heard" by the state as legitimate demands, while others are rendered illegible and illegitimate.[10]

While nonpayment was framed by activists as a political act during the antiapartheid struggle, over the course of the 1990s such acts of nonpayment were resignified and increasingly conceived as criminal or self-interested acts. In the latter half of this chapter I trace the protracted process of resignification that came to be at the heart of attempts at normalizing fiscal citizenship after the first democratic election in 1994. It is in such less evident, "merely" administrative spaces that the fault lines of the transition are negotiated and, at times, contested. In turn, it is in such forms and registers that the work of making liberal democracy unfolds.

FRAMING NONPAYMENT, FRAMING DEBT

While Johannesburg Water framed Operation Gcin'amanzi ("Save Water!") in a globally mobile language of sustainability, this elided the more complicated and distinctly local targets of the project. Johannesburg Water, as a newly corporatized utility, was tasked with "balancing the books." The most immediate motivation to embark on the project was that 70 percent of the water it was buying from the bulk provider Rand Water and reticulating to Soweto was "disappearing" every month—what is termed "unaccounted for water" in utility parlance—implying millions of rands in losses for the utility. "Unaccounted for water" was further subdivided into "technical" and "commercial losses," the former referring to leaks in reticulation pipes, the latter to any losses not traceable as technical, for the most part losses incurred through the apartheid-era unmetered flat-rate connections.[11] Given the absence of metering in Soweto, however,

9 I am here in part inspired by the problematization of representation that became central to Subaltern Studies after its poststructuralist turn (Spivak 1988; see also Chatterjee 1993). Within science studies, the question of representation has in a different way been crucial. Annemarie Mol, for example, describes "ontological politics" as "a politics about what there is in the world, what there might be in the world" (Mol 1999). See Redfield (2002) for an insightful discussion of the possibilities of thinking postcolonial studies and STS together.

10 Rancière (1999) suggests a distinction between "speech" and "voice" in his discussion of political intelligibility.

11 Flat rates were calculated on the basis of 20 kl per stand per month of water consumption. However, most households in fact consumed much more water, often in part due to leaks.

distinguishing the two was not an easy task. It was unclear to officials how much water was being lost in derelict apartheid-era pipes, how much was lost on each resident's property, and how much was "lost," in monetary terms, due to the nonpayment of water accounts.

Indeed, a large advertisement for the project on Old Potchefstroom Road, one of the main roads running through Soweto, showed a bucket of water heavily leaking through several holes, headlined "Soweto Leaks!" The banner faithfully, if unintentionally, reproduced the problem from the utility's point of view: water was being lost in what appeared as an unmapped and unmappable mass of technical malfunctioning and human unreliability—"wastage," broken pipes, the (unpaid) flat rate system, and neglected domestic infrastructure. In this way, what were in fact two separate problems—derelict apartheid-era infrastructure and the nonpayment of accounts—were merged into a generic problem of "unaccounted for water" to be met by an equally generic quest to "save water." By extension, the two main interventions of the project, the upgrading or repair of infrastructure and the installation of prepaid water meters—despite having substantially different targets—were presented as inextricably connected.

By thus conflating the two, the utility elided the drastic consequences the introduction of prepaid water meters would have for Phiri residents. At the time the project started, conservative estimates put the figure of nonpayment of service charges in Soweto at 87 percent with roughly the same percentage of accounts in arrears. For the vast majority of Soweto's residents, then, water was not only unmetered, but also de facto free. The installation of meters thus entailed the forceful introduction of a new economy of water consumption, a point I will elaborate in Chapter 5. More important, Johannesburg Water also elided the long histories of conflicts over service provision and payment during the antiapartheid struggle, which culminated in the rent boycotts from the mid-1980s onwards. By framing the project as one concerned with "saving water," the utility thus bracketed the issue of unpaid accounts altogether.

Indeed, although the question was often discussed internally, the question of nonpayment was initially not mentioned in any of Johannesburg Water's official brochures or pamphlets, and the utility's spokesperson repeatedly denied that it was a consideration in the project.[12] Johannesburg

12   Internally, however, officials often admitted that prepaid meters were aimed at creating what two of Operation Gcin'amanzi's planners termed the "acceptance of the user-pay principle." See Michael Rabe and Nico Singh 2005, "Creating Efficiency Using Prepayment as a Demand Side Management Tool," Presentation at the South African Prepayment Week (Cape Town, May 2005). In the aftermath of widespread protest, brochures increasingly conceded that the project was aimed at "the creation of an environment conducive for payment of water and sanitation services" (Johannesburg Water. n.d. "Everything you need to know about the upgrade and FreePay Meters: Operation Gcin'amanzi Public Education Manual", brochure obtained in 2004).

Water officials' reluctance to talk publicly about nonpayment was particularly striking given that for years there had been an intense preoccupation in urban planning and policy circles about what officials routinely referred to as a "culture of nonpayment," often said to be linked to a "culture of entitlement." Over the years, there had been many attempts by policy makers, development consultants, and government officials to establish the causes and motivations of nonpayment. Throughout the 1990s, numerous studies were carried out by individuals and institutions, often with widely divergent findings and policy prescriptions.[13] At the same time, in the course of Igoli 2002, the city-wide restructuring program, new techniques and modes of thinking and speaking about payments to the state developed. Globally circulating managerial concepts such as "credit control," "demand-side management," or "cost recovery" increasingly recast such payments as contractual exchanges. It is this attempt at reframing the question of payment from the ethical and political questions of the antiapartheid struggle toward a globally modular account of payment practices that ultimately failed as residents turned infrastructure into a public site of disagreement.

Given the high rates of debt in places like Soweto, there was much at stake in understanding why residents did not pay; indeed, answering this question itself became a political battleground. Understanding nonpayment was important because, as multiple educational campaigns asserted, without a paying citizenry, services were difficult to provide. Moreover, in a context of the rising popularity of commercialization amongst government officials and consultants, paying customers were an important asset to be traded in contracts or concessions. Beyond such practical worries, however, nonpayment was also a concern because it suggested that residents did not recognize the authority of the state. This preoccupation with residents' motivations becomes intelligible when we remember the stakes of nonpayment outlined by Mauss in the quote opening this chapter. Refusals to reciprocate heralded more than simply financial implications for the city; the mass nonpayment also produced larger worries about the relationship between citizens and the state and thus about the postapartheid order.

As Janet Roitman (2005: 73) observes, debt can be "socially sanctioned" creating bonds of obligation and reciprocity; the monthly cycle of billing for example is a socially sanctioned debt, one that depends upon and

---

13   For a sample see Gert Pienaar's (2003) study commissioned by Eskom. R. W. Johnson's study for the Helen Suzman Foundation is the most extensive argument for a "culture of nonpayment" (Johnson 1999). Other studies suggest that nonpayment is in large part a question of affordability; see the survey-based study by the University of the Free State and the studies by the Municipal Services Project at Queens University (see, e.g., McDonald and Pape 2002).

reinforces a relationship of trust.[14] In Phiri, as in much of Soweto, most residents had what is known in economics and in the Johannesburg City Council as "bad debt," that is, arrears owed to the city which they could never repay, a form of debt that made them guilty of a misdemeanor. Thus, debt no longer functioned as an instance in a larger system of reciprocity, but rather signaled a removal from the social contract. Via a semiotic mediation "debt" was thus perceived not merely as "theft" (Keane 2008: 33), but, following Mauss, as a "declaration of war." Much like the widely discussed lawlessness, then, nonpayment came to stand for a larger postapartheid problematic of how to make compliant citizens and how to establish (a liberal) order.[15] It is these questions—questions which the project sought to sidestep unsuccessfully—that I want to take seriously here.

If from the perspective of utility officials, development consultants, and city bureaucrats, nonpayment constituted an interpretive and practical problem, in Phiri and much of Soweto debt was a paradoxical state to be in. On the one hand, the vast majority of Soweto's residents were in debt to varying degrees, many so high it was impossible to even think about ever being able to pay them off. Often without dramatic repercussions, having accounts in arrears had thus come to be normalized. Moreover, as I elaborate below, the debt they had accumulated was also a form of de facto cross-subsidization, enforced from below. Although the apartheid state always officially held onto a policy of self-financing for the townships, residents' mass nonpayment for rents and services had forced white local authorities and the central state to break with this policy and to directly finance township services. Thus, nonpayment had brought about fiscal concessions from the state, extending often meager budgets on a regular basis.[16]

On the other hand, for many residents in Phiri, debt was a source of persistent anxiety bound up with a generalized uncertainty about the workings of the state. Many lived in fear that they might at some point get evicted or, if they owned their houses, that their services might be cut off. Debt also defined and structured many residents' relations to local bureaucracies. Having an account in arrears often meant that in many townships, residents could not join the local ward committee, which thus excluded

14 Gustav Peebles helpfully coins the term "credit/debt" to signal the "dyadic" nature of debt and credit relations (Peebles 2010). For my purposes here, one should also note the way in which specific modalities of credit/debt have come to be viewed as "empowering" within contemporary development programs. The ubiquity of microcredit schemes and the formalization of title deeds in order to enable collaterals for loans are two examples (Elyachar 2005; Mitchell 2009).

15 On the framing of crime in South Africa, see Comaroff and Comaroff (2006b), Jensen (2008) and Pillay (2008).

16 For an ethnographic account of the ambivalences of indebtedness in South Africa, see James (2014).

the vast majority of them from participating in the formal political process.[17] Beyond such obvious exclusionary practices, debt also structured urban citizenship and revealed the often fraught relation to the local state. Amongst the many conversations I had with residents in Soweto about debt and payment, one story stands out. Told to me by a pensioner in Phiri in a local *shebeen* (bar) in response to my question about his arrears, it elucidates how debt is experienced as a particular form of state power, defined by unpredictability and capriciousness, and, for this reason, by continuities with apartheid-era bureaucracy:

> You know what happened last year, they came suddenly at home, I was not there. I went to pay a sum of 360 rand. From that side, I came home and my daughter told me "Daddy, they were here, they said they were coming to cut this [electricity] off." I say "Why?" "They say that they want 2000 rand!" I still got that receipt. So I went into my bedroom, got it and ran there. [The clerk] said to me: The only thing you have to do is to consult this lady. I said "OK, I'll wait for them." I want to tell you, there is a big bottle store. . . . So I got myself a small bottle of dry gin, you know, to have power (loud laughter from the other pensioners sitting at the table). I'm telling you the facts; I don't want to tell lies. I got there and drank the gin (more laughter). . . . There is that one who knows me and she said to me "Friend, what's wrong? They cut your electricity." I said "I don't know. They want money." She said "Go inside. You'll get one of my friends there, she's a clerk there." So [still] I had to part with that 1000 rand, but every time I look at my account my 1000 is not there, it's not written there. . . .
>
> You know they forced me to have this prepaid. After going somewhere, I came back and it was already installed in my yard. Til now they didn't come [back], I am buying [prepaid credits], but they are still sending me account [statements]. I still owe them.

Debt here emerges not merely as a source of existential insecurity, but also comes to define a particular relation to the state in which residents often view themselves at once at the mercy of an unpredictable state bureaucracy and as being in a constant state outside the law. In several ways, this is reminiscent of the paradoxical relationship to the state that Adam Ashforth described in his account of Soweto in the early 1990s. While Soweto residents on the one hand experienced the state as incompetent and corrupt,

---

17 Ward committees are advisory bodies without formal decision-making powers. While they were supposed to be at the heart of "participatory governance" at local government level, de facto, many ward committees are ineffective and embroiled in relationships of various forms of dependence and patronage (cf. Atkinson 2007b; Jolobe 2014). In Phiri, most residents did not feel represented by the local ward committee. The exclusion of residents on the basis of accounts in arrears was recounted to me by Phiri residents, but was not confirmed by the local councillor.

on the other, they often felt a "sense of the supreme efficacy of the state" as a system of oppression (Ashforth 2005: 103). This legacy, as Ashforth predicted, continues to this day.

The power of debt was well recognized by Johannesburg Water. When the utility began the project in Phiri a couple of years earlier, a central argument that convinced many residents to agree to the installation of the meter had been the promise that debt would be written off over three years, if the meter had not been tampered with in the meantime. For most residents in Phiri, this was the most convincing argument for agreeing to a prepaid meter—getting rid of debt, and thus removing themselves from the relation of obligations they were often unable to meet.

PAYMENT, INFRASTRUCTURE, AND APARTHEID TECHNO-POLITICS

As Mauss (2002) suggests, relations of exchange are not simply instrumental, utility-maximizing processes, but are central to the production and maintenance of particular social relations of obligations and reciprocity. This is so not just in the nonwestern world, but also in a context of capitalist modernity, where numerous nonutilitarian monetary relations co-exist with relations of commodity exchange.[18] Similarly, fiscal transactions between the state and its citizens are invested with ethical and political content, including most centrally the rights and duties associated with citizenship.[19] While such fiscal relations are mediated by bureaucracy and thus often seem impersonal and "cold," much recent scholarship attests to the ways in which state payments can elicit affective investments and moral claims, and be associated with specific forms of belonging (Abelin 2012; Maurer 2007; Peebles 2011; Roitman 2005). Foremost amongst such payments is taxation, which is also bound up with particular conceptions of political community and allied with distinct governmental techniques.

Fiscal relations between citizens and the state have historically unfolded within particular regimes of power and in turn have often produced an attendant politics. In the early modern period, extraction was both the principal mode and the primary end of state power (cf. Tilly 1990; Foucault 1991). In the context of colonial rule, monetary extraction in the forms

18   This point has been illustrated by numerous recent studies (e.g., Guyer 2004; Maurer 2006, 2007; Zaloom 2006; Zelizer 1997).

19   As Joel Robbins (2009) has pointed out, Mauss's conception of reciprocity is akin to a Hegelian conception of recognition in that both reciprocity and recognition stress the centrality of mutual ties as preceding the self.

of taxes, fines, and tributes not only enabled a particular, colonial form of primitive accumulation that forced subsistence producers to enter into the colonial cash economy, but also became a central strategy to govern native populations. In this context, taxation was a "materialization of colonial power in fiscal form" (Roitman 2005: 10).

If in early modern Europe and in the colonies, such payments were closely linked with processes of extraction, domination and violence—what Achille Mbembe (2001: 66) describes as *fiscality*—with the rise of mass democracy, fiscal relations became not only regularized via bureaucracy, but also enmeshed with "population" and "security." The primary rationale for taxation and related payments was, at least in theory, no longer extractive; rather, with the rise of "population" as an object of state concern, taxation was tethered to the redistribution of risk and the establishment of interdependent relationships between citizens concomitant with a solidaristic notion of the "social" (Donzelot 1988; Ewald 1991). Thus, such payments became intimately tied to the building of a body politic often guided by sacrificial logics premised on the state's obligation of care for its population, now conceived of as a subject of need.

Parallel to this shift, the state increasingly became responsible for the provision of basic services, thus multiplying the relations of payment to include direct payments for networked services, such as water, gas, or electricity. Such payments, unlike taxation, appeared as a more direct relation of exchange more akin to the *quid pro quo* logics associated with market exchange. And yet they too were often tethered to an understanding of the "public," both via techniques like cross-subsidization and through symbolic associations with public works.

As rail tracks, cables, pipes, and wires increasingly connected all citizens in what Graham and Marvin (2001) have called the "modern infrastructural ideal," municipal infrastructure also came to materialize the biopolitical relationship between state and population. Water infrastructure, in particular, was seen as vital not only to public health, but also to the creation of an environment conducive to moral behavior (Joyce 2003; Osborne 1996). It is in this context that payment for insurance, taxes, and services became an ethical obligation tied to citizenship and a measure to distribute "risk" throughout society. If payments for municipal services established an immediate fiscal relation between the state and the individual household, the monthly or quarterly cycle of billing expressed a mutual obligation between citizens and the state. Given that here the provision of services preceded payment, it was based on a temporality of trust. Inscribed in mediating technologies like the credit meter or the monthly bill was a social contract, which, while violable, entailed the assumption of a regularized flow of provision and payment, and a citizenry both willing and able to pay.

In contrast to Europe where municipal infrastructures became increasingly associated with citizenship, in the colonies the history of the modern state followed a different trajectory. Here, the biopolitical connection between the state and its subjects often preceded the connection of political representation—"population" preceded "the people" as a juridical subject (Chatterjee 2004). From the outset, infrastructures in the colonies were primarily linked to extractive projects and to exigencies of control. Railways helped produce the colonial economy, in the process reconstituting space in the colonies (Goswami 2004). Electricity, gas, and water works operated via both spectacular and less visible biopolitical forms of power often rationalized in the idiom of public health and hygiene (Gandy 2004; McFarlane 2008; Prakash 1999). This close association of colonial infrastructures with modalities of rule also worked at a symbolic register, aimed at producing particular modernist sensibilities and dispositions, if often fissured by experiences of lack (Larkin 2008).

In South Africa, early twentieth-century infrastructure projects were primarily organized around colonial demands for security and extraction. Electricity provision was limited to private generation and distribution in the mines, while water and irrigation works were for the most part confined to large commercial farms.[20] Increasingly, however, infrastructures also became integrally linked to "native policy." Water and sewerage services were extended to urban locations out of concern for public hygiene, signalling the increasing centrality of a particular, racialized biopolitics in a context of urbanisation and rising labour mobilisations.[21] As Parnell and Mabin put it, in a larger discussion of modernist urban practices of segregation, "apparently boring and mundane activities of local government in the 1920s and 30s . . . represented radical new departures and affected the whole character of towns" with sewering and public housing particularly important (Parnell and Mabin 1995: 3; see also Swanson 1968). Rather than viewing race as a starting point for the making of policy "the creation of race [was] part of the intricate development of modern urban society" (ibid.). Indeed, the very idea of the race-based township—or what Jennifer Robinson (1996) termed the "location strategy"—was both premised on and produced by such mundane devices and techniques.

20   On the history of electricity in South Africa, see Christie (1984) and Veck (2000). For a social history of electrification and energy use in the townships around Cape Town see Lee (2006). On the history of Rand Water, see Tempelhoff (2003).

21   In an important article, Maynard Swanson described the "sanitation syndrome" of the early 1900s when forced removals and segregation were instituted in the name of public health (Swanson 1977). This centrality of public health in racist state projects is repeated with striking similarity in many places across the globe in the late nineteenth century and early twentieth century (Eichelberger 2007; Gandy 2004; McFarlane 2008).

If this imbrication of bureaucratic practice, material infrastructures, and race defined the period of segregation, it intensified with the beginning of the apartheid project. While the injustices of apartheid were most starkly represented in the battery of racist legislation passed in the aftermath of the National Party victory in 1948, in particular in urban areas apartheid was primarily brought into being and sustained through administrative rather than juridical forms of power including techniques of urban planning, bureaucratic procedures, and mundane infrastructures. While "native administration" from the beginning relied on repressive force, apartheid's specificity—and its endurance into the present—lay in its intricate accounting of and intervention into private lives via administrative means (cf. Evans 1997). This was especially true in urban areas, where native policy was exercised primarily through civil administration: "collecting rents, supplying public utilities, and planning transport routes" (ibid.: 9). Urban apartheid, materialized via a labyrinthine web of legal provisions and administrative regulations, thus directly shaped everyday life and in the process fashioned particular forms of urban sociality, sensory environments, and a distinct urban habitus. It is this intimate form of power that not only shaped resistance to it in specific ways, but also, I suggest, makes up its most persistent, if often least visible legacy today.

This centrality of civic administration in carrying out and producing the ideological apartheid project becomes obvious in the ways in which modalities of rule were materialized within infrastructures and space. From their establishment, townships were conceived as temporary dormitories rather than as urban places; Soweto, in particular, was an "unwanted city" (Kane-Berman 1978: 56). The townships were established far away from white metropolitan areas, making infrastructure provision more difficult and rendering means of transport over long distances a necessity. Their spatial layout was designed for purposes of surveillance and in ways amenable to policing—including radial roads, limited thoroughfares and exits, and a lack of places of congregation. Electricity was first extended to the townships in the form of tall light poles that enabled their surveillance at night. Domestic power connections were provided to the townships only much later.

Beyond surveillance, infrastructures also worked on the senses. In their history of Soweto, Phil Bonner and Lauren Segal depict newly built areas during the 1950s:

> [R]ow upon row of identical dirt streets radiating from a central hub, line upon line of drab, cheap, uniform houses, a colour-less, mind-numbing monotony. It is almost as if the government felt that through regimentation and uniformity it could establish a firmer control that could not be challenged" (Bonner and Segal, 1998: 34).

This experience of uniformity was reinforced by the absence of street names and addresses, which until the 1990s were indicated only by a number and the township (e.g., 2146 Phiri), clearly marking Soweto as a camplike space rather than an urban place made up of singular forms and distinctive parts.[22] Beyond the repressive power on which it rested throughout, apartheid thus also worked at numerous, and at times less visible, registers from the symbolic and the spectacular to the sensory and the mundane.

The high-apartheid period was characterized by the neglect of urban infrastructures, consistent with the grand-apartheid ideology of giving the black population "representation" in the Bantustans. As I pointed out in the previous chapter, in the post–1976 Soweto Uprising period, and in a context of economic crisis and shifting demands for labor, it became increasingly clear that the fiction of urban residents as "temporary sojourners" could no longer be maintained. From the mid-1970s, amidst systemic crisis, urban infrastructure became a serious concern for apartheid urban planners and increasingly integrated within the larger project of counterinsurgency that began with "total strategy" in 1977 and would ultimately usher in a period of intense militarization in the 1980s.

Importantly, especially for my purposes here, in the urban areas this techno-politics of infrastructure was also bound up with a particular fiscal politics. The racial welfare state enforced racial solidarity among whites while particularly insuring the Afrikaner population against poverty via job reservation, pensions, and the subsidization of housing, often by breaking up mixed areas and forcibly removing black residents to locations far outside the city. At the same time, throughout the apartheid period, township residents were often responsible for financing their own infrastructure, a kind of "cost recovery" *avant la lettre*, by which, for example, township residents were at times required to build their own housing via "site and service" schemes, and capital investments were often paid for by alcohol sales in the townships.[23]

22   And yet, as both Jacob Dlamini (2009) and Adam Ashforth (1996; 2006) have shown in different ways, township residents often turned such homogeneous spaces into particular places through practices of informal naming and minor transformations in yards and houses. Similarly informal modes of distinction are suggested by Krige (2011: 82) who shows that even the often minute differences in apartheid housing came to symbolize class differentiation.

23   In the course of the mobilizations and protests of 1976 and aftermath, the public beer halls were almost all destroyed, increasing the importance of rent as a source of revenue (Frankel 1979: 58; Seekings 1988b: 16). Insofar as the townships were made responsible for recovering the full cost of service provision, this was indeed an early form of "cost recovery." Here again, neoliberal techniques became enmeshed with the contradictions stemming from the crises of late-apartheid period. However, early on the establishment of the townships and their infrastructures was also funded through the 1952 Native Services Levy Act, which imposed levies on businesses that employed African workers (cf. Carr 1990; Frankel 1979).

Thus, while the link of political representation was supposed to extend back to the "homelands," the urban black population's fiscal link to the central state was constituted not via direct taxation, but through payment for tangible entities—rent for a plot, payments for water, sewage, and, later, electricity. Partly for this reason, taxation in urban South Africa was often less politicized than payment of "rent" for township residents' ostensibly "temporary" living arrangements and charges for basic services.[24] This specific form of fiscal apartheid was thus directly bound up with a racialized biopolitics of infrastructures, space, and territory. As such it was clearly distinguishable from universal taxation, which would have entailed the recognition of a common political community of obligation; a social contract expressed in fiscal form. Unlike taxation, payment for "rent"—which importantly encompassed both rent payments and service charges—was not a fiscal relation based on citizenship, but one that affirmed black residents as subjects rather than citizens, "population" rather than a political community.[25]

This fiscal policy, and the political tie between payment and infrastructure it produced, intensified during the 1980s when township administrations were increasingly forced to raise the funds for infrastructure provisions themselves. While until the 1970s white municipalities were able to selectively cross-subsidize services in the townships, the emphasis on fiscal "self-sufficiency" was increased in the early 1970s when the administration of the townships was taken over by the central state in the form of regional Bantu Affairs Administration Boards (BAABs) and, shortly thereafter, black self-governing structures were established in the townships. In 1982, as part of a larger set of "reforms," Black Local Authorities (BLAs) were introduced, designed to give the urban black population a semblance of political representation to defuse urban discontents.[26] Consistent with the crumbling logic of separate development, the apartheid state presented BLAs as self-standing bodies ostensibly mirroring and parallel to the white municipalities. It also shifted responsibility for the provision and financing

24   However, in the rural areas, taxation was often subject to intense contestation, in particular with the introduction of hut taxes in the colonial period (Beinart and Bundy 1987; Redding 2006).

25   And yet, being an account holder did give urban residents rights unavailable to unauthorized squatters and migrants. Although the term "rent" denoted both rental charges for public housing and charges for basic services, to residents these were not distinguishable as they appeared as one sum on residents' bills. As Chaskalson, Jochelson, and Seekings (1987: 53) suggested, the state attached importance to this distinction for political reasons.

26   As Hindson (1987a: 90) observed, in the new form of dividing urban from rural residents that began with the Riekert recommendations, "labour is to be discouraged from entering metropoles by linking provision of municipal services directly to the ability to pay local taxes."

of services to the new structures while ultimately retaining control over all decision-making functions, which continued to rest with the BAABs. Given that most township residents both worked and spent their money in the white areas, however, much of their finances, in taxes as well as spending, remained in and benefited the white areas. In the absence of a tax base, the BLAs resorted to raising the funds for their administration through rent and service charges, often by instituting sudden and steep increases.[27] The effects of what might be termed fiscal apartheid thus increasingly led to discontents and protests. From the beginning, the BLAs were regarded as illegitimate by township residents, as shown by the low turnout at elections, which hovered at around 10 percent in most townships.

South African scholars and activists at the time frequently analyzed such struggles over payment for basic services in Marxian terms as conflicts over collective consumption. Often inspired by Castells's *City and the Grassroots* (1983), they focused on the cost of social reproduction, involving the state, employers, and township residents qua laborers.[28] And yet these fiscal struggles went beyond material demands. The introduction of Black Local Authorities brought to a logical conclusion a gradual process, which had been ongoing since the late 1970s, of bifurcating political from administrative functions as outlined in the previous chapter. Fiscal and managerial responsibilities for services were thus given over to local authorities, while exerting a firmer grip on decision-making powers and securitization at the center. Increasingly, local government in the townships was tasked with the administration of daily life, while control was exerted indirectly and often more obliquely from the central government. It is this dynamic and the specific techno-political relation between township residents and the local state it produced that continues to haunt the present in numerous ways.

For much of the apartheid period, then, infrastructures—and the fiscal relations in which they were enmeshed—were the material embodiments of the apartheid state's shifting strategies for governing the townships. In the absence of political representation, infrastructure and the biopolitical and fiscal links to the state it constructed became, for the vast majority of residents, the only link to the state—short of repression. In the urban areas, infrastructure both attested to the reluctant acknowledgement of their presence and simultaneously signaled their disavowal and subjection.

27   Such inequalities were also written into tariff structures. Johannesburg could use the bulk supply of services from Eskom to subsidize private users, who as a result paid 38.6 percent less for electricity than Sowetans. Similarly, unlike Soweto, Johannesburg did not have to bear the cost of installing a new electricity grid (Beavon 2004: 235).

28   Castells's influence can be tracked in academic work at the time; see, e.g., Lupton (1993), McCarthy and Swilling (1985), but it had a similarly important influence on activists, in particular those associated with the activist planning organization Planact. From there, it also disseminated to the civic organizations and became part of activist idioms.

Beyond its often extreme violence, the apartheid state in its various guises was also the landlord of plots and houses, manager of services, and collector of rent and service charges. It is thus unsurprising that while the antiapartheid movement became most visible in its national campaigns for political rights, it was for the most part organized around localized protests and boycotts, which took infrastructure—and payment for it—as both the terrain and the object of struggle. While such localized struggles over payment and infrastructure had been important parts of resistance ever since the colonial period, they intensified during the 1980s culminating in the rent boycotts.[29]

THE RENT BOYCOTTS

On September 3, 1984, residents of the Vaal triangle townships, some thirty miles south of Johannesburg began protesting massive hikes in rates and service charges that had been imposed by the local authorities. The protests were put down with repressive force by the apartheid government, and sixty-six people were killed in the violence that ensued. In the aftermath of the massacre, residents of the Vaal triangle resolved to refuse paying their rent and service charges. This first localized act of fiscal disobedience soon spread to many townships around the country. Allied to other forms of resistance—including mass demonstrations, bus and consumer boycotts, and the formation of self-governing structures like street committees and informal people's courts—the refusal of payments to the state became an essential strategy of the liberation movement.[30] The "rent boycotts" and associated forms of resistance ushered in a period of successive states of emergency in the mid-1980s in which the primary goal of the liberation movement became "rendering the townships ungovernable." In the process, payment and infrastructure became inextricably tied to a series of practices through which township residents constituted themselves as the legitimate subject of popular sovereignty.

29   Indeed, boycotts of public transport, rent strikes, and pass book burning were already important forms of opposition in the 1950s (Evans 1997: 6; First 1957). In his account of the Soweto Uprising, Harry Mashabela recounts student mobilizations around rent hikes in Soweto, many of which were successful in forcing the council to drop the increases (Mashabela 2006 [1987]: 111ff). For an analysis of debates and protests around rents during the late 1970s and early 1980s, see, e.g., Work in Progress (1980).

30   At its height, forty-nine of the Transvaal's eighty-two townships were boycotting rent (Swilling and Shubane 1991: 224). On township politics of the 1980s see Mayekiso (1996). More specifically on the rent boycotts, see Seekings (1988a) and Chaskalson, Jochelson, and Seekings (1987).

Like many other aspects of the struggle, the rent boycotts are today often integrated within a linear nationalist struggle narrative in which they feature as a tactical tool within a larger story of liberation. Framed in this way, the rent boycotts are primarily viewed as a neutral instrument, rationally deployed in the service of the substantive aims of national self-determination. Here, I focus on a less linear history of the boycotts, emphasizing two aspects with particular relevance to the contemporary moment: First, the question of political intelligibility, that is, the discursive framing of the boycotts and their rendering within particular lines of causality and interpretive matrices, which were central to how the boycotts unfolded and to their performative effects. Second, I focus on the specific *forms* of political action they prompted, and the affective attachments and the stances of defiance toward the state they produced. Tracing the framings and forms of political struggle brings into view a more heterogeneous terrain in which ethics, politics, and technics often combined in a multiplicity of ways—from the spectacular to the mundane. It is this murky space—at once administrative and political—that, I suggest, is the less visible, if often more persistent and intransigent remainder, of the late-apartheid period.

During the antiapartheid struggle, a multiplicity of protests and acts of defiance became subsumed within the larger aim of national liberation. Many of them began not as explicit, direct challenges to apartheid, but with a host of different rationales and in a diversity of languages. In hindsight, the boycotts are often primarily associated with the leadership of the civic organizations, but their beginnings were frequently less organized.[31] Often, they began as acts of despair against the violence of everyday life under apartheid. At other moments, they were reactions to the intransigence of local bureaucrats or the capriciousness of administrative fiat. Many were initiated by ordinary residents and sustained by a diversity of local groups, only some of which were in the beginning linked to the main liberation organizations. In many instances, nonpayment for rent and services preceded the official boycott and only later became designated and integrated within the larger movement. Most national liberation organizations at the time were, as one civic leader put it, "trailing behind the masses."[32] Thus, the rent boycotts often developed independently, and for a variety of reasons, and were in many instances only later fused with explicitly nationalist demands for political rights.

---

31   The civics were a mass-based, primarily urban movement against apartheid that was central to the liberation struggle during the 1980s. It was later organized at a national scale through the United Democratic Front (UDF) and from 1992 onward as the South African National Civic Organisation (SANCO). See Mayekiso (1996), Seekings (2000), and Zuern (2011) for an analysis of its history.

32   This is how UDF leader, and member of the Soweto Civic Association (SCA), Popo Molefe put it (Seekings 2000: 120).

Partly as a result of this initial multiplicity, the boycotts were also framed in a diversity of languages and expressed in a multiplicity of forms. Activists in both the civic organizations and associated activist NGOs like Planact later framed their demands in a pragmatic, goal-oriented language, epitomized by the slogan, "one city, one tax base." And yet, in many townships, the campaign became known simply as "Asinamali! Asibadali!"—"We don't have money! We don't pay (rent)!"—a slogan that expressed a clear stance of defiance, but did not entail a clear political *telos* or agenda. The boycotters, then, were not apolitical, passive victims, but neither could they by definition be said to automatically share in the particularity of the political visions and dispositions of the wider nationalist movement.

If the boycotts were initially not necessarily bound up with explicitly articulated political goals, they could also not simply be seen as the result of material deprivation. Though they were clearly in most instances related to questions of affordability, often triggered by the council's raising of rates, in the beginning, the boycotts—and in particular their nondirected parts—often developed in administrative spaces in which technical and political questions were often fused indistinguishably. For example, residents often directed their demands at the administration boards, which in turn would argue that it was politically "neutral" (cf. Shubane 1987). As Alan Mabin observes, such localized actions were often focused on "struggles over the de facto ability (and right) to live, work or enjoy facilities in particular places; on struggles over access to urban life rather than merely on policies from above" (Mabin 1992: 23). Similarly, Jeremy Seekings (1988a: 201) located the grounds of resistance in the townships surrounding Johannesburg and Pretoria in "the 'physical landscape' of houses, roads and railways, factories and offices, parks and pavements, schools and sewage systems." This landscape exerted its power at a number of levels, not just in the daily reminders of deprivation, particularly in relation to the wealthy and well-served white areas in which many township residents worked, but also in its sensory and symbolic force. It is these less visible, infrastructural forms of power against which residents often directed an equally infrastructural form of resistance that was not always articulated in the register of political rights.

In Soweto, which in 1986 was late in joining the boycott, the first incidents of nonpayment took place far away from Soweto's older, more established townships, which were often the center of political organizing.[33] Here, the rent boycott was triggered by a sharp increase in electricity rates, which had been imposed as a result of the electrification program that had been initiated as a response to the 1976 Uprising. This monthly "electricity

33 Seekings (1988b) suggests a number of reasons for why Soweto's mobilization was less intense and later than in the Vaal, amongst them greater internal social differentiation and a longer history of cross-subsidies.

masterplan levy" was perceived as a form of "racial taxation" (cf. Veck 2000: 172n). Similar to other townships, in Soweto, the boycott was not planned by the civic association, but emerged in a largely uncoordinated way, for the most part in areas of Soweto that did not have any links to civic organizations, in particular in Naledi, Chiawelo, and Jabulani (Shubane 1987). Indeed, the first instances of nonpayment began without explicit nationalist goals and were only later forced on the agenda of the Soweto Civic Association (SCA) by residents themselves. As an activist evaluation suggested in retrospect:

> The rent boycott was not initiated from above by the SCA or any other formal township-wide or national structure. It was initiated from below in poor working class areas. Ordinary people, mainly women, got up from the floor at mass meetings called by the civic to discuss other matters and urged those present to support the rent boycott.[34]

The Soweto Civic Association, which started out as a relatively conservative organization, thus needed to be pushed into more radical demands by ordinary residents (cf. Seekings 1988b; Shubane 1987; Zuern 2011). Even after the civics became involved, it was difficult to control the boycotts, as different demands issued from different townships within Soweto. It was only after widespread nonpayment had already occurred that the SCA articulated its formal demands, many of which, following in the footsteps of the United Democratic Front (UDF), were articulated in national terms.[35] And while later on the civics—especially including its local structures, the street committees—would come to play an important sustaining role, they also saw themselves as disciplining more unruly elements. This initial disjuncture between localized actions and the civic leadership that would come to represent them continued to define township politics during the 1980s and into the postapartheid period.

Striking, and important for my purposes here, is the *form* that such struggles took and their close relationship with infrastructures of various

---

34 "SPD Evaluation" (n.d.), Planact Collection 21.5.19.1, Department of Historical Papers, University of the Witwatersrand.

35 Swilling and Shubane (1991: 233) note the shift from more localized "socio-economic" demands to "political" demands. A survey found that most residents supported the boycotts "because people think that housing and services are inadequate" (ibid). Thus, "the rent boycott enjoyed wide-spread support because it was perceived as the best way of resolving socioeconomic conditions" (ibid). While Swilling and Shubane conclude from this that the boycotts were about "socio-economic conditions" rather than "political considerations," this rendering ultimately relies on a definition of the political as always already articulated at the national, rather than the local level, a distinction that, as I suggest in this chapter, should be rethought (see also Chipkin 1995).

kinds. Evictions often became the sites of militant mobilization as residents were let back into their houses by activists. Residents carried night-soil buckets and emptied them in front of council offices. Petitions circulated to contest the procedures for electricity billing. Mass meetings to oppose rental and transport fare hikes became crucial organizing grounds (Murray 1987; Zuern 2011). Often, electricity boxes were painted with slogans or in ANC colours. In his memoir, a former Soweto administrator noted at the time that buses were stoned or burned by residents "who regard the very existence of these buses as part of the 'system', i.e. as part of the machinery of apartheid oppression" (Grinker 1986: 42). He also noted the "large number of street light poles which have been damaged to the point of no longer being functional" (ibid.: 50) which according to Soweto officials was due to impatience with the electrification scheme.

Political actions thus unfolded at a number of different registers ranging from symbolic defiance to persistent, if less visible, stances of noncompliance, evasion, or sabotage. These less explicit forms of defiance also included squatting land, growing arrears, and illicit connections to services (Seekings 1988a: 201; 1990). Beyond the articulation of moral-political stances, then, there was also a less perceptible habitus of quiet refusal and evasion bound up with the very forms of life that apartheid had brought into being. In these various ways, the politics of the struggle took a number of different, at times less visible, forms.

The boycotts were also defined by the distinctive temporality of the late-apartheid period marked, on the one hand, by the futures of liberation anticipated by the antiapartheid movement, but more immediately by more heterogeneous temporalities ranging from present and recurring concerns of everyday existence to dramatic emergencies in which everyday experiences of time were thrown into disarray. Indeed, it is these distinct temporalities—of long-term future expectations, on the one hand, and the more cyclical, daily pressures of the present, on the other—that the local state often appealed to when it suggested that even if residents stopped paying rent in protest, they should continue to pay for service charges to keep services running on a daily basis. Nonpayment and the end of the cyclical fiscal relationship with the state thus also signaled the rejection of a common future with the apartheid state and simultaneously gestured toward the larger horizon of a future after apartheid.

Government attempts at breaking the boycotts took a number of forms and hinged largely on how it interpreted the boycotts. While there were internal disagreements about the causes of the boycotts, early on apartheid bureaucrats often claimed that nonpayment was based either on ignorance or on intimidation by "agitators." By extension, measures to quell the boycotts often either sought to "educate" residents or to shield them from presumed targeting by activists. Thus, for example, pay points were installed in downtown Johannesburg, so that residents could make payments out of sight from the prying eyes of neighbors or movement-affiliated activists. (They were hardly ever used.) Throughout, councils insisted that they were not ideological arms of the apartheid state, as activists suggested, but merely "apolitical providers of services" (Shubane 1987: 53). Propaganda campaigns included the distribution of pamphlets and newsletters, often with technical information. Rent statements were redesigned to include a breakdown of charges, thus explicitly splitting "rent" from "service charges" in an effort to convey to residents that payments for services did not go to the maintenance of an oppressive state, but rather that they were apolitical quid pro quo exchange transactions required for the continued provision of services. In another such reframing tactic, government tried to make employers deduct rent payments directly from residents' paychecks, a measure that was opposed by both business and workers' organizations. In yet another version, the missing payments were covertly "built into housing prices."[36] In a great variety of ways, strategies of counterinsurgency thus took shape at an administrative register and in an often technical language. The responses to such tactics frequently took a similarly technical form, ranging from illicit reconnections to services to activists taking legal action against evictions on technical points, such as the lack of official documentation by councils, improperly served summonses, or faulty court orders.

In the course of the increasing militarization of the state in the late 1980s, infrastructure became ever more closely associated with security concerns, including a wide range of counterinsurgency strategies. Following the institution of the National Security Management System (NSMS), the military was granted immense new powers that bypassed parliamentary oversight, what Swilling and Phillips (1990) at the time termed the "emergency state." As a result, the townships witnessed an unprecedented militarization via the establishment of Joint Management Centers (JMCs), covert military bureaucratic installations that linked the administration of the townships directly to the central military apparatus, stationing military offices in each region with outposts in each municipality (cf. Selfe 1989).

Under the aegis of NSMS, and in a context of rising resistance, the government embarked on the Winning Hearts and Minds (WHAM) campaign, a counterinsurgency strategy that combined fierce repression with attempts at meeting township residents' perceived material grievances. The campaign was based on the assumption that if "agitators" were eliminated, and township residents' economic and social demands were met, the larger political question would disappear. As Swilling and Philipps (1989) noted at the time,

36   "Memorandum for the Meeting between a Delegation of Soweto Residents and the Executive Community of the Soweto City Council" (1988) in Planact Archives/Mark Swilling Collection, Department of Historical Papers, University of the Witwatersrand.

the shift from "total strategy" to WHAM was a shift from the political terrain of reform (e.g., through the establishment of local government representation) to the terrain of "civil society." In other words, the target of counterinsurgency now became the very environment in which political claims took shape, including centrally its infrastructural, material forms.

The centerpiece of WHAM's "soft" side was the selective upgrading of the townships, what came to be known as the "oil spot" program that would supplement existing projects by private organizations (Boraine 1989; Jochelson 1990). The program targeted thirty-four townships that were particularly politically active, amongst them Soweto. Apartheid officials here drew on the increasing centrality of infrastructure and development in U.S. counterinsurgency doctrines, which often focused on the building of roads, irrigation schemes, schools, and so forth (Swilling and Phillips 1989: 144). In Soweto, as in many other townships and informal settlements around South Africa, this strategy took a distinctly urban form, focusing primarily on housing and basic infrastructure upgrades.[37]

This dual strategy of security and welfare represented two distinct modalities of counterinsurgency, but often the two were linked very closely. Indeed, while the organization of the emergency state was murky, the linking of infrastructure, payment and security it produced often happened in plain sight. As part of WHAM, the military forces became intimately entangled in development work. This close tie between security and development can be seen, for example, in the direct involvement of South African Defense Forces (SADF) personnel in the selling of housing to township residents. As one SADF official put it in 1987, this focus on development work was necessary in order "to contain the total onslaught and beat the rent boycott" (as cited in Cock and Nathan 1989: 9f). At the same time, evictions for nonpayment became so militarized that "at times there [was] hardly a person in sight dressed in civilian clothes [or] resembling a messenger of the court" (Shubane 1987: 55). Often the army went door to door in the early hours of the morning to collect payments while "balaclava-clad men" issued receipts to those able to pay. In other cases, hundreds of army and police personnel raided the townships officially as part of "crime prevention exercises" designed to intimidate people into paying rent. The council also instituted individual and collective cutoffs of electricity. While individual cutoffs were often reconnected by breaking the padlocks on the electricity boxes outside on the pavements, blanket cutoffs of entire townships within Soweto could last for months.[38] Increasing policing powers in

37   See here also the work on the important case of Crossroads in which infrastructure and housing became similarly central (Cole 1987; Robins 1998).

38   A Memorandum from the Soweto People's Delegation (SPD) notes the collective cutoff of Tladi, Naledi, Zola, Emdeni, and Orlando West, which was only lifted after two months when Helen Suzman and Transvaal administrator Danie Hough intervened.

the form of *kitskonstabels* (auxiliary police forces), council-sponsored vigilan-
tes and "community guards," were also granted to the Soweto Council and
often used to police unauthorized shack settlements and protest activities.

Despite this diversity of often intensely coercive tactics, the boycotts
continued. By the late 1980s, many Black Local Authorities were fiscally
in crisis, and it was increasingly difficult to carry out disconnections or
evictions in the militarized townships. In Soweto, illegal reconnections
abounded. By 1988 meters were no longer read, and the council stopped
sending out bills altogether (Veck 2000). Because the boycotts had spread
to many urban areas, with local negotiations happening haphazardly, it was
clear that payment for rents and services would remain subject to political contestation in the years to come. As I elaborate in more detail in the
following chapter, it was in the context of this stalemate that apartheid-era
municipal engineers increasingly began to search for large-scale technical
solutions to nonpayment, and it was at this moment that prepaid meters
were first developed and tested in South Africa.

NEGOTIATIONS

In the late 1980s and early 1990s, after a stalemate and increasing moves
toward national reform, local-level negotiations began in municipalities
across the country. In the Transvaal alone, there were sixty-seven negotiations taking place in many municipalities.[39] By far the most important negotiations took place in Soweto (Swilling and Shubane 1991). They involved
officials from the provincial government, the Soweto Council, utilities, and
the Soweto People's Delegation (SPD), a group of prominent Sowetans
who represented the civics and, in turn, the residents. Interesting for my
purposes here is the techno-political form these negotiations took. If part
of the struggle over payment was an interpretive battle over how to assign
meaning to the boycotts—whether to deem them "political" or "apolitical";
whether to classify nonpayment as an administrative, criminal, or socio-
economic problem—this politics of framing continued during the negotiations. First, unlike the famous national constitutional negotiations that
would begin later, the local negotiations were for the most part concerned
with addressing apartheid's techno-political effects, that is, with beginning the reform of the "apartheid city,"[40] including addressing questions of

39   Olaus van Zyl, then chairperson of the Transvaal Provincial Administration (TPA),
interview, December 1, 2004.
40   The term "apartheid city" emerged from Planact's research and became widely used
to indicate the specific spatial form produced by apartheid urban planning (Smith 2003; Swilling, Humphries, and Shubane 1991).

taxation, service provision, infrastructure upgrades, and housing backlogs. For this reason, a central role within these negotiations fell to experts— planners, development consultants, and engineers—whose knowledge of urban processes allowed them to make concrete reform proposals.

While the Transvaal Provincial Administration (TPA), which repre- sented the apartheid state in these negotiations, had an arsenal of expertise at its disposal, the civics were supported by NGOs, including most cen- trally the NGO Planact, which in 1989 had tabled an influential report on the Soweto rent boycott (Planact 1989). This centrality of expert knowl- edge during the negotiations on both sides shaped not just the outcome of the negotiations, but the very terms in which they were held. The exper- tise required for such negotiations, and the technical language in which they were conducted, de facto excluded the civics' constituency of ordinary residents and, at times, the civic leaders who represented them in these meetings. Indeed, as Alan Mabin (1994: 6) in his personal recollection of the negotiations showed, the civics confronted a "phalanx of expertise . . . which they found impossible to match." Much agency thus devolved to the "technical" consultants on each side, such that "the people on the ground have not really been able to influence this process—and little democracy has been realised in the effort to reshape the city" (ibid: 10).[41] As a later document produced by Planact noted, the state tried "to depoliticise the content of the negotiations by making them as 'technical' as possible."[42] Thus, for example, in the Soweto negotiation the TPA insisted on setting up a separate "Joint Technical Committee" in which political issues were redefined as technical ones and the civics' participation was limited.[43] Here, again, then, the very act of framing particular questions as technical or political became a central strategy of negotiation.

41   Mabin quotes a civic leader: "Agreements were made in the Chamber in such a way that only the technical people and 1 or 2 executive committee members really understood the issues. We allowed the Johannesburg City Council to set the pace and were mostly having to respond in a reactive way, rather than being proactive. We were then forced into a situation of having to 'sell' the agreements to our constituency and the Soweto public, rather than being involved" (as cited in Mabin 1994: 6–7).

42   "Generalising the Negotiating Experience," p.10. Mark Swilling collection, Depart- ment of Historical Papers, University of the Witwatersrand.

43   The national liberation movement at times noted the limits of such technical nego- tiations; however, they often did so on different grounds. Both the ANC and the South Afri- can Communist Party (SACP) were worried that this negotiation of administrative questions might bypass and become a substitute for the necessary larger political negotiations at the national level. More generally, the ANC was often ambivalent about these localized struggles and negotiations, and aspired to bring them more tightly into the national fold; see, e.g., "Struggles at the Local Level" *Mayibuye* (December 1990). Similarly, as the SACP's journal *Umsebenzi* put it, "While urban apartheid is a national policy, negotiating it has become a local issue" ("A New Deal at Local Level?" *Umsebenzi* 7, no. 1 (1990).

Outside the meetings, in the municipalities and townships surrounding Johannesburg, a different technical politics was taking shape, which more directly involved the provision of services and infrastructure. In the course of ongoing boycotts, many individual white municipalities refused to enter into negotiations, particularly those controlled by the right-wing Conservative Party. Instead, they often simply cut off entire townships from water and electricity services—actions which the civics interpreted as a "declaration of war against black people."[44] Similarly, the ANC argued that in the context of ongoing negotiations, "it is clear that the decision to cut services is a political one."[45] Thus, blanket cutoffs became a tool to interfere with the ongoing negotiations—an infrastructural politics of sabotage from above.

The local negotiations had several other consequences. In the early 1990s, and before the first general elections, the civics and the old government in many townships reached individual agreements to end the rent boycotts; the Soweto Accord in 1990 being the most influential one. Often negotiations ended by means of a compromise that would include the cancellation of debt and a commitment on the part of residents to pay a small flat rate for services. These arrangements drastically lowered residents' charges, again forcing the government to cross-subsidize via payments of "bridging finance." Here, the boycotts achieved very tangible results in that they formally established a politics of cross-subsidization prompted by and enforced from below by boycotting residents.[46] At the same time, from the point of view of utilities and municipalities, small payments could be seen as a kind of pedagogical achievement in that even if the amount was too low to cover the cost of service, residents would be rehabituated to regular payment and, it was hoped, tariffs could be increased in due time. And yet, despite the official end to negotiations and agreements between civics and local authorities to resume payment, in most townships, the civics' calls to resume payment went unheeded, and nonpayment continued.

The rent boycotts were one of the most important and effective tools of the liberation struggle. They fused expressions of discontents about material neglect by the apartheid state with its symbolic rejection. Through nonpayment, the boycotts also enforced cross-subsidization from below in the form of a continuous flow of "bridging finance," thus forcing the state to allocate monies to the townships despite an official policy of self-financing.

---

44   Pat Lephunya cited in Louise Burgers, "Civic Bodies Warn of Fresh Boycotts over Services Cuts" *The Star*, October 19, 1990.

45   Ibid.

46   This is testified to by the R1.1 billion in "bridging finance" that the central state had transferred to the townships of the Transvaal by 1990; of this R791 million went to Soweto (Swilling and Shubane 1991: 224).

Beyond such immediate material effects, the boycotts identified the bio-politics of infrastructure as a political question, thereby dramatically challenging the distinction between the political and the administrative spheres tenuously maintained by the apartheid state. Simultaneously, the boycotts challenged the fiscal relationship on which that subjection was constituted—a challenge captured by the slogan, "one city, one tax base." In the process, the rent boycotters' struggle on a fiscal and infrastructural terrain turned township residents into moral-political subjects in relation to an illegitimate state. Here, the refusal to meet fiscal obligations was, indeed, as the opening quote by Mauss suggests, "tantamount to declaring war."

And yet, beyond their instrumental importance and more obliquely, the boycotts were also essential in the establishment of a less visible terrain of politics defined by stances of defiance against and nonrecognition of the apartheid state and its local iterations. The modalities of fiscal disobedience that emerged here constituted its own terrain defined by its own logics, tools and habitus that at times overlapped with, but was irreducible to the nationalist *telos* of liberation articulated by the African National Congress and other Charterist organizations. It is this governmental-administrative terrain that is part of late-apartheid's "debris," the late-apartheid state's less evident but more durable remainders that at times come back alive in the present.

WRITING OFF THE DEBT, MAKING A NEW (FISCAL) SOVEREIGN

In 1994, ten years after the beginning of the rent boycotts and shortly before the first democratic elections, the ANC announced that all debt residents had accumulated during the boycotts would be written off. The debt write-off was a double settling of accounts. On the one hand, as a symbolic public act, the cancelling of debt signaled a break with the apartheid era and thus inaugurated the new ANC-led government as the legitimate embodiment of "the people." On the other hand, viewed from within each individual household, the debt write-off was intended to mark the beginning of new fiscal citizenship whereby residents would recognize payment for services as a moral and political obligation in the context of a new social contract that emphasized national solidarity premised on mutual recognition. This production of postapartheid fiscal citizenship entailed a number of semiotic operations. First, it required resignifying residents' debt within a moral economy of civic obligation. Secondly, it mobilized a sacrificial economy by which individual payments became allied to the larger temporality of the new nation—each citizen's fiscal contribution today would be required for the transformation and thus the future of the "New South Africa."

Accompanying the write-off was the assumption that because township residents now had political rights and representation in a legitimate state, the boycott would end and residents would automatically resume payment.[47] And yet, about a year later, national debt for service charges had again risen to R810 million while payment rates had only increased from 17 to 31 percent.[48] In an effort to understand this serious miscalculation on the part of the liberation movement-turned-government, many, especially left-wing commentators, suggested that the ANC was out of touch with its constituency. The ANC's assumption that it would be possible to simply "switch on" payment was, they argued, in part a misunderstanding of the extent to which services were simply unaffordable, especially given increasing unemployment. But there was, I would suggest, another, perhaps more significant misreading by the ANC concerning the history of the struggle—one that becomes visible against the backdrop of the history of the rent boycotts.

The ANC, like most modern movements of self-determination, was working with an assumption of the citizen as emerging seamlessly from the liberation struggle in the aftermath of oppression, an assumption which as David Burchell (1995) has shown, is part of a romantic tradition going back to Rousseau, in which citizenship epitomizes the true nature of human expression. During the struggle, a large variety of stances and behaviors were deemed ideologically principled political acts by the liberation movement. And yet many such acts began without a fixed *telos* or clearly articulated set of demands, and often became part of a larger nationalist project only after they were already in process. Much as the subaltern studies tradition has shown, in the history of anticolonial struggle, multiple, heterogeneous forms of anticolonial expression were often overwritten by a more singular nationalist discourse. In turn, this nationalist discourse often relied on a specific, normative figure of a political actor and thus on a particular understanding of the legitimate grounds, forms, and motivations for political expression.[49]

47   This assumption that "local government structures would hold sufficient moral currency to sway people who had not been paying in the past" is testified to most starkly by the fact that local budgets were drawn up with the assumption that payment levels would be at 100 percent (Corrigan 1998: 13).

48   Gaye Davis "From Boycott Leader to Boycott Buster," *Mail & Guardian* (Johannesburg), March 3, 1995.

49   Dlamini (2009) describes this enrolling within an ANC-dominated liberation narrative with the example of the widespread use of the term "sites of struggle" to refer to a diversity of locations of resistance to apartheid (the factory, townships, etc.). Terming all of them

In the postapartheid period, such ascriptions of political agency also produced a fundamental misapprehension on the part of the new government of how the postapartheid transformation would unfold. The ANC's assumption that payment could simply be "switched on" in the aftermath of apartheid was thus not merely a sign of the ANC elite's distance from its poorer constituents; rather, and perhaps more significantly, it could be seen as an indication of a misreading of the rent boycotts themselves, based as it was on a purely rationalist-instrumentalist understanding of the politics of the antiapartheid struggle. This misreading provides insight into the specificity of the political terrain that is at stake here.

In the aftermath of the unsuccessful debt write-off, the ANC-led government launched the Masakhane Campaign (Let us build together), a large-scale national project to encourage payment. From the very beginning, the imperative of paying for services was couched in a moral language of "empowered" and "active" citizenship. In turn, nonpayment came to figure not only as a cognitive problem, but also as a behavioral one. Concomitant with the widespread notion of a "culture of nonpayment," nonpayment was seen here as emerging out of a "sense of entitlement," a particular "attitude."[50] Having identified the problem in this way, the Masakhane Campaign sought to encourage payment by framing it in a moral-pedagogical language aimed at reforming the "culture" of township residents and most centrally changing—or indeed establishing—their conception and practice of civic virtue.

The Masakhane Campaign, launched in February 1995 by President Nelson Mandela himself, was conceptualized as "part of a drive to normalise governance and the provision of basic services at the local level."[51] It explicitly linked payment for services to the creation of "a new culture of democracy and a new consciousness" (NEDLAC 1996: 19). The campaign

---

"sites of struggle," Dlamini argues, "allowed the liberation movement to suppress local, regional and other differences by focusing on what ostensibly united every corner of South Africa. Labelling places that were different in composition and history 'sites of struggle' allowed the liberation movement to project its vision of a post-apartheid South Africa onto 'sites' that were there, ready for new construction once apartheid was defeated" (Dlamini 2009: 154).

50   The 1994 *White Paper on Water Supply and Sanitation Policy* stated the problem in this way: "An insistence that disadvantaged people should pay for improved water services may seem harsh but the evidence indicates that the worst possible approach is to regard poor people as having no resources. This leads to people being treated as the objects rather than as the subjects of development. . . . A key element influencing a household's willingness to pay for an improved water supply is the households' sense of entitlement . . . and their attitude toward Government policy regarding water supply and sanitation. In general, communities are reluctant to involve themselves in countries where the perception prevails that it is the Government's responsibility to provide services" (Department of Water Affairs and Forestry 1994: 7).

51   Valli Moosa, Deputy Minister for Provincial Affairs and Constitutional Development, *Hansard*, Tuesday, 23 May 1995.

initially proceeded without large-scale evictions or blanket electricity cut-offs and focused instead on changing residents' perception of their relation to government. Unlike previous initiatives to encourage payment, it did not involve the civic organizations, but was initiated by the national government, which the civic organizations, now united nationally as the South African National Civic Organisation (SANCO), viewed as symptomatic of the ANC-led government's increasingly top-down mode of relating to township residents. In large part, Masakhane was a costly media campaign including expensively produced TV advertisements featuring iconic figures like Archbishop Desmond Tutu exhorting citizens to help in the reconstruction effort. Walking around Soweto in the mid-2000s one could still see occasional remnants of this project. Close to the Phiri/Senaoane local government office, for example, a fading sticker exhorted residents:

YOUR RIGHT TO SERVICES = YOUR RESPONSIBILITY TO PAY.

First called Operation Self-Reliance and only later renamed Masakhane, the campaign sought to fuse the existing discourse of nation-building (often articulated through an idea of collective overcoming and shared victim-hood) with a discourse of "active citizenship" suggesting that national reconstruction was only possible if all citizens realized that while liberation had given them rights, it had also imposed duties on them. Although the invocation of nation-building and civic virtue pointed to a modality of citizenship-formation reminiscent of many postindependence governments in Africa and elsewhere, Masakhane from the beginning ambivalently resonated with a neoliberal logic in which a notion of (individual) self-help came to conceptually overlap with (collective) self-determination. As a local Gauteng organizer for the campaign told me, Masakhane was aimed at remedying a "dependency syndrome" stemming from the apartheid era, a diagnosis reminiscent of neoliberal characterizations of the welfare state: "Black people were not allowed to be creative, they were used to waiting for others to do something for them. That's why now, we need to be creative. So we said: let's take every person in the country as an asset." He went on to emphasize that the campaign was about teaching people how to "balance freedom and responsibility."

Following this logic, the Masakhane Campaign shifted the meaning of "people-driven development" de-emphasizing democratic participation and instead stressing each citizen's fiscal responsibility toward the nation. Similarly, "freedom" now tended to be aligned with individual autonomy and the promotion of responsible behaviour. In this way, the Masakhane Campaign signaled a more general shift within postapartheid nationalist discourse. "The people" now signified not only an aspirational insurgent subject and the foundation of popular sovereignty, as articulated most explicitly in the Freedom Charter's principle that "the people shall govern"; it was also imagined as a pedagogical subject in need of reform.[52] Central to this process was the displacement of the formerly dominant rights-based discourse of the antiapartheid movement and the reconstitution of the citizenry as a fiscal subject allied to a quest to "normalize" the fiscal relationship between citizens and the state. The act of payment, and thus of *recognizing* one's obligation to the state, was posited as the prerequisite for recognition as a legitimate member of the new political community. As a public project of political resignification, Masakhane thus intentionally and explicitly catapulted the question of nonpayment into the public sphere.[53]

This politicization of payment in public discourse took a number of unexpected forms. Coinciding with Masakhane, a different type of fiscal disobedience emerged amongst wealthy white suburbanites in Johannesburg. On coming into office, the newly elected local ANC government began imposing higher municipal rates and property taxes in wealthier white areas, partly in order to subsidize the upgrading and rollout of infrastructure services in the townships and informal settlements, and to compensate for nonpayment in places like Soweto. In response, white residents and businesses in Sandton, Johannesburg's wealthiest suburb, began a widely publicized payment boycott.

Sandton, which had been a separate municipality prior to 1995, had kept rates low by spending relatively little on public infrastructures such as parks, bus service, or street lighting. Most of its white residents drove cars and were not dependent on public buses or street lighting. Similarly, instead of parks, many residents had large gardens or access to expansive private country clubs. As with many wealthy white suburbs, public street life was, and continues to be, limited to the black domestic workers and gardeners employed in Sandton's households gathering on street corners during break times. Infrastructure (with the exception of roads) was here often effectively privatized and racialized, primarily serving individual

---

52   On this double meaning of "the people," see Agamben (2000).

53   White government bureaucrats who had remained in their positions since the late-apartheid period I spoke to often perceived the campaign simultaneously as an effort to "educate" the new ANC-led government. As one utility manager put it to me:

> When the new government came in, they didn't act promptly to say to people "pay your bills now." The big cry at the time was 'It's fine not to pay, because you're not giving us a decent level of service." In hindsight that was a foolish thing. We lived with them, we were in council in those days, 95/96. The politicians were still revolutionaries, they were still preaching resistance. . . . We were treated as corrupt local officials, because we came from the previously white local authorities. . . . They said, "We don't have to pay, because you're not giving us service" . . . that's why they're not paying and that came back and bit them. That's the legacy we live with today.

white households, but not the public; indeed here the lack of infrastructure reflected the absence of a (nonracial) public.

The Sandton rates boycott threatened to put the city government even further into crisis. It was eventually resolved, though not until a legal challenge launched by the Sandton Ratepayers' Federation was struck down by the Constitutional Court. In adopting the tactics of the antiapartheid struggle, white ratepayers did more than simply protest what they perceived as unfair taxation. Linked to this was an often racist concern over the "chaos" of an ANC–run government, its "lack of capacity," and the threat of "centralized planning." Their protest thus needs to be read as an expression of much larger anxieties about the transition and as a refusal to be part of the new nonracial social contract. [54]

Although many ANC council members argued that white residents had a larger economic and moral debt toward the black population, Sandton residents relied on well-worn arguments absolving themselves of any responsibility for apartheid-era inequalities. Most Sandton residents, they argued, had had nothing to do with the apartheid government and, on the contrary, had always been active in charitable work for the black population. Here, again and in a performative reversal, fiscal relations—and the infrastructures to which they are tied—were bound up with a particular vision of South Africa's public and its futures.[55]

THE TECHNO-POLITICS OF A NEW FISCAL RELATION

As a nationalist project of "cultural reform" and as a project to produce an ethos of virtuous citizenship, the Masakhane Campaign was a spectacular failure. Nonpayment rates remained at similar levels, a fact several consultants I spoke to retrospectively attributed to the campaign being "not community-based enough," and too reliant on advertising as a mode of communicating with residents. In Johannesburg, continued nonpayment in the townships coupled with increasing fiscal crisis led to a dramatic change in strategy. In 1997, the Gauteng head of the Masakhane Campaign

54 As Andy Clarno argues, the Sandton Rate Boycott also needs to be seen as "an effort to articulate a new relationship between race, class and space in the northern suburbs" (Clarno 2013: 1198).

55 These political implications of state payments by white wealthy South Africans are also apparent in Bill Maurer's (2007) exploration of amnesties for "tax minimizers" who had illicitly transferred money abroad during the transition. While his focus is on the ways in which such amnesty payments are bound up with "the active process of forgetting the legacies of apartheid" (Maurer 2007: 134), they could thus also be seen as central to the process of making postapartheid citizens who recognize the (new) state's authority.

concluded: "Persuasion hasn't been taken seriously, so we are now at the stage of coercion, and it's paying dividends."[56] Initially, "coercion" meant the cutoff of services, for the most part in the form of large-scale electricity disconnection drives, but also in some cases of water.[57] In at times dramatic raids, tens of thousands of residents in arrears were cut off—cables pulled out and destroyed (to avoid illegal reconnection). Many residents were evicted from their houses for nonpayment. Perhaps unsurprisingly, the strategy of cutoffs, evictions, and repression, reminiscent as they were of the 1980s, led to massive protests and sometimes violent retaliation and fights within communities. In Soweto, residents formed the Soweto Electricity Crisis Committee (SECC), which would later become the largest affiliate of the Anti-Privatisation Forum (APF), and increasingly gained in strength in the context of widespread disconnections. Apart from organizing protests, the SECC launched Operation Khanyisa (Light Up) that would help residents illegally reconnect to the electricity grid.

The shift from "persuasion to coercion" was also reflected in the public discourse addressed to noncompliant residents. While Masakhane had still held onto a moral language of attachment to the new nation, in the campaigns launched by municipalities and utilities from the late 1990s onwards, "tamperers" and "nonpayers" were increasingly depicted as "criminals" outside the social contract. One of the most talked about and most dramatic campaigns was Eskom's Izinyoka Campaign, which was targeted at people tampering with meters, illegally reconnecting electricity, and stealing copper cables.[58] The campaign primarily consisted of highly visible advertisements against cable theft and illegal reconnections. The slogan touted in TV spots, radio ads, and newspapers was "Beware Izinyoka!" (Zulu for "snakes"). One particularly prominent TV advertisement, for example, portrayed cable thieves or tamperers as snakelike creatures intent on doing harm to the community. It ended by urging residents to "help Eskom put these *izinyoka* where they deserve to be . . . *in a hole*."[59] Such advertising campaigns overlapped with previous initiatives like Masakhane insofar as they sought to convey that individual acts of pilferage would affect others,

56   Sicelo Shiceka, then Gauteng Local Government MEC and head of the provincial Masakhane Campaign, quoted in "Gauteng Switch-Off Brings in R500m in arrears payment" Sapa press report, August 13, 1997.

57   For studies on the effects of these disconnection drives in Soweto and on the rise of the Soweto Electricity Crisis Committee (SECC), see Fiil-Flynn (2001), Khunou (2002), and Egan and Wafer (2004).

58   Copper cables would be cut and sold, reportedly at the time costing Eskom over R90 million a year. Illegal connections similarly were widespread, as I elaborate in the next chapter.

59   See "Eskom Izinyoka," https://www.youtube.com/watch?v=n8vjq-dD0EU. See also the depiction by Gareth van Onselen, "Eskom and the Izinyoka," http://www.politicsweb.co.za/opinion/eskom-and-the-izinyoka.

and to draw the connection between individual acts and a larger whole. In all other respects, however, the public discourse that became prominent here entailed a significant departure from previous exhortations of civic virtue and fiscal duty toward the nation. Masakhane had appealed to a collective project of overcoming and civic virtue still energized by the tropes of the antiapartheid struggle and the recent first elections. By contrast, the Izinyoka campaign operated on a visceral register that mobilized fear rather than common affective investments of belonging. By extension, it no longer equated morality with the law, but presented the law as primarily an instrument of vengeance, while excluding noncompliant residents from the community of rights-bearing citizens altogether.

In presenting cable thieves and people making illegal use of electricity as *izinyoka*, Eskom not only established them as outsiders to the communities, but as *particular* outsiders associated with evil, unpredictable forces and with the unseen. The snake symbolism deployed by the campaign hinged on and conjured up the traditional centrality of the snake in beliefs in invisible forces that can cause harm or misfortune. As Adam Ashforth argues, the postapartheid period has been defined by a widespread sense of "spiritual insecurity" that is a "condition of danger, doubt, and fear arising from exposure to the action of unseen forces bent upon causing harm" and a concern about the flourishing of interpretive authorities (Ashforth 1998: 63; 2005). In such contexts, a snake is the central unseen actor threatening communities and causing explanatory dissonance. Against this backdrop, Eskom's imagery is striking, especially since the postapartheid state has repeatedly been faced with the conundrum of dealing with witchcraft accusations and, indeed, with collective violence against perceived witches (Ashforth 2005; Niehaus 1993). Eskom thus mobilized this economy of accusation for its own purposes, all the while realizing that it ran the risk of encouraging and legitimating violence.

Eskom's campaign can be read as emblematic of a larger transformation in public discourse in which actions previously deemed part of the antiapartheid struggle became increasingly resignified as illegitimate and often criminal acts. In the course of the 1990s and in the aftermath of the failure of campaigns like Masakhane, the question of nonpayment was increasingly removed from the public sphere and shifted to an administrative terrain. Here, the question of nonpayment was primarily viewed as a technical problem subject to administrative rather than political action or considerations of public morality, while its management was given over to the domain of utility officials, engineers, and local bureaucrats.

This reframing of nonpayment as an administrative, rather than a political question also took shape against the backdrop of a global shift toward liberalization and commercialization, including techniques like "demand side management" and "cost recovery" promoted by international institutions like the World Bank and the increasing popularity of "new public management" in South African urban planning circles.[60] Because Johannesburg was increasingly moving toward corporatization and commercialization, understanding the causes of nonpayment was of wider importance, especially since paying customers are a central asset traded in the privatization of basic services. In a larger global context of widespread deregulation in the 1990s, a veritable industry of "willingness to pay" studies emerged, designed to produce what could be termed a sociology of payment practices, usually in rational choice terms.[61]

In the course of my many visits to the offices of development consultants, the City, Johannesburg Water, and meter manufacturers, the question of nonpayment and "credit control" emerged centrally and without fail. What became apparent throughout the various renderings I heard during interviews and conversations was the importance of ascriptions of intentionality and the epistemologies through which they could be made. Establishing why residents did not pay was seen as crucial for the development of solutions to the problem. Crucial to this process was how nonpayment and debt were framed (Keane 2008). *When* a debt becomes "bad" or when nonpayment becomes a "problem," and through which epistemologies and interpretive grids such determinations could be made thus became the objects of new forms of knowledge production. Various typologies were developed to understand and establish the precise causes of nonpayment. One, for example, which I was first given by an employee at the Water Research Commission (WRC), differentiated between "no payment" and "nonpayment." "No payment" implied a willingness, but inability to pay, what the consultant called "the true poverty situation." "Nonpayment," on the other hand, referred to people unwilling to pay. Distinguishing the two, he conceded, was not always an easy task, but they were developing research tools to establish precise causality.[62]

In line with the popularity of rational choice approaches, nonpaying residents were often characterized as rational actors evading payment for

60   See, for example, the World Bank report on infrastructure, which emphasized the "more efficient, more user-responsive and more environmentally-friendly" service provision to be created by "manag[ing]" infrastructure more like a business" including setting tariffs to "cover costs" (World Bank 1994).

61   "Willingness to pay" studies were first introduced and popularized by the World Bank in the 1980s in a larger move from supply-side provisioning to demand considerations (cf. Rogerson 1996). See also Karen Bakker's (2003a) discussion of the "willingness to pay" concept in relation to water privatization and commercialization.

62   This concern with distinguishing between different kinds of reasons for nonpayment or debt accumulation has been similarly observed by Peebles (2013: 704f) in his analysis of debates around the reform of debtor's prisons in nineteenth-century England. Here, too, distinguishing between "malfeasance and misfortune" became a crucial concern.

their own individual benefit—free riders—hiding behind those who could not pay. And yet simultaneously, and paradoxically, residents were often depicted as creatures driven fundamentally by "habits." Here, the primary problem was identified as a "culture of nonpayment" inherited from the antiapartheid rent boycotts of the 1980s, the wider implication being that residents had failed to develop the "cultural" capacities to become democratic citizens. If nonpayment in various forms had been a problem for the South African state for decades, throughout the 1990s, in a context of a larger shift toward "cost recovery," payment was thus increasingly analyzed in individual, rational-choice terms and presented as a question to be solved by municipal management.

It is in this context, defined, on the one hand, by the failure to "normalize" the fiscal relationship between citizens and the state by means of nationalist exhortation, and, on the other, by increasing imperatives for "cost recovery" that projects like Operation Gcin'amanzi and the widespread use of prepayment meters and similar technologies became increasingly attractive.[63] Indeed, as one engineer involved in the planning of Operation Gcin'amanzi argued, payment in South Africa had to do with deeply ingrained behaviors and "socio-economic problems" that could not be changed very easily. The deployment of prepayment technology, he suggested, would avoid having to institute a harsh credit control program of regular meters, bills, and water cutoffs later. Given the various, mostly unsuccessful approaches to nonpayment in the past, he suggested, prepayment metering was seen as "the solution to nonpayment."

As I elaborate in the next chapter, Operation Gcin'amanzi, and the wide deployment of prepaid meters more generally, thus emerges as one instance within a much longer history of ongoing, often techno-political struggles over payment and, as such, over the kinds of relations that can be established between the state and its population. Prepayment technology at once materially mediates a biopolitical relation to the state (in the form of provisions of basic services), *and* a juridical, civic relation (based on rights and duties of citizenship). Thus, in the specific postapartheid context, prepayment technology can be seen as a techno-political device that both embodies and reforms fiscal citizenship.

At the same time, the meters also entailed a shift in the medium through which payment was to be achieved. If the Masakhane and the Izinyoka Campaigns had relied on the creation of a paying public via the media, from billboards to TV and newspaper ads, and thus on the creation of a collective consciousness of one sort or another, with the introduction of

---

63 A similarly technical intervention widely deployed around South Africa during this time is the "trickler" a small plastic disc with a tiny opening that reduces water flow to a trickle, forcing residents to calculate the time it takes to fill a bucket in advance of actual usage.

the meters, nonpayment could be individually managed via a technical device. In other words, the exhortation to pay for water was here *transduced* to the meters themselves, much like in Latour's famous example of the "sleeping policeman" (or speed bump), which replaces moral considerations and calculations about driving too fast with a material obstacle that forces drivers to slow down (Latour 1992). The imperative to pay for services thus became materialized in the technology itself. In the process, the quest to create a paying citizenry turned from appeals to a new postapartheid moral economy to individual enforcement and behavioral adjustment via a technical instrument, thus giving up on and forgoing the question of civic morality entirely.

If the credit meter expressed a mutual obligation between citizens and the state and established a temporality of cyclical payments that was based on trust, materially inscribed in the technology of the prepaid meter is also the abandonment of the project to produce civic virtue and national attachment. Payment for services here is no longer a moral act affectively binding citizens into a mutual relation with a larger collective vision; instead paying for water or electricity is an individual transaction premised upon an immediate exchange and ultimately enforced by a technical instrument. Indeed, it is this ethos and this subject that the technology itself anticipates and reinforces, even if its effects are often uncertain.

And yet, as I elaborate in Chapter 5, Operation Gcin'amanzi also came with a new moral project, now articulated in environmental terms. "Saving water" and individually managing one's water supply thus came to overwrite previous projects of fiscal citizenship that had appealed to solidarity and individual sacrifice in a context of national reconstruction. It is this attempt at transforming the ethical and political questions of payment into an administrative-technical issue that failed as residents turned the project into an object of political demands.

CONCLUSION

In May 2005, twenty years after the beginning of the rent boycotts and ten years after the general debt write-off, the City of Johannesburg announced a second debt write-off that would cancel the arrears accumulated since 1994. This write-off was no longer universal, but was targeted at specific population groups and part of the newly introduced "Special Cases Policy" by which residents who were registered as "indigent" would be eligible for free basic "lifeline" provision of water and electricity, if they agreed to have all services delivered via a prepaid meter.

Unlike the debt write-off in 1994, this one arrived with relatively little fanfare. On the day the write-off was launched, lines stretched outside and around the local Phiri/Senaoane council office. They were largely made up of older women, some sitting on makeshift benches in the shade in the backyard of the office. Most looked tired, having come here at 5:00 am in the morning. The women who could not find a bench waited in the sun. All of them had come to apply for the new indigency program that had been announced by the city via pamphlets and radio programs. All qualifying residents—those who could provide all the documentation required (ID book, statement of rent and an affidavit)—would have their debts written off, provided they had consented to the installation of a prepaid meter. Many held their bills in their hands, some with debts of over R20,000. A general sense of hope and despair, uncertainty and fear, was in the air. Many people queuing up were not entirely sure what the debt write-off was about or whether they would be eligible.

The first write-off in 1994 had marked the ritual inauguration of a new postapartheid social contract. By contrast, the write-off in 2005 was a decidedly less flashy, more bureaucratic affair. Rather than designed to build a universal social contract, this write-off separated South Africa's population into those who could be trusted to pay their monthly bills and those who would have their connection to the city's flows mediated by a technical instrument. For this latter section of the population, it was no longer possible to accumulate "bad debt," a fact that many residents appreciated. And yet, it was also no longer possible to enter into a relationship of "sanctioned debt" with the state and the specific fiscal modality of belonging produced by regular cycles of payments.

Prepayment meters and practices of prepaying are by now ubiquitous in Phiri and in townships all over South Africa. Many have interpreted this explosion of prepayment devices as a consequence of the neoliberal imperative of "cost recovery" and, therefore, as related to larger global processes of privatization and commodification. As I elaborate in Chapter 5, such analyses are not entirely wrong. And yet, in their understandable focus on a larger, global story of commodification, such analyses risk closing off the space for an appreciation of the distinctly local political targets and consequences of the meters. Read in more historically contingent terms, prepayment emerges as an intervention into an ongoing techno-political struggle over fiscal citizenship. If, as anthropologists have long suggested, relations of payment produce and reproduce particular social ties and are invested with ethico-political content, we might reread prepayment as a particular instance through which the dynamics and logics of postapartheid citizenship are being reconfigured.

But the history I have traced here also tells a somewhat different story about the shape of the political in the present. Infrastructures and the fiscal relations in which they are embedded became a key political terrain during the 1980s, when seemingly technical operations were turned into an important arena of the antiapartheid struggle. Such battles over payment and infrastructure were also often battles over signification; indeed, the very act of distinguishing the technical from the political became a site of negotiation and struggle. This flourishing of epistemic claims and attributions did not end in 1994. The more recent history of the protracted series of reforms and measures to deal with nonpayment over the course of the 1990s and early 2000s shows that such significations are still unsettled and often unruly. Although the question of nonpayment increasingly disappeared from public discourse and was turned into a technical, administrative matter, this did not end these battles and the ties between payment, belonging, and citizenship. Instead, it was increasingly delegated to a technical terrain and materialized in the infrastructure itself.

We might then also return to the intensity of protest with which Operation Gcin'amanzi was initially met. It was perhaps no accident that the project's name echoed the militant and military language of the anti-apartheid struggle and of developmentalist projects of an earlier era, rousing the people to action in the name of the common good. Against the backdrop of the techno-political terrain created during the 1980s, Operation Gcin'amanzi appeared as just one amongst a series of interventions designed to reform fiscal citizenship. Given the long histories of "technical" interventions in Soweto and the ways in which such interventions became crucial sites of struggle, it is unsurprising that this politics of infrastructure continues in the present, when for many residents the sphere of national government appears far removed and when it is local relationships between residents and local bureaucracies through which urban citizenship is experienced and given substance. Here, the administrative domain again becomes the site at which ethical and political questions are often de facto negotiated. Ostensibly technical projects such as the installation of prepaid water meters are then also spaces in which civic pedagogies take shape outside the official spheres of civic engagement. And yet, as I elaborate in the next chapter, the meters were ultimately unsuccessful in achieving these goals; indeed, it is precisely in such spaces of seemingly total depoliticization that such questions are continually negotiated, albeit in different forms.

Chapter 4

THE MAKING OF A TECHNO-POLITICAL DEVICE

In July 2011, in the midst of a particularly cold South African winter, a violent protest occurred in Chiawelo, a poorer area of Soweto, close to Phiri. For hours, hundreds of residents blocked one of Soweto's main thoroughfares and protested outside local government offices, in the process igniting a car and burning down the houses of two local councilors. Like the many so-called service delivery protests that have been making regular headline news in South Africa in recent years, the protest in Chiawelo bore an uncanny resemblance to the scenes of spectacular violence in the townships during the 1980s. In an apparent effort to dispel such uncomfortable associations, government and ANC officials were quick to condemn the protests as "acts of anarchy" by "mobs" and "rogue elements." Meanwhile, the media, scrambling to understand what was going on, had identified the cause of the protest as a set of prepaid meters that had recently been installed by the electricity parastatal Eskom. The meters had automatically cut residents off from electricity service, leaving them cold and in the dark.

This was not the first time that prepaid meters emerged as protagonists in large-scale protests. Over the past fifteen years, such protests have occurred at regular intervals, primarily in urban areas. Throughout my fieldwork, I had often seen the meters—pulled out from walls and backyards and dropped at the gates of local government offices—take center stage at demonstrations, and such protests continue to make headline news now and then. And yet, despite such periodic protests, for the most part the meters sit quietly in residents' homes. Given the ubiquitous use of prepayment technology—from cell phones to electricity and now water provision—"living prepaid" with an always precarious connection to flows of water or electricity has become an increasingly normalized condition.

At the same time, many residents in Soweto and other urban areas have bypassed their meters, rendering the meters useless and giving residents de facto free water or electricity. As a result, there is an ongoing low-intensity battle between residents tinkering with the technology and utility officials trying to secure it. This chapter tracks this technical micro-politics involving residents, engineers, and utility officials in a seemingly perennial struggle over the enforcement and evasion of payment. This politics does not take conventional political forms of public demonstration, disagreement, or deliberation, but takes shape at the level and in the language of technology itself.

Via a genealogical exploration of the travels of the meter on the one hand, and an ethnographic account of the contemporary metering industry in South Africa on the other, I chart the political life of the meter as it is deployed within a diversity of ethical regimes and techno-political assemblages. This chapter thus takes the contemporary conflicts surrounding prepayment as a starting point for a broader conceptual reflection on the relationship between ethics, politics, and technics. What is the relationship between technology and the constitution of particular forms of agency and subjectivity? How do devices such as the prepaid meter mediate the relationship to the state, and how might political histories become materialized and sedimented within material objects? And, finally, how might what Madeleine Akrich (1992) termed the "de-scription" of technology enable us to read particular configurations of power?

A TRAVELING TECHNO-POLITICS

The previous chapters traced the broader historical and political horizon against which infrastructure became a political terrain in South Africa; here, I focus specifically on how technical devices, like the prepaid meter, are enrolled within particular ethical regimes and political projects. I examine how in their very design, such technologies are inscribed with and come to reflect specific ethico-political projects, targets, and expectations (De Laet and Mol 2000; Redfield 2012). As engineers develop devices, they "script" their innovations with specific assumptions about their users, with injunctions to act in particular ways, and thus with specific "programs" of action (Akrich 1992; Latour 1992). As Soweto residents bypass or destroy the devices, they negotiate and at times subvert these semiotic-material scripts. In the course of such techno-political innovation, questions that were central to the liberation struggle—about the limits, entitlements, and obligations of citizenship—are delegated and transduced to novel forms, media, and idioms.[1] In this material battle, I suggest, technologies and infrastructures

1 See Stefan Helmreich's discussion of the concept of transduction (Helmreich 2007). Latour (1992) uses the concept of "delegation" to understand the process by which specific programs of action become part of technical processes.

are not merely symbols or tools for political expression; rather, technology itself is turned into a political terrain for the negotiation of moral-political questions that were at the heart of the antiapartheid struggle and that continue to animate the forms of life left in apartheid's wake.

My focus in this chapter will be on understanding the semiotic-material *work* through which technologies travel and come to inhabit new contexts. This genealogical investigation of the "travel" of technologies across time and space opens up conceptual and methodological space for an exploration of forms of the political outside its conventional locations and mediations, while simultaneously focusing our attention on the specific ways in which the technical is always already mobilized within specific ethico-political conjunctures.[2]

Partha Chatterjee (2004; 2011) has suggested that in much of the post-colonial world, popular politics takes shape not in what is conventionally thought of as the formal political sphere; rather, it is at the register of administration and population where "rules may be bent and stretched" (Chatterjee 2004: 60) that political questions are often de facto negotiated and resolved.[3] It is here, he suggests, that we should locate "political society." While Chatterjee is primarily concerned with recalibrating our understanding of the sites of the political in the postcolony, this chapter focuses on the *techno-political forms* of political society and the multiplicity of its terrains. As the previous chapter demonstrated, in South Africa this politicization of the administrative has a long history and has also taken a specific fiscal and infrastructural form. Here, I explore a less visible, material micro-politics concerned with the shaping of subjectivities, ethical dispositions, and political agencies; in the technical politics of meters, pipes, or wires, infrastructure itself becomes a terrain on which central questions—of civic virtue, basic needs, and the rights and obligations of citizenship—are negotiated and contested.

Two linked lines of inquiries guide this chapter. First, I trace a genealogy of the prepaid meter as a techno-political device. My aim is not to provide an exhaustive social history; rather, my focus is on two historical moments

---

2   While social studies of technology have opened up conceptual space for a rethinking of technology in less deterministic terms, particularly in the focus on the vernacular uses of technology, such approaches have often focused less on extending these insights to theorizations of the political. On the "user heuristic," see, e.g., Fischer (1994); and Bijker, Hughes, and Pinch (1987). As I detailed in the introduction, compelling work on the imbrication between the technical and the political within science studies includes Akrich (1992), De Laet and Mol (2000), and Winner (1980). More recently, much work has argued for the rethinking of concepts of the political in more material terms (Barry 2013; Marres 2012; Mitchell 2011).

3   In a critique of Chatterjee's distinction between civil and political society, James Holston (2009) suggests that citizenship and governmental processes overlap in numerous ways. I hold on to Chatterjee's theorization, then, mindful of the multiple, historically situated forms that "insurgent citizenship" can take (Holston 2008; see also Gupta 2012; Zeiderman 2013).

at which prepaid meters suddenly proliferated on a large scale and became enrolled within distinct ethico-political projects. First, in late-nineteenth-century Britain, the meter was invented to provide gas to the working classes and became integral to the Victorian project of moral reform. Second, this chapter explores the conceptual and practical labor of translation as the meter moved to late-apartheid South Africa, when it came to be deployed as a device of counterinsurgency to end the antiapartheid rent boycotts. In each moment, the meters became integral to the constitution of specific techno-political terrains.

In the final part, I draw on my ethnographic work with engineers in the metering industry to examine how prepaid meters come to be *rescripted* as they are deployed in the aftermath of apartheid and in a context of neoliberal reforms.[4] In following engineers' seemingly perennial quest to develop ever-more-secure metering devices, I describe a technical war of position in which minute technical innovations become crucial tactical moves dependent on engineers' capacity to mobilize local knowledge and interpretive skill.

FOLLOWING THE LIFE OF THE PREPAID METER

When I arrived in Johannesburg to carry out my fieldwork, Operation Gcin'amanzi and the installation of prepaid water meters in Soweto was at the forefront of activists' concerns and the primary cause of protests.[5] And yet, concerns about prepayment metering had already been raised some years earlier when Eskom had begun installing prepaid electricity meters in Soweto on a large scale. While less legally and morally fraught than prepaid water meters, prepaid electricity meters had been one of the primary rallying points of the new social movements, in particular the Soweto Electricity Crisis Committee (SECC) that had been formed in a context of the utility's increasingly repressive policing of cost recovery. Apart from organizing protests, the SECC was also directly involved in reconnecting residents to services. During Operation Khanyisa ("Light Up"), SECC-affiliated "struggle electricians" reconnected residents to electricity supply if they had been manually disconnected and also bypassed or removed prepaid meters.[6] Thus, they turned illicit reconnections and meter by-

---

4   See Madeleine Akrich's and Bruno Latour's work on this semiotic-material conception of inscription (Akrich 1992; Callon 1987; Latour 1992).

5   For work on prepayment technology in South Africa and elsewhere, see Guy and Graham 1995; Harvey 2005; Loftus 2006; Ruiters 2007; van Heusden 2009; and Veriava 2007, 2014.

6   On the electricity crisis and the social movement activism that has developed around metering, see Egan and Wafer 2004; Fiil-Flynn 2001; Khunou 2002; McDonald and Pape 2002; McDonald 2009; Naidoo 2007; Naidoo and Veriava 2009.

passes into a public spectacle and mobilization tool. While such protests continue to flare up periodically, most of the time, prepaid meters are an unremarkable part of life in Soweto. And yet, the bypassing or "bridging" of meters continues silently on a large scale, often without any link to social movement organizing or a public, "political" language. Indeed, while the protests against Operation Gcin'amanzi would eventually subside and the utility argued that its surveys showed a 98 percent satisfaction rate, in 2011 utility officials told me that 30–40 percent of the prepaid water meters they had installed had been bypassed and needed to be retrofitted with new security features. By 2015, Johannesburg Water officially announced that "most" of Soweto's 131,000 meters had been bypassed.[7]

To have their meters bypassed, residents may individually pay a skilled person—often a utility employee earning a side income—or a skilled family member or SECC-affiliated technician might do it for free. The decision to bypass is determined by multiple calculations—often both pragmatic and moral—and is also subject to disagreement within households. While the social movements linked the meters to larger concerns about neoliberal reforms, residents often have a multiplicity of concerns that are less clear cut and more ambivalent. On the one hand, prepaid meters frequently come with the promise to erase debts, which most Soweto households had accumulated over years of not paying for services, and to prevent the accumulation of new debts in the future. At the same time, the meters raised larger worries about affordability especially in a context in which, for years, the vast majority of Soweto residents had not paid for basic services and thus money for water or electricity was often not part of household budgets. Electricity is particularly difficult to afford in poor areas of Soweto, where unemployment is high and many households rely on grants and pensions as primary income.[8] A particularly cold winter, for example, can dramatically increase costs for topping up credit and often multiplies cutoffs and blackouts. Importantly, the meter affords no room for negotiation should money to buy credits be in low supply. An unpaid monthly paper bill will not result in an immediate disconnection, and thus enables residents to delay payment until money has come in. The prepaid meter, on the other hand, automatically cuts the connection without regard for context or special circumstances.

But there are less immediately apparent reasons for opposition to the meters. As I showed in the previous chapter, in South Africa, and in Soweto in particular, infrastructure has never been merely a neutral conduit for the

7   Olebogeng Molatlhwa "Sowetans Sabotaging Water-Saving Efforts," *Times* (Johannesburg), June 23, 2015.
8   Despite the nationally mandated free provision of 50kWh per month, in 2004, poor Soweto households often spent large parts of their monthly income on basic services (Nefale 2004).

provision of services, but has always been bound up with questions of belonging and citizenship. Part of the promise of liberation was an end to the everyday violence of apartheid. Similar to other postindependence projects, the extension and improvement of basic services—from education or health to electricity and water—was seen as central to national reconstruction. Often bound up in objections to prepaid meters are larger concerns about the limits of this promise in the paradoxical context of postapartheid neoliberal reforms, where services are often extended and restricted at the same time (cf. Ferguson 2007; Mains 2012). Prepayment technology in South Africa is thus coded in very specific terms that may differ widely from other places where the technology has been deployed more recently. Indeed, my point here is precisely that technologies are enrolled within ethical and political assemblages in historically specific ways that may or may not "travel" elsewhere and that may shift over time.

THE PREPAID METER AS A COMMODITY

"We've developed a system that requires absolutely no human intervention" said the engineer with a certain amount of triumphalism. "No chips, no pads, no nothing," he added, pointing to a small plastic device mounted high up on the ceiling of his stand. The sole representative of an Australian metering company, his stand was in the far back of the large exhibition hall crowded out by the imposing multinational, South African–based company stands in the middle aisles. He was one of many engineers and manufacturers who had come to attend South Africa's fourth Annual Prepayment Week. A large-scale international industry conference organized in conjunction with the African Utilities Week, it brought together nearly 800 delegates from all continents to exchange industry news, present innovations, and sell their products. Held in Cape Town's glitzy International Convention Center, the conference was designed to "showcase prepayment as the technology continues to revolutionize utilities' ability to collect revenue" and would "provide an opportunity for water, electricity and gas utilities to exchange knowledge and best practice on revenue management options."[9] Organized annually by Spintelligent, a South African company founded in 1995 with the aim of providing spaces for publicity and exchange of expertise for the domestic and international metering industry, it is the first international conference dedicated exclusively to prepayment technologies.

---

9 Spintelligent, press release, May 13, 2005.

The proceedings took place in large conference rooms upstairs with utility and industry representatives giving papers on recent innovations and presenting case studies from particular municipalities. Downstairs, a large exhibition hall brought together the major companies and manufacturers in the industry, many South African or multinational companies with a base in South Africa, but also company representatives from as far as India and Argentina. The conference interpreted prepayment technology broadly. While the emphasis was on metering technology for electricity, gas, and water, major South African cell phone companies also had stands at the conference, promoting new technologies for prepaid cell phones. In the exhibition hall, meters were neatly lined up according to functionality and level of sophistication. Brochures and manuals stacked on the sides or on adjacent tables provided descriptions of each meter, and most stands were flanked by a number of representatives—many corporate representatives wearing suits, others in less formal workman outfits. Large multinational companies were easily distinguishable from the smaller, less flashy local stands.

I had come to Cape Town after spending a lot of time in Soweto yards with residents looking at, debating, and complaining about the prepaid water meters installed in their front yards, analyzing their functioning (and malfunctioning), the intricacies of bypassing techniques, or seeing them carried on women's heads at the most recent protests against Operation Gcin'amanzi. The conference required a shift in perspective. In the exhibition hall, meters were no longer objects of anger and complaint, but rather displayed to promote the desire of their would-be buyers. Far from dusty township grounds and unconnected to the pipes or wires for which they were designed, the meters were neatly lined up according to functionality and level of sophistication—shiny, disentangled objects, next to and in competition with their peers. Here, the social life of prepaid meters was clearly in its commodity phase (Appadurai 1986). But what kind of a commodity was being marketed here? What made the meters valuable in the eyes of manufacturers and prospective buyers?

Industry fairs and conferences, much like academic ones, present finished products, disentangled from all the practical, intellectual, human and nonhuman labor and obstacles that accompanied their emergence. They enable the *performance* of technical expertise; that is, it is here that "technology" is produced by separating it from all the nontechnical processes that enabled its emergence. It is perhaps not surprising that the only major international industry fair for prepayment metering technology was being held in South Africa. Prepayment technology has over the previous ten years become the dominant mode of connecting township residents to infrastructures. From the chip in the cell phone to upload airtime credits, to the increasing provision of electricity and now also water via prepaid meters, prepayment technology is a familiar aspect of daily life for many residents of urban townships and informal settlements, and the increasingly multinational market in prepayment technology is booming in South Africa. The magnitude and large international participation in the event furthermore testified to South Africa's status as an international leader in prepayment technology innovation. It is not only the country with the largest number of installed prepaid meters in the world, but the international standard transfer specification (STS) for the technology now registered with the International Electrotechnical Commission (IEC) was also developed and first used by South African prepayment meter manufacturers. Over the past decade, South Africa had also become a major exporter of prepayment technology and expertise not just to the rest of the continent but to other places in the global south.

My attending the South African Prepayment Week entailed entering a world often inaccessible to researchers and despised by the social movements. Throughout my research in Johannesburg, I had been trying to interview meter developers and manufacturers, but often my efforts had been unsuccessful. Given the rise in protests against prepaid meters, many metering companies were suspicious of researchers, believing them—often correctly—to be allied with social movements or NGOs opposing prepayment metering. I had come to the conference in part to learn more about the history of the meters, and to fill the gaps of my archival research. Many of the original developers, it turned out, were still in the business, though today mostly working for multinational companies. Many had been engineers during the apartheid era, sometimes with previous employment in military and security industries. During conversations with various delegates, I was repeatedly directed to Peter Clark, who was described to me as the South African "pioneer of prepaid metering."[10] A man in his early sixties and an electrical engineer by training, he had developed the first meters in the mid-1980s and continued to be a central figure in the industry. As we sat on a bench outside overlooking the bustling convention center, Clark seemed happy to talk about the early trials—South African prepayment technology was an international success story in which he had played no small part.

Like many of the engineers I had talked to earlier in the day, Clark explained to me that the widespread antiapartheid rent boycotts in the townships during the 1980s had increasingly become a fiscal problem and that engineers had begun to look for "technical solutions" to the crisis of nonpayment. Having first seen prepaid meters during travels in Britain, Clark had a meter shipped to South Africa. Demonstrating its size with

10   Following anthropological convention, I use pseudonyms for all individuals named in this book, apart from public figures or those who are already visible in the public domain.

his hands, he described the meter as "a huge metal box" with "very rudimentary technology." It was coin-operated and thus easy to bypass. This, he maintained, had worked in the UK, since, as he put it, "people there are polite." In South Africa, where, he argued, "people get involved in energy theft, and things like this," this meter would not work and would have to be re-engineered from scratch.

Clark's offhand comment about the character of South African and British users sheds some light on the labor of translation required for a technology to be made operational in new contexts, a point I will return to in the next section. More important, his association of prepayment technology and "politeness" encodes a key problematic that goes to the heart of the *kind* of techno-politics I will be concerned with in the rest of this chapter. While the concept of techno-politics has been productively used in relation to large engineering projects and expertise (Hecht 2009; Mitchell 2002), the remainder of this chapter tracks a techno-politics that operates less spectacularly on a more micro-political terrain and that is centrally preoccupied with the relationship between subjectivity, ethical dispositions, and the technical. Like Mitchell and Hecht, I am interested in understanding the ways in which the technical is both shaped by and shapes the social world, with often unintended effects; more specifically, however, my focus is on the techno-political modalities through which subjects are formed and dispositions fashioned. It is at this more micro-political scale that the technical and the infrastructural become a location in which ethical and political questions are materially assembled, mediated, and negotiated.

THE "AGENCY OF THE PENNY-IN-THE-SLOT METER" (LONDON, 1888)

The prepaid meter began its career in Britain in 1888, late in a century that had witnessed the proliferation of machinery and technical devices, not just in the production process, but also increasingly saturating social life outside the factory. Indeed, the rise of the "social" itself was only possible by means of the knowledges produced by new techniques of enumeration, statistics, and other administrative technologies of accounting (Donzelot 1988). What Ian Hacking (1990) described as the "avalanche of numbers" was, one might say, produced by an avalanche of technical devices. Such technical instruments shaped ways of knowing the social and introduced new modalities of identifying targets of governmental intervention; they also, as I want to explore in more detail here, became allied with particular civilizational projects and central to the production of particular subjectivities.

As perhaps the first to point to the importance of technology in the formation of modern subjectivities, Marx described how factory machinery quite literally produced the worker. He described the factory as a "lifeless mechanism" that turned workers into "its living appendages" (Marx 1990: 548). Machinery materialized the capitalist relation; it rendered "technical and palpable" the inversion of control between workers and the instruments of labor. Machinery to Marx was on the one hand parasitical and extractive—it "exhausts the nervous system to the uttermost," it "confiscates every atom of freedom, both in bodily and intellectual activity," it "soaks up living labor-power" ultimately leading to the "technical subordination of the worker to the uniform motion of the instruments of labor" (ibid).[11] On the other hand, machinery was habituating, pedagogical, and thus *productive* of particular subjectivities inextricably linked to bodily comportment: working at a machine, Marx suggested, required the worker to "learn to adapt his own movement to the uniform and unceasing motion of an automaton" (ibid: 546). Machinery thus "transforms the worker, from his early childhood, *into a part of a specialized machine*" (ibid: 547, my emphasis).

While factory machinery was seen by Marx as a disciplinary apparatus aimed at the production of docile laboring bodies; throughout the nineteenth century a flurry of technical devices increasingly structured spheres outside the immediate domain of production. In a famous essay, E. P. Thompson showed how the production of work discipline was unthinkable without devices of time measurement—clocks, bells, watches, devices for clocking workers in and out—that would produce "time-sense in its technological conditioning and . . . time-measurement as a means of labour exploitation" (Thompson 1967: 80). Importantly, such techniques of time measurement were designed to produce a more calculative spirit amongst the working classes. Calculative practices, it was thought, could be "induced by the use of machinery":

> A machine worked so many hours in the week would produce so much length of yarn or cloth. Minutes *were felt* to be factors in these results, whereas in the Potteries hours, or even days at times, were hardly felt to be such factors (as cited in Thompson 1967: 75, my emphasis).

In other words, here machinery not only measured the commodities produced, but also, and in the process, made time *sensory*; minutes could be

---

11   This subordination was often unsuccessful. Marx cites Ure's complaint about the "difficulty . . . in training human beings to renounce their desultory habits of work, and to identify themselves with the unvarying regularity of the complex automaton. . . . Even at the present day, when the system is perfectly organized and its labour lightened to the utmost, it is found nearly impossible to convert persons past the age of puberty into useful factory hands" (Ure as cited in Marx 1990: 549).

"felt" rather than merely registered cognitively. An ethics of calculation could be produced through a transformation of bodily sensation and comportment which in turn was dependent on the intervention of machinery and other technical devices at a somatic and sensory register.

This close link between technology, bodily comportment, and new forms of subjectivity, while most acutely observable in the factory, was in the latter half of the nineteenth century increasingly extended to other domains. The squalor of working class life became a matter of concern, often expressed in the register of public health and addressed by disciplinary institutions from the poorhouse to the hospital.[12] Similarly, with the increasing focus on urban planning and civil engineering, the latter half of the nineteenth century witnessed a thorough reorganization of space, most centrally introducing new topographies of the public and the private (Joyce 2003; Otter 2008). An emphasis on openness and visibility in the city's spatial layout—larger avenues, more open spaces—was matched by the increasing privatization and nuclearization of the family.[13]

Although gas lighting had been invented in the eighteenth century, throughout much of the nineteenth century its domestic use had remained limited to wealthier households. Working-class homes had remained excluded from networked grids and instead relied on candles, oil lamps, and coal for lighting and heating. The darkness of the working-class home was increasingly seen as a problem, in particular given the growing emphasis on public hygiene and concerns about the time spent by workers in better lit and warmer pubs (Daunton 1983). Infrastructures—and the circulation of water, electricity, and gas they enabled—were seen as central in the effort to produce the domestic conditions on which a new moral order could be founded (Joyce 2003).[14] As Schivelbusch has argued, domestic infrastructures while often providing more comfort, for many consumers signaled a loss of autonomy—infrastructures were perceived to be "sending out tentacles, octopus-like, into every house" (Schivelbusch 1988: 29). This feeling was not unfounded as the extension of infrastructure was an instance of a larger process of the gradual decline of the "total household," that

12   See here in particular Foucault's depiction of the disciplines: "Over the whole surface of contact between the body and the object it handles, power is introduced, fastening them to one another. It constitutes a body-weapon, body-tool, body-machine complex" (Foucault 1977: 153).

13   Working-class housing, for example, was reorganized from barracks with shared space, toward nuclear family units with separate infrastructure connections and enclosed backyards.

14   Chadwick's report recommended "that the removal of noxious physical circumstances, and the promotion of civic, household, and personal cleanliness, are necessary to the improvement of the moral condition of the population; for that sound morality and refinement in manners and health are not long found co-existent with filthy habits amongst any class of the community" (Chadwick 1842: 372). Chadwick's "sanitary city" became the model not just in the metropole, but also in the colonies (cf. Gandy 2004; McFarlane 2008; Swanson 1977).

is, the self-sufficient, producing household, replacing it with a household that was increasingly connected to and dependent on a larger whole, the national *oikos*.[15] What Hannah Arendt (1958) and after her Foucault (1978) described as the entrance of biology into political life, thus became materialized in city infrastructures and, indeed, within individual households.

It is in this context of the rise of biopolitics and its technics that the "penny-in-the-slot meter" was invented and dramatically changed the politics of infrastructure. Within ten years, over 60 percent of Londoners had domestic gas connections via the slot meter, and the number of gas consumers increased from two to eight million. As one engineering report noted at the time, many dark working-class areas had thus "become illuminated through the agency of the penny-in-the-slot meter."[16] Although the slot meter enabled the integration of the whole city within a networked grid, it simultaneously divided its population into two sets. A first segment, mostly wealthier households that could be trusted to pay monthly or quarterly bills and hence would have a contractual relationship to the utilities, and a second segment, mostly the working classes, who would have their connection to infrastructure regulated by a technical device, and were thus more precariously located outside of such contractual relations. Unactivated, the meter would automatically disconnect them from the city's flows.

As with other practices of metrology and automation during the nineteenth century, prepayment technology became closely bound up with distinctly modern moral anxieties about the blurring of human and technical agency.[17] On the one hand, the automated mechanism of the meters aroused suspicions about the morality of machinic agency, much like the newly invented vending machines that had come into use to sell tobacco or sweets. Numerous accounts of the time depict such "automatic machines" as "immoral," tempting users to cheat and in turn prone to cheating the users, laying bare the uneasy coincidence of an unprecedented exaltation of the autonomous human agent and her increasing, but surreptitious dependence on technical instruments.[18]

---

15   Energy sources, for example, became increasingly centralized in large technical systems (Hughes 1999). While candles and paraffin were available from various sources, gas or electricity was usually only available from one source via a fixed network of pipes or wires.

16   Association of Gas Engineers and Managers. 1895. UK, *Report of Proceedings 1895*, p. 302.

17   On the moral economies of measurement, see Gooday (2004) and Wise (1995).

18   See, for example, the satirical depiction of "automatic machines" by nineteenth-century humorist Jerome K. Jerome:

[I]t is not only in his pocket that [automatic machines] ruin a man. They damage his immortal soul. They warp his moral nature. . . . You see, when doing business with an ordinary human tradesman, various considerations occur to you, causing you to pause before

On the other hand, much like the devices of scientific objectivity studied by Daston and Galison (2007), penny-in-the-slot meters were invested with human virtues such as patience, preciseness, and continuous alertness; virtues, which ironically most humans were now seen as lacking. The meters—alongside other domestic measuring devices such as thermometers, scales, or clocks—were seen as capable of eliciting and shaping certain habits, subjectivities, and dispositions. Indeed, they became integrated within a set of larger moral-political concerns that defined the late Victorian era (cf. Otter 2008). First, the slot meter, in its ability to extend gas services, was seen as aiding in the "moral upliftment" of the working classes by improving domestic sanitary practices and encouraging domesticity by simplifying the cooking of warm meals and thus discouraging men from frequenting pubs. Gas was perceived to be a "sanitary" force that, as one leading member of the gas industry suggested, would be a "measure of moral reform" (Daunton 1983).

A second moral political concern was the constitution of the worker not only as a producer, but also as a judicious consumer, in particular in a context of the increasing centrality of credit and consumption to economic life (Poovey 2008). Consumer culture had emerged in the 1840s largely involving the middle and wealthier classes. Here exhibitions and show rooms lured buyers, providing the spectacles of the commodity fetish, so acutely described by Benjamin (1999) in his Arcades Project. During much of this period the working classes had remained at the margins of consumer society and were viewed as prone to "preindustrial" forms of consumption and irrational money-spending. In many reports of the time, prepaid meters were perceived as devices that would aid in the production of a more rational attitude to spending, most centrally through the encouragement of an ethos of budgeting. As an advertisement by a prepayment meter manufacturer put it shortly after its invention:

The benefit to the Small Consumer is evident, as he has no calls nor collectors dunning him for the payment of the Gas bill. When he used his pennyworth, he

---

endeavoring to rob him. You think of his wife and children, or you reflect that he may possibly catch you at it, and give you in charge. But from a deal with a cast iron automaton all such elevating influences are entirely absent. . . . The thing seems to be made to be robbed. The first one I ever saw stirred all the thieving instincts within me that had been lying dormant for years. . . . The virtue of the nation is being drained into their capacious slots. . . . Very often . . . the machine robs the customer by taking his pennies away from him and giving him nothing in for it. In consequence of this, folks who might otherwise be honest are compelled, in sheer self-defense, to try and cheat the machine on every possible occasion; and thus a general spirit of guile is fostered through the land. Personally, there is nothing . . . arouses more sinful thoughts in my bosom, than being done out of my money by one of these soulless automata" (Jerome 1892: 601–603).

can always drop in another penny and start afresh. He need not fear having his Gas cut off; he pays as much as he can or likes, consumes what he pleases, and becomes his own master so far as his Gas supply is concerned.[19]

While the benefits of the meters were widely touted in engineering journals of the time, the actual process of their introduction was beset by problems. In the beginning, meters tended to be imprecise. Often the collections of coins from households would find a discrepancy between the gas used and the coins emptied from the meter by the collector, which, as one report put it, tended to "destroy the confidence of the user in the penny-in-the slot meter."[20] A Belfast columnist, pondering the impending introduction of prepayment meters in 1890, similarly expressed the fear that the meter would exhibit problems similar to confectionary or tobacco dispensers: "But the annoying part of the business is that in about eight cases out of ten the recalcitrant 'automatic' refuses to disgorge that modicum of its contents which it is supposed to be prepared to part with in return for the coin of the generous would-be purchaser."[21] And while engineers were certain that improvements in the technology would eliminate any doubts about the meter's accuracy, this could never quite be established in the user's mind. To "lie like an automatic gas meter" soon became a popular metaphor to express habitual mendacity.

It was not only the meter that posed obstacles to the smooth operation. The introduction of gas via the prepayment meter into working class homes was not a forgone conclusion, but required the creation of demand.[22] A perhaps even greater challenge was to make the user respond to the new device in expected ways. Meters were broken into, coins were inserted on a string, and foreign coins would get stuck in the meter, leading one engineering report to soberly note that the meters could only

19   The Prepayment Gas Meter Company (Limited), Advertisements & Notices, *Birmingham (England) Daily Post*, April 1, 1895.
20   Report, Association of Gas Engineers and Managers, 1896: 307.
21   "The Automatic Gasmeter," *Belfast News-Letter*, March 7, 1896. Despite these worries, the columnist, like most of his contemporaries, goes on to hail the meter as much safer than other automatic devices.
22   In this endeavor, again, the introduction of further technical devices—a further extension of the socio-technical network—provided a solution. While advertising, canvassing, and exhibitions in the nineteenth century were central to the production of a consumer society, a more successful strategy adopted by gas companies was the provision of appliances to households free of charge or for a small hiring fee. Gas cookers would, for example, be installed with the prepayment meter, thus guaranteeing a certain level of gas consumption and making gas a regular and soon to be indispensable feature of housework. This linking of new domestic devices with the prepaid meter not only produced a new way of doing and relating to housework, but also drastically transformed the household economy (Clendinning 2004).

be deployed in "localities where people were exceptionally honest."[23] In the initial stages of the invention, enormous trust had to be placed in the penny collector, who was also prone to help himself to coins from the piles he collected daily. But, in the end, for many engineers it was again technology that would solve these "human" problems. As one report put it, "both the penny collector and the householder may be dishonest; but, unlike the human heart, the metallic mechanism of these automata cannot be demoralised."[24]

In the early years, then, the problem of innovation in prepayment technology lay in gauging *how to distribute agencies*. Could measurement be left to the meter, or would the penny collector have to double-check? Could the collector be trusted not to serve himself? Would consumers be trustworthy or, as Clark might put it, "polite" enough not to tamper with the meter? The meter and the user thus needed to be co-constructed.[25] Importantly, however, these co-constructions were inspired by and became allied with a liberal project. Indeed, it could be argued that the engineers' worries spoke to a larger liberal conundrum of distributing agencies and responsibilities: how to avoid governing too much, which population groups to include as reasonable members of the social contract and which to designate as in need of tutelage. This continuous redistribution of agencies, or what one might call *agencement* (Callon 2007), took the shape of an ongoing techno-political battle in which the technology itself became the terrain on which such ethical and political questions were negotiated. The autonomous self-governing citizen, so central to the liberal imagination, here emerges as a precarious socio-technical achievement, a figure unthinkable without the work of tools, devices, and infrastructures.

What Clark identified as British politeness, then, was not a forgone conclusion, but had to be painstakingly manufactured and was always prone to failure. And yet Clark was correct in assuming that the meters would not simply travel smoothly to South Africa. The transfer of expertise, as Richard Rottenburg (2009) has shown, is predicated on a labor of translation. How a technology moves from context to context and what travels with it and what stays behind is thus an open question—once they leave their makers, technologies are "unstable objects" (Larkin 2008). And yet, as technologies move to new contexts, they also become restabilized: harnessed to new projects and anchored to new ethical regimes. It is this semiotic-material *work* that goes into making devices functional within specific ethico-political assemblages that I explore below.

23 "Penny-in-the-Slot Gas Meters," *Western Mail* (Cardiff, Wales), November 8, 1898.
24 "Penny-in-the-slot meters," *Liverpool Mercury*, June 19, 1893, p. 5.
25 See Woolgar (1991) on the "configuration of the user."

BUDGET ENERGY CONTROLLERS
(JOHANNESBURG, 1988)

As Clark himself was well aware, the context in which the prepaid meter came to be deployed in South Africa was quite different from late-nineteenth-century Britain. South Africa in the 1980s, he suggested, was "in a mess" because of "that political thing." For him, as for many other engineers I spoke to in the course of my fieldwork, talking about "politics" was not part of their job description and was often accompanied by frowns or pained expressions. Many had been in the business since the apartheid period and were at best uncertain about how to incorporate the antiapartheid struggle into the narration of their professional biographies.

As I showed in the last chapter, the antiapartheid struggle became known to the world outside South Africa through its campaigns for political rights, which for the most part were articulated at a national scale, but it often took the shape of localized struggles that involved the more tangible, if less visible administrative connections to the apartheid state. During the "rent boycotts" in the 1980s, township residents all over South Africa withheld payment for rents and service charges as part of the effort to make the townships "ungovernable." Such acts of fiscal disobedience became both symbolic and material tools of insurgency—with dramatic effects—disabling township administrations and turning disconnections from services and evictions into sites of political struggle. It was in this increasingly militant and militarized context of the boycotts that engineers began the search for technical solutions to the problem of nonpayment.

At the same time, there were increasing moves toward the electrification of the townships by Eskom, South Africa's powerful electricity parastatal. Over the course of the 1970s and 1980s, it had become clear that "urban Africans" would not "return" to the Bantustans as grand-apartheid ideologues had envisioned. This realization prompted an increasing interest in the black urban population as an untapped market and as potential consumers of electricity and electrical appliances, particularly given that Eskom had an overcapacity of electricity generation at the time. It had also become increasingly clear to local officials that the disparity of services between black and white areas had become a major cause for urban protest. While white areas were fully electrified, in most townships there was either no or minimal domestic electrification. In 1988, Eskom thus embarked on its "Electricity for All" program that sought to extend electricity to all black households. It was in this profoundly paradoxical context of planned large-scale electrification and simultaneous politicized nonpayment–of "reform" and counterinsurgency—that prepaid meters emerged.

As Peter Clark told me, in 1986 he and a colleague developed the first South African prepaid meter and tested it in the Bantustan QwaQwa that had also been hit by widespread nonpayment. Much as for engineers in Britain, one of his primary tasks was to construct a functional assemblage of device, consumer, and utility. Clark transformed the original technology primarily in two ways. First, in order to "protect" it from South African users, he replaced the coins with a magnetic card and nontransferable "tokens." In this way, credit would be linked to a specific household, and the cash transaction would be limited to the local pay point. Second, the protective box around the meter needed to be made of cheaper, yet sturdy material to discourage residents from selling it as scrap metal. Apart from making changes in the technology, however, and similar to utilities in nineteenth-century England, Eskom needed to configure its users. One crucial issue, for example, was the creation of demand for electricity, particularly in a context of cheaper energy alternatives, a problem the utility sought to solve by providing residents with free basic appliances, such as lamps or hotplates. And yet, as several engineers told me, when visiting individual households at the time, they would often find the prepaid meter box blackened from the smoke emitted by a fire burning from a wood stove underneath, the electric hotplate not being used at all.

By the late 1980s, and in a context of both large-scale electrification and simultaneous nonpayment, prepaid meters began to be commercially produced by South African companies on a large scale.[26] Then variously known as "Budget Energy Controllers," "Econometers," "E-Kard electricity dispensing system" or simply "Electricity Dispensers," prepaid meters were hailed as "the next major technological breakthrough following the invention of the computer" since "at one stroke the twin problem of unpaid electricity accounts and meter reading are eliminated."[27] Similarly, it was argued that they would aid in "the elimination of bad debts, meter reading and disconnections/reconnections."[28] For yet another supporter, prepaid meters would "allow the supply of electricity to communities previously considered unsuitable."[29] The political implications, while not often openly admitted, were also clear to manufacturers. It was, as one

26   The biggest prepayment electricity meter company, Conlog, emerged out of a venture established during the 1980s between the Israeli group Elron and the company Control Logic owned by the South African mining corporation Anglo-American (Hunter 1986). In many instances, the companies that took on the commercial production of prepayment meters had previously been primarily involved in manufacturing security technologies and military electronic equipment.

27   George Malan, "Budget Energy Controllers Can Solve Non-Payment of Water Accounts," *Municipal Engineer* 20, no. 10 (October 1989): 58.

28   Herman Bos, "Prepayment Electricity Dispensing," *Municipal Engineer* 22, no. 4 (April 1991): 21.

29   Conlog, "Prepaid Metering: A New Concept," *Municipal Engineer* 21, no. 4 (April 1990): 2–3.

engineer put it in retrospect, the result of efforts "to solve the problem of non-payment for electricity by means of a technology intervention."[30] Ten years earlier, another South African manufacturer had suggested more explicitly that "the development of prepayment technology . . . will help to depoliticise the supply of electricity such that energy does not become a pawn in the ideological struggles which the country is bound to face in the years ahead."[31] By 1992, prepayment was explicitly mentioned in a report by the Presidents' Committee on Economic Affairs on a new urbanization strategy. The report argued for the investigation of "prepayment schemes" "to eliminate administrative and other difficulties with regard to payment for services" (RSA 1992). In a conversation I had with a key representative of the apartheid state during the 1980s Soweto negotiations, he suggested that the prepayment meter during the 1980s was a "political tool" to deal with nonpayment.

The political target and effects of the invention became most apparent in Clark's depiction of the early trials, during which engineers began simultaneous negotiations with the white municipalities and the rent boycotters in the adjacent black townships. In the late 1980s, Clark, by then employed by a meter manufacturer, started marketing the meters to individual municipalities *specifically* as devices that would enable breaking the boycotts and thereby eliminate the need to access the townships directly to institute disconnections. Simultaneously, he marketed the meters to the boycott leaders, who desired electricity for the townships, but were unwilling to negotiate with the white municipalities. As Clark put it:

> We realized that we needed to go straight to the community. We . . . approached [the civic organisations] and said: "Look, we understand that you have a war, but we know you want electricity. With [prepayment], you will have both— electricity and no contract with the government. Nobody will ever come in again to disconnect you." There was a lot of psychology involved.

Although Clark was eager to tell me about the successes, often such negotiations with the civics failed. As one observer from the civics-aligned NGO Planact noted in 1992, prepaid meters were "fast becoming dangerously discredited" and had become "a source of real controversy in many townships, while some civics refuse to even discuss them" (Cobbett 1992: 5f). Indeed, as one document produced by the civics in the context of the ongoing negotiation argued, "to date, electricity supplies to Soweto

---

30   J. Groenewald, "From Legacy to Legendary: Migration of Prepayment Vending Systems in South Africa," *Energy Supply Industry (ESI) Africa* 18, no. 1 (April 2002).

31   See the account by a representative of an early prepaid meter manufacturing company, Plessey Tellumat SA Ltd (Stevenson 1992).

have operated as if electricity was virtually a pure public good. . . . This in turn defined consumers as a collectivity which in turn created the basis for organized social mobilization." Eskom's various reform proposals, the document went on, "involve a series of complex mechanisms designed to break down this mode of provision and hence the material basis for opposition . . . the new metering technology will facilitate the provision of differential quantities of electricity at metered unit prices to each individual consumer—metering cards would be the extreme version of this break down of collectivity."[32]

During the 1980s, prepaid meters were thus invested with the capacity to delink questions of payment and infrastructure from larger claims to citizenship and to re-establish and materially enforce the boundary between the administrative and the political, a fact that was well recognized by activists. In this way, the meters were harnessed to a late-apartheid techno-politics that combined piecemeal "reforms" with a fierce defense of minority rule.[33] However, partly as a result of such contradictions and failures, many projects stayed at the trial phase and only relatively few prepaid meters were in fact deployed in the 1980s. It was thus ironically only in the aftermath of apartheid that prepaid meters deployed on a mass scale.

While the meters began their life as tools of moral improvement in the era of Victorian liberalism, in their move to late-apartheid South Africa they were thus reassembled as devices of counterinsurgency. In both moments, specific ethical and political projects were delegated to technology, and technology itself became a terrain on which such questions were expressed and negotiated. What joined the two moments, and what "traveled" with the meter, is the ability to delegate protracted ethico-political questions—of belonging, civic virtue, and indeed the limits of citizenship—to a technical terrain. The meters, as technical forms of "political society," thus produce what might be termed a graduated social contract by which citizenship is *de facto* mediated on an administrative terrain. And yet, even in a context of seemingly radical depoliticization, technical devices are constitutive of a material politics in a variety of ways and open to a diverse set of ethical claims and affective investments.

In contemporary South Africa, this material politics has taken several, seemingly counterintuitive forms. In a context of continued widespread nonpayment in townships like Soweto and a neoliberal imperative for "cost recovery," prepayment technology has become the default mode of

32   "An Assessment of Eskom's Proposals for Resolving Problems Related to the Supply of Electricity to Soweto" (on behalf of the Soweto People's Delegation) (n.d.) Planact Collection AL 2666 21.5.16.3, Wits Department of Historical Papers.

33   Ironically, it is the legacy of apartheid techno-politics that in part accounts for South Africa's contemporary status as a "global" leader in prepayment technologies.

connecting poorer township residents to services, in the process often cutting previously unmetered access to services. Here, this graduated social
contract maps onto the racial legacies of apartheid and is often experienced
as punitive. Thus, prepayment metering becomes the terrain for an ongoing techno-political struggle over the limits of citizenship. Simultaneously, the meters are sometimes deployed to *extend* services to residents
of informal settlements. Here, they enable the connection of residents to
the grid for the first time, while simultaneously rendering this connection
precarious. Finally, there has also been an increasing demand for prepaid
meters, often from wealthier residents who mistrust municipal accounting
practices and see the meters as devices to wrest control from unaccountable city officials. Indeed, implicit in such demands for prepaid meters is
often a desire to withdraw from the contractual relationship with a local
state that is perceived as biased and untrustworthy. In an ironic reversal,
this too produces a graduated social contract, although one initiated and
demanded by residents themselves. Thus even in this context, the meter
becomes the object and terrain for ethical and political questions of trust,
belonging, and civic obligation. As prepaid meters increasingly become the
default way to connect all residents to infrastructure,[34] yet other ways of
assembling ethics, politics and technics may emerge.

BAD PAYERS, SMART METERS, AND "TECHNICAL" INNOVATION

After about an hour, my conversation with Peter Clark was interrupted by
the Annual Prepayment Award ceremony that had been scheduled for that
night. Sponsored by South Africa's largest cell phone company, the award
is given each year to the company with the most innovative prepayment
concept. The invention that won the award this year was a device called
the Information Link at Point of Delivery, short InfoPOD, developed by
Peter Clark's employer, the multinational company Actaris Metering Systems. The Minister of Minerals and Energy, Phumzile Mlambo-Ngcuka,
had been invited to the ceremony to present the award. In her speech, she
thanked Actaris for their tireless efforts for development and infrastructure
in South Africa.

Although prepayment technology was presented at the award ceremony
as the transparent result of technological progress and South African

---

34   In 2011, Johannesburg mayor Parks Tau announced that Johannesburg will become a
"prepaid city." Less than two years later, in April 2013, City Power, Johannesburg's electricity
utility, announced plans to install prepaid meters for all of its users.

ingenuity, throughout the conference this linear narrative had steadily unraveled. Earlier in the day, a group of protesters had gathered outside the convention center armed with placards reading, DOWN WITH PREPAIDS! This was not particularly surprising to the delegates, who, after numerous demonstrations and a looming legal challenge, were well aware of the multiple objections to prepayment, especially for water. Meanwhile, inside the conference rooms, a less visible kind of politics emerged, which involved the design of the technology itself. In the course of a host of PowerPoint presentations, what emerged was an industry in constant struggle with "nontechnical" problems—government intrusions, legal hurdles, problems of standardization and financing, and centrally a variety of noncompliant consumers, who emerged as the protagonists in a seemingly perennial conflict over payment for services.

Despite the end of apartheid in 1994, many township residents had never resumed payment for services. Campaigns urging residents to pay for services in the name of national reconstruction had failed spectacularly, and in places like Soweto nonpayment had in fact increased. Manual cutoffs from services and illegal reconnections were widespread, often aided by residents' organization such as the Soweto Electricity Crisis Committee. At the same time, many municipalities began instituting neoliberal reforms and thus the pressure to institute "cost recovery" had grown dramatically. It was against this backdrop that prepayment technology came into wide use: this time, a technical solution to the failure of nationalist interpellation. In the ten years following the end of apartheid, five million households had thus been fitted with prepaid meters. Within a few years, however, many of these meters had been bypassed by residents, rendering the meters useless and giving residents illicit access to electricity. This in turn had left Eskom with the impossible task of manually checking and disconnecting each account. And it was *this* problem of the bypassed meters that preoccupied many presentations at the conference. I will focus here on two of the proposed solutions in order to illustrate this techno-politics of innovation.

As an arena of technology development, municipal engineering is in many respects unique, in that it is addressed primarily at populations and not merely at individual users. Infrastructure developers are often centrally concerned with constructing and managing particular relations to utilities and the state, albeit relations usually conceived of as administrative rather than political. Indeed, in many of the presentations, what emerged most saliently were the relationships that could be established between the user and the technology, and how these relationships would in turn mediate the population's relation to the utility or municipality. The value of the meters could only be established after an indication about how well it would fare in the establishment and durability of such relationships. This in turn required engineers to demonstrate not just knowledge of basic demographics, but also knowledge of a sociological kind, including a certain interpretive skill. For example, engineers needed to be aware of the history of payment practices in a particular area, which in turn was often bound up with the political histories of the townships. They needed to demonstrate how they had gone about testing the meters, which potential obstacles they had considered, or what kinds of "social interventions" would be needed to ensure "user acceptability." Presentations thus often included the results of field trials or pilot projects that could demonstrate a certain *local* knowledge. The importance of this mobilization of local knowledge became most obvious in the disjuncture between international and local presenters.

The day started with a presentation by a French representative of a large global infrastructure technology company who introduced the concept of "Automatic Meter Management" (AMM), a combination of prepayment and "smart" metering technology that would enable remote communication between the meter and the utility. The novelty of this technology was its claim to universal usability, that is, as the engineer put it, its ability to flexibly respond to "*global* challenges." In outlining each of these challenges, he created a peculiar map of the world from the perspective of the global trade in infrastructure technology that divided the world according to distinct "customer bases" with a diversity of needs, various levels of trustworthiness and sophistication, and a range of more or less predictable behavior patterns. In the "first world," for example, the meters needed to be compatible with internet services to enable online billing or to offer customers flexible tariffs. In "third world" contexts and in places like South Africa, he argued, AMM would enable the "constant monitoring" of consumption and thus help eradicate bad payment, illegal connections, and theft.

Standard metering, the engineer argued, was insecure and thus required constant auditing by utility employees. In a PowerPoint slide he summarized the resulting problems in the following way:

"1000 Inspectors with 1000 dogs" can visit any account at least once a year . . .

- If they were to know where to go . . . without political biases
- If they are let in . . .
- If this does not create political repulsion against the Utility . . .
- Frauds can be reinstalled a day after the visit . . .
- Evidence about frauds may be insufficient to recover past losses
- . . . and why could not the readers execute this fraud eradication program before?
- . . . and would anyone replace a dumb old electromechanical meter with a new, still dumb, electromechanical meter bound to be tampered with soon?

It is in PowerPoint slides such as this that the process of "delegating" scripts to technology becomes explicit. Older, "dumb" meters require a municipal official to audit the meter. This in turn opens the door for all sorts of problems. As the engineer suggested, residents may decide not to let the meter reader in, he may become the target for "political repulsion," or he may be unreliable himself. Even with the aid of a dog, meter readers would be under threat, as demonstrated by another PowerPoint slide showing a cartoon meter reader getting a brick thrown at his head. AMM would *delegate* the functions of auditing the meter from humans to technology. Measuring, meter reading, surveillance and disconnections could now be performed by one technical device. Thus, the meter itself would "provide ways to bring [such] behaviors back to law and help dealing with the political issues of these customers." The technology would not only eliminate the unreliability of the municipal official and the possibility of bypassing the meter, but also the space for negotiations or protests left open by the presence of an official. Thus, the technology would, the engineer argued, perform "political" operations. AMM then was *one way* in which disputes over payment could be delegated to technology.

Having outlined the problem in this way, the engineer proceeded to propose a "massive installation of new electronic meters [to] create a fraud-free installed base." Once operational, the "smart" AMM meters would enable the continuous monitoring of energy flow, producing an "auditable track record of consumption patterns" that could be used to track down residents trying to defraud the meters. This, he argued would be the "most systematic" solution to end nonpayment and theft.

The presentation seemed to garner limited interest from South African delegates. It was quite clearly a costly solution that didn't speak to the financial constraints faced by South African utilities. More important, in the absence of evidence from a field trial, the engineer was unable to generate the *kind* of authority that would convince the other delegates. As one South African delegate argued, "Consumers will for some reason accept a technology type in one country, but in the next they will not accept it all. This behavior is unpredictable and will ruin your venture and your investors' trust in your solution." What was required, in other words, were mechanisms that would limit the unpredictability of consumers' responses. And this, in turn, required a more sociological kind of knowledge and, indeed, a *thicker* description of the relations between communities and the local state.

It is here that the award-winning Information Link at Point of Delivery (InfoPOD) raised the interest of the other participants and quickly cast aside "global" solutions. In his presentation, the InfoPOD's developer, a local representative from Eskom, laid out the problem. Eskom could ill afford to replace its entire existing "dumb" prepaid meter base. On the other hand, many of the installed meters had been bypassed and had thus become

useless. The InfoPOD, which had been piloted in the past year, would provide the solution. The InfoPOD—described by its developer as "a walk-by,
non-intrusive, non-contact system to collect information from prepayment
meters"—is a small radio device that can be attached to existing prepaid
meters to enable officials to track tampering by accessing the meter re-
motely without needing physical access to residents' premises. Retrofitted
with the InfoPOD, the old meters would, as it were, become "smarter."
Rather than having to enter the premises, utility employees could now
drive or walk through the township with a radio receiver and automatically
collect information from the meters at a distance.

Importantly, his presentation also included a discussion of the potential problems that could be expected during the introduction of the new
devices. Asked how it would be possible to make people agree to such an
installation, the engineer suggested: "When you come there, you don't
only tell them that [the InfoPOD] is there to detect tampering. You tell
them about the nice benefits. You have to be strategic, if I can put it that
way." The success of such "technical" innovation thus relied centrally on
engineers' local knowledge and on their capacity for thick description and
strategic intervention.

Viewed from this perspective, the InfoPOD was only the latest install-
ment in a series of strategic measures to enforce payment—from appeals to
civic virtue to the compulsions of a technical device—and thus to fashion
a new relation between the local state and its citizens. It was an "antiprogram," to use Latour's term.[35] As I showed in the previous chapter, exhortations had failed to convince residents, so prepaid meters were originally designed to do the job, cutting nonpayers off once credit had run out. Many if
not most householders, however, had within a few years of the meters' life
bypassed them, rendering the technology useless and necessitating meter
readers to come and check each meter's functionality, often at some personal risk.[36] What made the InfoPOD valuable, then, was its capacity to
strategically intervene in an ongoing conflict over payment, albeit one that
was now carried out in the *form* of technology and at an administrative
register. It was just *one move* within an ongoing techno-political battle.

35 In coining the terms "programs of action" and "antiprogram," Latour (1992) suggests
that actions may be inscribed or anticipated within technical artifacts. These may, however,
in turn be obstructed by other programs of actions, or antiprograms. Thus, an artifact can be
"de-scribed" according to its programs of action (or antiprograms).

36 As the editor of the Cape Town–based industry journal *Metering International* had explained to me a few months earlier somewhat hyperbolically: "One of the beauties of AMR is
that it makes tampering very easy to detect . . . without having to visit the site. You see, visiting
the sites and checking for tampering can result in lynch mobs. The community, if they see the
inspectors coming round, are very unhappy, because they have been tampering with their meters, and they know the inspectors is going to cut them off if they discover that the meter has
been tampered with. And there has been violence, I'm sorry to say, in more than one instance."

At the end of the conference, a delegate from Johannesburg told me epic stories about the various obstacles that had to be overcome by engineers throughout the history of prepayment technology in South Africa. Finally, he suggested, "You know, the providers thought that people are uneducated, but in fact, a lot of innovation happens through them. If it wasn't for people regularly subverting the meter, we all wouldn't be here." And indeed, while much of this chapter has been concerned with the experts at the conference, its absent protagonists were the "users," the "cunning water thieves," the "economic saboteurs," the "bad payers," "tamperers," "electricity poachers," and the residents with "political problems." Prepayment metering in South Africa is an industry that *requires* constant innovation, because the latest technologies are quickly out of date, having been pulled out, bypassed, broken, or rewired. New antiprograms are thus required on a regular basis: "smarter meters," "security seals," tools that "audit," "track," "monitor," and "enable remote disconnections." Here, then, technical expertise is produced in constant conflict with a form of technical counterexpertise.[37]

Importantly, my point here is not to tell a story of small acts of resistance to rationalization, neoliberalism, or modernity;[38] rather, my goal has been to map a techno-political terrain that often remains invisible in the common analytic focus on the public and on immaterial speech. Indeed, invested in the "technical" transformations I traced above are strategic scripts and counterscripts—interventions in an ongoing series of low-intensity conflicts that have become materialized within the technology itself. Such a micro techno-politics concerns central moral-political questions about civic virtue and postapartheid citizenship, albeit in a dramatically different form. In this context, infrastructure is not merely a tool or a symbol *for* the political, nor *merely* a conduit of power; rather, infrastructure itself is a political terrain. Indeed, this is a politics of nonpublics, inscribed within pipes, wires, and technical devices as much as in the more visible protests that continue to make headline news on a regular basis in South Africa.

CONCLUSIONS

The South African story of the prepaid meter is, of course, in many ways specific. As the meter travels on, many different stories can surely be told. And yet, we might discover a similar *kind* of techno-politics in a diversity of locations and forms. Prepayment technology is only one of a host of

---

37   In this sense, this is an instance of what Michel Callon (2009) calls expertise "in the wild," that is, an instance in which the knowledge of lay people outside the laboratory setting comes to challenge the "secluded research" by professionals.

38   A point that was made by James Scott (1985) thirty years ago.

other new technological innovations dealing specifically with the financial transactions of the poor. There is today an unprecedented investment in developing sometimes highly sophisticated technologies for the poor and their presumed condition.[39] In much of the world, such technical devices increasingly mediate relationships between populations and the state or NGOs. Such technologies are often alternatively invested with a magical power to radically improve the lives of the poor or decried as tools of domination or surveillance. What I have suggested here is that seemingly neutral technical mediators come to do work within a diversity of ethico-political projects beyond their apparent pragmatism. Tracking the travels of such technical devices and ethnographically following the work of their inscription may thus enable us to "de-scribe" a politics in unfamiliar places and in unexpected forms. In turn, it might expand the conceptual and imaginative horizons of how we study and conceive of the political.

In a context in which the formal political sphere appears increasingly inaccessible, such material links often become the location at which political and ethical questions are negotiated and contested. Questions concerning citizenship, belonging, or civic virtue may here be expressed by flicking a switch, cutting off a wire, or by installing a smarter meter. This is a politics far removed from the modern political imaginaries of a transparent, unencumbered sphere of public deliberation. Of course, at certain times, as during the protests in Chiawelo with which I began, and in the many protests and debates I describe in this book, this material politics does become public, transforming technics into a "matter of concern" (Latour 2004). But even here, looking more closely, "public" protest is often intimately tied to the more invisible forms of techno-politics I have outlined in this chapter.

Returning to the protest in Chiawelo, it became apparent later that the protest was spawned, at least in part, by a new technical counterscript. Indeed, residents of Chiawelo had already had prepaid meters for a long time, but, as in other areas of Soweto, many of the meters had been bypassed. The protests, it emerged, were prompted by a pilot project, begun a few years earlier, to install a new type of "split meter," an innovation that divides the meter into two parts: a touchpad to enter in the credit code located in the house and the actual meter now located outside on the pavements in unbreakable, "tamperproof" green steel boxes—a new

39 Not all of these are technologies designed for use by the poor, but most are developed specifically for the global south. See, for example, the development of biometric devices to distribute social grants in South Africa, which are increasingly also used elsewhere (Breckenridge 2010, 2014; Donovan 2015); informal finance and banking technologies (Maurer 2012,); biometric identification of refugees (Fassin 2011); or, more broadly, humanitarian design (Cross 2013; Redfield 2012).

antiprogram, one even more secure than the InfoPOD. And yet, three months after the protests, in October 2011, an audit by Eskom found that residents had opened the "unbreakable" green boxes with the help of grinders. Thus, the meters had been bypassed yet again, setting the stage for the development of new antiprograms in a seemingly endless cycle of innovation and subversion.

Chapter 5

MEASURING LIFE

Living Prepaid and the Politics of Numbers after Apartheid

Joyce Mofokeng had a little notebook scribbled with columns and lines of numbers. A few times each month, she pulled out a tiny three-legged plastic chair and sat down to open the water meter box that had been lodged in her front yard since the previous year when the water utility began installing prepaid water meters in Phiri. She opened the meter box with the plastic key and placed the chip tag onto the touch port next to the green LCD screen of the meter. The by now familiar series of flashing numbers and letters appeared showing her how many liters of water she had used this month and how much credit remained before the meter would automatically cut off her supply, thus alerting her that she needed to buy further credit at the local pay point. Each time Joyce flipped open the meter box to audit the meter, she wrote down all of the numbers in the tattered notebook, tabulating them into neat rows and columns. Receipts of her water credit purchases were tucked into the back of the book.

Joyce was measuring her household's water use and computing numbers. And yet, unlike her neighbor who also checked her meter a few times each month, she did so not primarily in order to budget her family's water consumption, but rather to establish an archive of numbers that could be used as evidence against the utility that had installed the prepaid meter in her yard as part of Operation Gcin'amanzi. And Joyce was not alone. In Soweto backyards, just as in academic offices and social movement centers in Johannesburg, numbers were being collected, analyzed, recalculated, and disputed. Some activist academics calculated the most equitable modes of cross-subsidization, and members of residents' groups tracked the incidence of water cutoffs, while others surveyed the township to record household size and water consumption. Activists and social movements in South Africa have been centrally preoccupied with measurement and establishing quantitative knowledge.[1]

In certain respects, this activist preoccupation with numbers is not surprising. Numbers saturate the public imagination in postapartheid South Africa. From crime statistics and unemployment figures, to HIV/ AIDS rates, numbers are displayed daily like stock market columns in newspapers, often designed to represent what are unrepresentable crises (Comaroff and Comaroff 2006b; Morris 2008). For some, this flurry of numbers is not new, but a continuation of the "mania for measurement" that defined the apartheid era; the postapartheid state, Jeremy Seekings writes, "has taken the passion for numbers to new heights" (Seekings 2006).

And yet, numbers and quantification per se don't tell us much about the work they do. As Helen Verran (2001, 2008) reminds us, numbers are not always and everywhere the same, that is, *what kinds* of numbers are collected, by whom, and to what end—all these matter to the kinds of labors numbers are to perform.[2] Numbers also depend on a particular semiotic ideology, that is, on a set of assumptions about "what signs are and how they function in the world" (Keane 2003: 419). While certain kinds of numbers work to fix things or people in place, others enable movement (of, say, goods and people). While some establish aggregates, others individuate. Similarly, the practices of quantification Joyce engaged in are not the same as those of her neighbor who also checked her meter regularly in order to budget the household's expenses. Both in turn are different from the kind of water accounting practices assumed or actively encouraged by Johannesburg Water. While each is an act of measurement and involves a meter audit, each has different ends and is invested with different meanings and, in turn, shapes different subjects.

In this chapter, I explore how specific sets of numbers were mobilized and came to do work as the metering project unfolded in Soweto. Operation Gcin'amanzi, I suggest, was a project to institute a new "metrological regime" (Barry 2002) that sought to make Soweto and water provision legible in new ways and to encourage new modalities of accounting amongst

---

1   For academic and activist calculations of water cutoffs, cross-subsidization and related numbers, see, e.g., Bond 2002; Coalition Against Water Privatisation 2004, 2005; McDonald and Pape 2002; Municipal Services Project 2001. More broadly on evidentiary practices in South African social movements see Chari 2008; Robins 2014; Storey 2014.

2   Recent literature has sought to broaden the range of performative possibilities of numbers by looking more closely at the multiple uses and semiotic-material registers of numerical practices (Bowker and Star 2000; Espeland and Stevens 1998; Guyer 2014; Guyer, Khan, and Obarrio 2010; Lampland 2010; Lampland and Star 2009; Zaloom 2006).

residents.[3] In turn, it was opposed by residents in similar metrological ways, as they produced countermeasures to oppose the numbers introduced by the utility. Taking the activist preoccupation with numbers as a starting point, I focus on the specific ways in which numbers and measurement became central, both to the planning and implementation of Operation Gcin'amanzi and to its opposition.

Although the use of numbers by activists has been discussed in a diversity of contexts, less attention has been paid to the conditions of intelligibility of such forms of making political claims and to the specific logics mobilized and summoned by numbers as activist tools.[4] Timothy Choy has argued persuasively for the importance of understanding how knowledge practices are articulated to become politically efficacious (Choy 2011: 100ff). While Choy is primarily concerned with the discursive possibilities and the metapragmatic effects of specific speech situations, in the following, I want to broaden his understanding of articulation by analyzing the larger techno-political terrain within which such numerical activism takes shape. I suggest that in order to understand how numbers become politically effective, we need to look more closely at the semiotic-material contexts within which they come to signify, how they are rendered semiotically stable, and how they come to be constituted and deployed within historically specific conjunctures of knowledge and power. If the performative force of numbers is dependent on pre-existing matrices of knowledge, it thus becomes crucial to attend to *how* numbers take on a political life, via which forms and with what uses. In order to understand Joyce's "countermeasures" and what her numbers "do," we need to first establish the context that gives her action meaning and renders her claims intelligible.

If in Chapter 4, I suggested that the prepaid meter can be understood as a techno-political device whose precise working and effect is always contingent on the specific ethical and political assemblages within which it comes to operate; here, my focus will be more specifically on how prepayment metering became part of a larger set of neoliberal reforms at the heart of which was the introduction of new epistemologies and targets for intervention and reform. What animates the current "mania for measurement," and how does it differ from apartheid forms of calculation and measurement?

---

3   Andrew Barry (2002) uses the term "metrological regime" to refer to the standardizing measures introduced by state actors to achieve certain forms of calculability, for example, ecological standards. Such regimes are always fragile, subject to, and often the product of, political disagreement.

4   On the deployment of numbers and other forms of evidence by activists, see Appadurai 2001; Ballestero 2012; Hetherington 2011; Rose 1999; Verran 2010.

What work do numbers perform today and toward what end? What are the *qualities* of quantification?

Perhaps the central claim often authorizing neoliberal reforms—and privatization and corporatization in particular—is that they will enable a more efficient allocation of resources through new and better forms of knowledge. Importantly, this claim hinges on a secondary claim; that privatization and corporatization enable different kinds of calculations that will allow actors to respond to new numerical incentives, from "price signals" to "performance targets." While processes of "marketization" are often viewed primarily as new modalities of pricing—both in critical accounts of commodification and in neoliberal arguments for liberalization—the creation of new modes of valuation and economization requires numerous interventions and semiotic-material transformations (Çalışkan and Callon 2009). Such processes of requalification are rarely friction-free and are often bound up with ethical and political questions (Miyazaki 2005). In Soweto, Operation Gcin'amanzi, and the new metrological regime on which it came to rest, required a myriad of large and small interventions; in turn, this metrological terrain became a site of contention on which much larger questions of civic virtue, the rights and duties of citizenship, and, in turn, the postapartheid condition were articulated.

This chapter explores three related points. First, I examine how Operation Gcin'amanzi emerged as part of a larger metrological project that parceled Johannesburg, Soweto, and its households into specific "spaces of calculability," thus materially and semiotically delimiting the frames within which new forms of calculation and accounting could occur (Callon 1998). The corporatization of water provision was more than merely an institutional transformation; it required work at a number of registers, not least at the level of each individual household. Second, the chapter explores how corporatization, as a particular technique to produce new modalities of calculation, ultimately came to rely on a figure of *homo economicus* that looked quite unlike the male entrepreneurial figure commonly pictured in that role. Indeed, rather than a male, disembodied calculating actor, at the center of the spaces of calculability produced by Operation Gcin'amanzi were often older women—pensioners and grandmothers—whose management of the households was dependent on the mobilization of affective capacities, everyday resources, and existing relations. Finally, I return to the question of the political terrain shaped by numbers to explore how activists deployed and resignified the numbers introduced by Operation Gcin'amanzi in making claims on the state. Here again, infrastructures and the measures through which they are rendered legible became a techno-political terrain for the negotiation of much larger questions.

A "MANIA FOR MEASUREMENT":
RACE, BUREAUCRACY, AND AFFECT

While numbers have been central to political modernity throughout, their precise functions in political life were often subject to intense debate (Hacking 1990; Porter 1996). Such disagreements about the precise role and capacity of numbers were in turn often bound up with the epistemological question of what and how the state can know. A crucial conceptual difference between Keynesian and neoliberal understandings of state intervention was a disagreement about how best to produce knowledge and what kinds of labor such knowledge could perform. The centrality accorded to the state in socialist and Keynesian regimes was based on a belief in the state as a knowing actor, in society and economy as intrinsically knowable and quantifiable and in numbers as capable of representing reality in an unambiguous way.[5] On the basis of this trust in numbers, the means and ends of state intervention became calculable. It is this set of epistemological assumptions that became the central target for neoliberal critique. Beginning with the Socialist calculation debate in the 1920s, neoliberal thinkers primarily disputed the capacity of the state to know and, by extension, its ability to intervene in social and economic processes.[6] Instead, they placed epistemological trust both in the individual and its "tacit" knowledge and in the market as a privileged site of truth (cf. Foucault 2008).

Concomitant with such epistemological premises, neoliberal reformers often relied on *different kinds* of numbers. Rather than large, collective numbers, such as statistics, that would make society and economy the object of direct intervention, they were focused on smaller, individual numbers to establish the conditions for the "self-ordering capacities" of the market to take effect and to bring *homo economicus* into being by indirectly enhancing his (or, more rarely, her) calculative capacities. According to Hayek (1945), for example, it was "price signals" that would provide individuals with the conditions to become effective market participants and thus to constitute order.[7] Here, numbers come to do a rather differ-

---

5   See here Timothy Mitchell's account of the making of "the economy" (Mitchell 2002, 2011) and work on the making of the social via statistics and other forms of numerical representation (Donzelot 1988; Ewald 1991; Hacking 1990).

6   In his seminal contribution to the debate, Hayek (1945), following an earlier argument by von Mises (1981 [1922]), suggested that knowledge is impossible to centralize. As I elaborated in Chapter 2, this antirationalist critique provided the foundation for the conception of the self-ordering capacities of the market as a "spontaneous order" constituted by the individual's "tacit knowledge." Such epistemological practices, Hayek argued, could not be captured by numbers and hence were unavailable for state intervention.

7   While Hayek's conception of "price signals" is one example, such numbers would take a diversity of forms, from what Michel Callon (2007) terms "market devices" to what Stephen Collier has more recently called "microeconomic devices" (Collier 2011).

ent kind of performative work. If in statist regimes numbers were seen as enabling the framing of a particular sphere for external intervention (e.g., via the census, population statistics, or, in South Africa, through labour bureaus), in neoliberal thought numbers are regarded primarily as subjectivating devices, that is, as central to shaping and delimiting the environment in which *individual* agencies and calculative capacities could be enhanced. It is from this divergence in the understanding of both the production and the capacities of numbers that most other conceptual differences between neoliberal and statist regimes follow.

In South Africa, as I elaborated in Chapter 2, this epistemological disagreement became closely intertwined with race. Apartheid, like many of the modernist state projects taking shape at the same time, was a regime that relied on an epistemological trust in numbers and the interventionist powers of the state. What Deborah Posel (2000) called the apartheid state's "mania for measurement" was primarily though not exclusively aimed at the formation of a particular racialized order, including a racialized labor regime. Here, numbers were primarily deployed to render legible and thus to *objectify* the targets of governmental intervention.[8] Via this centralized use of numbers, the black population—classified demographically, channeled via labour bureaus, and identified by passes—was turned into a part of the larger machinery of "the economy." Importantly, as Posel shows, this claim to objectivity was closely bound up with particular affective investments.[9] This affective dimension of measurement—what she terms a "frenzy," a "fervor," or a "demented rationalism"—emerged from the combination of modernist bureaucracy with an obsessive preoccupation with race. Such passions of measurement targeted, and indeed constructed, the black population as an object of intervention to be classified, moved, and recorded by statecraft. Viewed via such objectifying numbers, the black subject could be held at bay, its subjectivity disavowed;[10] indeed, in apartheid's machinery, the black worker became an inanimate puzzle piece within a larger statist economy of "racial Fordism" (Gelb 1991).

8   Keith Breckenridge (2014) has convincingly argued that the apartheid state often worked without a "will to know," and that attempts at total surveillance often failed, though this appears to be less true for urban areas. Here, passes and other modes of accounting for persons, such as municipal accounts, did function as effective, if clearly not total, means of control.

9   Much as Ann Stoler (2010) suggests, such "affective states" were often central to seemingly "cold" bureaucratic processes. See here also Daston and Galison on the affective dimensions of "objectivity" in scientific measurement (Daston and Galison 2007).

10   Indeed, as Seekings (2006) notes, there was very little data collected on the black population before 1994 that was not either bound up with the labor market or designed for purposes of counterinsurgency. However, as I argued in Chapter 2, this began to shift in the 1970s, in the aftermath of the Soweto Uprising, when urban data collection became a priority for both urban reformers and antiapartheid activists.

The modernist metrologies of the apartheid era did not go uncontested. Perhaps most spectacularly, the mass burning of passbooks—the most iconic local instantiation of this racial logic of accounting—explicitly defied the objectifications of the apartheid state. Less visibly, statistics on poverty compiled by allies of the antiapartheid movement were used to disprove the apartheid state's numerical claims; here, as Grace Davie has shown in her work on the Student Wages Commission, numbers became "a means of speaking back to the state" (Davie 2007).[11] Most prominently in Soweto during the 1980s, as discussed in Chapter 3, the NGO Planact carried out wide-ranging research on the apartheid city to support the civics in their negotiations with the state. In these various ways, apartheid metrologies, and the techno-science on which they rested, were politicized, and the "countermeasures" produced by the antiapartheid movement and its allies became part of the arsenal of political mobilization.

The resurgence of numbers in the postapartheid period emerges in part from the remainders of these apartheid-era metrologies and the legacies and traditions of such antiapartheid countermeasures. And yet, the contemporary moment has also been defined by novel logics of measurement, bringing to the fore different epistemologies and semiotic ideologies of number. Indeed, what is perhaps most remarkable about the widespread uses of numbers today is that they reflect both the democratization of numbers and, in many instances, fulfill new functions associated with neoliberal reforms such as corporatization, on the one hand, and with new modalities of social provisioning aimed at meeting "basic needs," on the other.

There are a number of facets to the contemporary ubiquity of numbers. First, measurement has been deracialized, democratized, and at the same time often privatized and depoliticized. In South Africa today, many different institutions count and countercount, and numbers flow from many sources. Although the numbers produced by the apartheid state were always subject to countermeasures, the liberalization of the postapartheid period has witnessed an unprecedented proliferation of numbers and the state's increasing inability to authorize its numerical claims (Comaroff and Comaroff 2006b). Moreover, democracy itself is increasingly expressed in quantitative terms, as numbers have become important not just in relation to political representation, but also to gauge and fulfill the biopolitical imperatives of the postapartheid state. Finally, and most important for my purposes here, in a context of neoliberal reforms many of the numbers generated by the state today are addressed at different targets and deployed to accomplish different goals. They do not necessarily always seek to establish centralized, total knowledge; rather, today's numbers are often also

---

11   Other groups that countermeasured during apartheid included, for example, the Black Sash or the South African Institute for Race Relations.

designed to work on individual capacities and dispositions, including numbers that audit, benchmark, incentivize, provide performance targets, or enable other forms of self-regulation akin to what Marilyn Strathern has described as "audit cultures" (Strathern 2000).

Thus, many of the contemporary numbers and attendant passions in South Africa are reliant on distinct epistemologies and concerned with measuring—and bringing into being—new realities. As I elaborate below, these new numbers in turn spawn new countermeasures that are often not merely concerned with contesting the accuracy of numerical representations, but also with the forms of subjectivity produced by acts of counting and accounting. Before returning to Joyce and her prepaid water meter, it is important to explore how such numbers became central to Operation Gcin'amanzi and the semiotic-material labors that were required to make them do performative work.

FROM BUREAUCRATS TO MANAGERS: CORPORATIZATION AS A TECHNIQUE OF CALCULABILITY

As is often noted, unlike other countries on the continent affected by structural adjustment programs, South Africa was not forced to introduce neoliberal policy measures. The neoliberal 1996 Growth, Employment and Redistribution (GEAR) strategy was, as Patrick Bond (2000) put it, "homegrown," though developed with heavy advice from the World Bank. As the ANC-led governing alliance came into power, it was increasingly clear that providing all residents with a basic level of infrastructure services would present a massive challenge. The World Bank, which had been in contact with members of the liberation movement since the early 1990s, drew up a plan that would aid the new government in the task of infrastructure "delivery." Called the Municipal Infrastructure Investment Framework (MIIF), it squarely made the case for the restructuring of existing basic services and for the centrality of the private sector to the provision of services in the future. In a candid article, influential urban development consultant Richard Tomlinson (2002), who was involved in the program at the time, details the strong influence of World Bank and USAID advice on the development of policy in the early years. "International best practice," he suggests, became a buzzword among local government officials and consultants. USAID not only provided teams of experts, but also funded the Municipal Infrastructure Investment Unit (MIIU), a think tank designed to "help municipalities package projects for private financing" (Tomlinson 2002: 384). Staffed largely by international experts drawn from a private U.S. consultancy and officials from the Development Bank of Southern Africa, MIIU with the help of USAID was central in "in helping to establish a market for Municipal Service Partnerships" (ibid.). At the same time, as Ivor Chipkin (2011) has shown, new globally circulating managerial concepts derived from New Public Management approaches became popular in South African policy circles.

In the late 1990s, and in a context of fiscal crisis, the City of Johannesburg announced Igoli 2002, a wide-ranging restructuring program. Aided by national legal reforms, advice from a variety of local and global think tanks, and "emergency powers" granted by the Johannesburg City Council, Igoli 2002 would enable the city "to be run as a business" (GJMC 1999).[12] As one official put it, the plan would "implement the concept of 'biting the bullet.'"[13] The most crucial and contentious reform introduced by Igoli 2002 was what the city council, following international development terminology, called the "corporatization" of basic service provision. This involved the creation of independent companies with the City as sole shareholder. Instead of the apartheid era's technical departments, which had been integral parts of the city administration, now the services were unbundled into corporate utilities whose tasks would be regulated via contractual agreements and an independent Board of Directors appointed by the Mayor. Corporatization divided the city into smaller, ring-fenced spaces within which new forms of calculation could flourish. Thus created were fourteen corporate entities, among them three concerned with basic services—Metro Solid Waste turned into Pikitup, Metro Electricity into City Power, and Johannesburg Water Pty Ltd was created as a private company whose shares were held by the City. Each company thus continued to be publicly owned; however, this ownership was no longer direct, but mediated by shares. All of them were now also managed with private sector principles. These entities were, as Laila Smith (2005) argued, "neither public nor private"; they operated *as if* they were companies. Achieving this peculiar form of market mimesis required multiple forms of labor, as I elaborate below.

The key transformation brought about by corporatization was a "reframing" of state practices that disentangled the provision of services such

---

12 For a detailed history of Johannesburg's restructuring and a critical analysis of the discursive mobilization of "fiscal crisis," see Beall, Crankshaw, and Parnell 2002. For further analyses of neoliberal reforms in Johannesburg and their effects, see Barchiesi 2007; Murray 2011; Samson 2010. While more recent city policies, such as indigent programs and social development packages, have moved away from the more openly neoliberal documents like Igoli 2002 and Johannesburg 2030, the corporatization of Johannesburg Water and the subsequent promulgation of Operation Gcin'amanzi have to be seen as part of this earlier paradigm. On these shifts in development discourses, see Hart (2006).

13 Anna Cox, "Johannesburg to get 'Survival Budget'," *Star* (Johannesburg), June 23, 1999.

as water or electricity from a larger complex of relations to make it visible and thus calculable in a new way; in this sense, corporatization should be seen as primarily a technique of calculability modeled on idealized market formations (Callon 1998). Two aspects of such a reframing were particularly central, and often talked about by city and utility officials. First, one key advantage of corporatization was, as an influential World Bank report had put it, that it would establish "the quasi-independence of public entities and insulate infrastructure enterprises from noncommercial pressures and constraints" (World Bank 1994). The new companies created by Igoli 2002 were no longer directly accountable to the City; instead, they were often regulated by "service delivery agreements" and an independent or municipal regulator. Being "at arm's length" from the city council, they were no longer subject to direct political directives or demands; indeed, politics, now understood as "noncommercial pressures and constraints," could, at least in theory, be taken out of a company's decision-making processes. A second advantage that, reformers argued, would flow from the first was that corporatization would enable new and more efficient forms of knowledge production. Parceling up the city into corporatized, "ring-fenced" entities could produce a set of numbers on the basis of which managers of the utility could assess costs and benefits in a new way.[14] Indeed, the advantages they associated with corporatization were primarily to do with the new modes of calculation they enabled. The city was thus *reframed*, making processes within it legible in a new way, while rendering others obsolete.

In the aftermath of apartheid and in a context of neoliberal reforms, trust in centralized numbers had rapidly diminished, and such numbers increasingly came to be viewed as one of the primary problems facing the city. As one senior city official put it to me during a conversation, postapartheid Johannesburg was "one big jumble," amassing data on a diversity of now often irrelevant matters, while failing at basic accounting tasks, like billing, and collecting no numbers that could be used by officials to measure their own effectiveness.

14 It was also on these two points that most contention emerged. Igoli 2002, and the nondemocratic way in which it was decided upon, led to massive protests and strikes by the municipal workers' union (SAMWU), as well as to the formation of the first social movements that positioned themselves explicitly outside the older liberation organizations. Several members of the ANC and the South African Communist Party (SACP) were expelled from party membership for their outspoken criticism of the program, and subsequently became leaders in the new social movements. The increasingly coercive "cost recovery" measures of disconnection and eviction of township residents led to the formation of several grassroots organizations, such as the Soweto Electricity Crisis Committee (SECC) and the Anti-Privatisation Forum (APF). For histories of the formation of this diverse group of constituencies within the new social movements, see, e.g., Dawson and Sinwell 2012; Naidoo and Veriava 2005, 2009; and Wafer 2008.

In the case of water, the corporate utility Johannesburg Water was created, and a team from subsidiaries of the French water multinational Suez was awarded a five-year management contract in order to introduce new management practices inspired by the private sector. As it turned out, in large part such new management practices rested on the introduction of numbers that could produce more clearly defined spaces of calculability through which water provision could be properly accounted for and organized more efficiently.

The consequences of this more narrow frame of calculation introduced with corporatization were explained to me by Thomas Gardner, a top-level manager of Johannesburg Water, himself a seasoned city official who had been employed by the Johannesburg council for years. Like many officials remaining from the apartheid era, Gardner was a civil engineer by training, but had, unlike many others, enthusiastically supported the shift from "municipal engineering" to "urban management."[15] When I asked him to tell me about the changes brought about by running water provision like a company, rather than as part of the city departments, his face lit up in excitement. Working in the new environment was "Wonderful!" he exclaimed. One key advantage of corporatization, he suggested, was the ability to separate "social conscience from delivery." The utility's task, he explained, would be to "deliver" via a "profit and loss mechanism" while the profits would "go back into the body that is responsible for social conscience," the city council. This, he suggested, was a much better solution, since before utility officials couldn't tell if they were "fish or fowl." "We had to deliver," he continued, "but we also had to be sorry for the poor and just didn't have any priorities."

Similarly, the utility was now fenced off from "political interference," which, he continued, was a great advantage, since politicians were not experts and were potentially driven by ideological motives that would irrationally delay or prolong decision making. As he put it, politicians "could be housewives or revolutionaries" without any technical or managerial knowledge of how to operate a utility. After corporatization, utility managers no longer had to subject their decisions to ethical or political considerations introduced by a larger set of numbers, but were guided by a general contractual framework that governed the newly created company and concerned with a smaller set of numbers directly pertaining to the operation of the utility.

---

15   This shift can be traced at all junctures when navigating the offices of the City of Johannesburg. It can also be gleaned from a look at the discursive shifts in municipal engineering literature. For example, the South African journal *Municipal Engineer* in the 1990s changed its name to *Urban Management*. See also Lindsey Bremner's account of what this entailed for the public-turned-private utility employees (Bremner 2004: 89–91).

Gardner's excitement was shared by many utility and city officials I spoke to during my fieldwork. Often they described the perspective enabled by corporatization as more entrepreneurial and thus as "broader."[16] And yet, ironically, this shift in vision was made possible by a narrower set of numbers that rendered their tasks and targets calculable in a strictly delimited field. To explain this transformation to me, utility officials often drew a comparison between managers and bureaucrats. Unlike bureaucrats, for whom efficiency had been measured in terms of rule-following behavior and whose primary responsibility had been to follow set processes, managers were primarily driven by performance targets, benchmarking, and individual incentives and thus made decisions within a more narrowly framed sphere concerned primarily with "balancing the books." This narrower set of numbers not only enabled new modes of calculation, it also produced an attendant shift in the temporal experience of work. Unlike the continuously recurring completion of bureaucratic tasks through "enduring time," the managers' work was now defined by a punctuated temporality, parceled by deadlines to meet and targets to reach, from quarterly reports, to levels of "buy-in" achieved, and liters of water saved.[17] Numbers were important not merely to count and amass data, they also, and often more importantly, operated by spacing time and work. Thus, a crucial transformation introduced with corporatization was the strict spatial and temporal delimitation of the frame of calculation in which numbers could do a new kind of work.

Importantly, city officials and utility managers like Gardner often described such numbers as producing a shift in affective dispositions. As one supporter of corporatization in the city council reiterated, managers were "not so much bureaucrats." They were "much more aggressive, they want to achieve a target." Thus, corporatization enabled an insulation from ethical or political considerations and the affect they induced ("feeling sorry for the poor"), but also encouraged other affective and behavioral stances ("aggressively pursuing a target"). Indeed, aggressiveness was *enabled* by the particular set of numbers and the strict delimitation of priorities.

While the affective states of apartheid-era bureaucrats—their mania for measurement—were generated by the twin concerns of racial purity and modernist statecraft, and thus by the close connection of instrumental tasks

16   Ivor Chipkin discusses the changing roles envisaged for bureaucrats in South Africa elaborating on some of the contradictory consequences of this shift: "Whereas the bureaucratic model delineated clearly between analytical, managerial, administrative and financial skills, the imprecise job descriptions associated with New Public Management often require them to be found in the same person" as a result leaving them "without clearly defined roles and tasks" (Chipkin 2011: 47). NPM, Chipkin suggests, thus de facto often produced a weakening of the local state.

17   See Jane Guyer's discussion of "enduring" and "punctuated time" (Guyer 2007).

with a larger ideological vision, in the new calculative framework of the city, managers' frames were refocused toward the achievement of more narrowly circumscribed "performance targets," which in turn meant that they could and indeed should be agnostic about larger ethical or political goals. In turn, the role of numbers here was not primarily to delimit a field of intervention. Rather, the main labor performed by numbers was that they would work on individuals—training their minds, habits, and actions on one set of numbers only and providing the conditions within which new actions became thinkable and calculable. These numbers, then, were explicitly designed as *subjectivating* numbers and aimed at the creation of reflexive persons with particular dispositions.

Although Gardner and many other city officials often described this transformation as "revolutionary," it is important not to overdraw this distinction between the old and the new uses of numbers, as they often overlapped in a variety of ways; "new" management techniques often rely on the intransigent socio-technical legacies of older metrological forms that still govern many of the city's policies.[18] Often this unwieldy patchwork of numbers meant that officials had to "muddle through" without a clear sense of what they were doing (Lipietz 2004). As in so many other cases of restructuring, the reforms moreover produced unexpected results. Crucially, the fact that the newly corporatized entities were staffed with highly paid managers, many of whom had been drawn from the private sector, meant that they often had skills that the city officials, who were supposed to regulate them, lacked. Several city officials complained that, as a result, regulating these entities was extremely difficult. The "insulation from noncommercial principles" thus ran the risk of creating companies that increasingly acted autonomously and potentially with little accountability.

Moreover, the affective dispositions and calculative subjectivities that were supposed to be produced by the new numbers did not always materialize. Pierre Mercier, one of the French managers who had been seconded to Johannesburg Water by subsidiaries of the Suez Group, complained that the introduction of a new management ethos had been extremely cumbersome. Clearly exasperated, he recalled that older staff members, mostly remaining from the apartheid era, were reluctant to make changes to old work processes. "Ooh!" he exclaimed, dramatically mimicking such recalcitrant officials, "now I have to change the way I do things!"

18   On this notion of intransigence and its relationship to neoliberal reforms, see Collier (2011). One instance of the intransigence of apartheid techno-politics is described in Breckenridge's history of biometrics (Breckenridge 2014).

Others, he argued, were blatantly sabotaging the new management culture brought in by the Suez team of experts.

INSTITUTING A NEW METROLOGICAL REGIME IN SOWETO

It was not only the managers' dispositions that were to be shaped by new kinds of numbers; a similar transformation was expected for the world outside the utility offices. However, much like the water utility before corporatization, the outside world did not yet fit this new metrological regime—it had not yet been mapped with facts that could be used to determine where reforms would stick. And, as it turned out, it proved to be even more resistant to the institution of a new metrology. Rather than a few recalcitrant employees and an intransigent bureaucracy, here everything—from water pressure and messy accounting and billing, to leaking apartheid-era infrastructure and residents unaccustomed to the habits of regular payment—combined to produce an undifferentiated mass of obstacles that militated against the introduction of new forms of measurement and calculation. It was this illegible mass of problems that came to be referred to as "unaccounted for water."[19]

One of the most pressing problems encountered by the new corporatized water utility was that it did not in fact have the numbers required to precisely account for losses and profits. In Soweto, as in many other townships during apartheid, water had rarely been metered, and the flat rate charged for water, though calculated to cover 20 kiloliters, meant that residents had a de facto unlimited supply. Simultaneously, there were massive water losses throughout Soweto's water system, and it was not easy to track how much water disappeared through crumbling infrastructure, how much was lost on residents' plots by broken toilets or dripping taps, and how much was in fact used by residents. Moreover, many residents had not paid for basic services in years, which utility officials interpreted as a persistent "culture of nonpayment" and a related inability to "properly value water." Utility employees regularly complained that for Soweto residents "water does not have a value" and that they were dealing with the perception that water should be free.

Part of the problem, they suggested, was that while water in South Africa in general was scarce, in Soweto, water had never been experienced as scarce. On the contrary, given the flat rate connections and

---

19   See Chapter 3 for a discussion of "unaccounted for water."

perennially leaking pipes, water had flowed everywhere and in unlimited supply. Much of Soweto's formal housing stock was built in the 1950s by the apartheid state, and the largely identical houses were each fitted with individual water piping and flush toilets in the yard and some with indoor plumbing.[20] There were also taps in the street, and water flowing through streets out of leaking pipes or dripping taps was a common sight. A central task outlined to me by one utility official was thus to make residents understand what "[they're] actually paying for, *what value [they] are actually getting*." For the new metrological project to succeed in Soweto, the challenge was twofold: first, to make Soweto measurable and legible by introducing new metrological techniques that could produce the necessary sets of numbers and, secondly, to introduce forms of calculability and modes of valuation that would convince or, indeed, force residents to pay for water.

The prepaid meter became crucial in addressing both of these tasks. Most obviously, the meters were designed to eliminate nonpayment, or so it was hoped. Households were provided with the nationally mandated 6000 liters of water per month for free; thereafter, however, payment was enforced without exception by the automatic disconnection mechanism embedded in the meter.[21] In the absence of credit to "top up" the meter, water flow simply stopped. The meters thus became the capillary ends of the larger metrological project that sought to map Soweto's water infrastructure, and thus render water flows measurable and legible to the utility. The numbers produced by the meter would, at least in theory, radiate in two directions. First, projecting outwards and collectively connected to a central database, the numbers produced by the meter and then aggregated by the database could enable the utility to compose a picture of Soweto as a space of water consumption. Whereas during the flat-rate system water had flowed without limit or measure, now each household's consumption could, at least in theory, be accounted for in minute detail. Each of the meters in theory had the ability to communicate with a centralized database that could then adequately calculate how much water was pumped into Soweto and how much was in fact used by each household, which, in turn, would enable the kinds of calculations the newly ring-fenced utility had been tasked with.[22]

---

20   Amongst the several models of housing built by the apartheid state, two dominated, each with 4 rooms: Type 51/6 with the toilet in the yard and Type 51/9, slightly larger and with in-house plumbing (Mandy 1984: 178f.).

21   The 6000 liters of free basic water provision were calculated on the basis of an eight-person household to reflect 25 liters per person per day (cf. Loftus 2005).

22   This mechanism of two-way communication was not initially deployed, as it required a much greater technical effort. It has, however, been activated more recently in the aftermath of large-scale bypassing.

Second, the numbers would project inward to each household via the LCD screen of the meter, providing residents with real-time updates of their consumption. Placing the "token," a small chip key, onto the "touch port" located next to the LCD screen produced a flashing series of numbers and letters, which included the free basic water amount, any monetary credits remaining, a cumulative figure of water consumption to date, and the current tariff band—thus giving residents the most important coordinates to calculate their daily and monthly water consumption. For the many meter developers, utility employees, and consultants I spoke with, it was this series of numbers that would enable residents to think differently about water and, thus, to change their consumption behavior. As the editor of the local industry journal *Metering International* told me, the meters provided "price signals." With the meters, she suggested, "you can *see* those numbers ticking down, you are actually aware of what you are doing." Similarly, as Johannesburg's mayor, Amos Masondo, would put it some years later during the legal case against the project, a primary task of the meters was to "ensure that demand reflected a cost benefit analysis on the part of the consumer."[23] The prepaid meter, now in its capacity as a semiotic instrument, was designed to both produce and mediate numbers, which, in turn, would enable a more reflexive stance on the part of residents. Thus, the introduction of prepaid water meters in Soweto was imagined to bring about a transformation of calculative capacities and, by extension, a new regime of valuing water. Indeed, residents who had a meter installed, including Joyce, now needed to read the meter regularly to check how much credit they still had and how this translated into liters and price.

And yet, the process did not go as smoothly as envisaged. One of the first obstacles encountered by utility outreach staff was that the numbers did not quite do the subjectivating work that had been expected. Throughout the early implementation phase, many of the local staff members complained that residents had no idea how much 6000 liters of water was. The numbers, they argued, didn't *mean* anything to residents. Thus, the utility embarked on a "social intervention" program that was in part designed to introduce a numerical pedagogy aimed at rendering visible and tangible the relationship between measure, form, and substance. In order for water to be valued "properly," and for the numbers to do performative work, a host of interventions were required, many of which involved "requalifying" water (Callon, Méadel, and Rabeharisoa 2002).

<hr />

23   Masondo Affidavit, *Mazibuko and Others v City of Johannesburg and Others* 2008 (4) All SA 471 (W), 28.

MAKING THE NUMBERS DO WORK

While Operation Gcin'amanzi's beginnings remained murky and shrouded in secrecy, in the aftermath of the massive protests and public debates that had met the announcement of the project, the utility embarked on a large publicity campaign. Suddenly, the project was visible everywhere. Large banners exhorted Sowetans to save water, minibus taxis sporting the slogan were a common sight, and the utility circulated pamphlets to residents. Meanwhile, local government offices now also often functioned as water pay points; in the case of Phiri, a blue container building had set up shop next to the local government offices, suggesting that one could BUY WATER HERE! Meanwhile, the utility began to refer to the prepaid meter as "free-pay meter" to emphasize that the meters were not punitive devices to force residents to pay, but that they would allow for the 6000 liters of free basic water to be dispensed every month. Johannesburg Water also started training contingents of local residents to act as door-to-door "peer educators" who would explain the project and collect the signatures required, thus gathering local "buy-in" for the project. Over time, such banners, murals, and signs also increasingly included numbers. One banner, for example, suggested that the meter would provide 6000 LITERS WATER FOR FREE! Others broke this figure down to twenty-five liters per person per day.

Such projects of publicity went to great lengths to demonstrate the units of measurement graphically (and preferably three-dimensionally), linking specific amounts of liters to concrete examples: a truck carrying thirty 200-liter water barrels was displayed to render the free monthly allowance of water imaginable. A combi taxi, a colorful brochure suggested, could be filled twice with 6000 liters. Many households were also given a twenty-five-liter measuring bucket to make sure residents were aware of their daily use.[24] At the same time, murals along Soweto streets as well as pamphlets distributed to households showed cartoons of Soweto residents, explaining how to use water "wisely" and graphically demonstrated to residents how daily water consumption could be organized in order to remain within the free basic water amount.

This numerical pedagogy often went into great detail. One pamphlet proposed this daily allocation of water to residents: "20 litres of water for cleaning, 6 body washes per day, 6 flushes of the toilet per day, 2 kettles of water per day, 1 sinkful of dishes per day, 1 clothes wash every second day, 12 litres of drinking water per day = 6000 litres of water usage for the

---

24   As one local outreach staff member put it, "in many communities they use these buckets, and we would say 6000 liters is equivalent to 200 liters [per day] and that comes to eight 25 liter buckets [per household per day]."

month."[25] On the back of the pamphlet, tariffs listed the price for additional water credit purchases. The pamphlet thus entailed several translations: one from metric volume of water into its price; and another, more important one from metric volume into specific consumption practices. The use value of water was thus graphically translated into a series of equivalences that transformed water into a measurable substance and, by extension, into an exchangeable object. In the process, Sowetans were encouraged to subject their daily consumption practices to metrological scrutiny. Life itself became the subject of measurement and intervention to be carried out not by an invasive state, but by residents themselves.

This pedagogical effort at producing calculability was also integrated into the technology of the latest generation of meters. Engineers often spoke proudly about the meter as a "small computer" whose abilities went far beyond those of a regular water meter. The meters were programmed to provide 6000 liters per month, after which residents would have to walk to the local office to buy further credit in order to avoid being automatically cut off. By accessing the meter with the chip key, and looking at the by-now familiar flashing of numbers and letters, residents were able to check how much water they had used and how much credit remained. Prepayment technology itself here became a semiotic instrument that could translate and materially mediate the commensuration of daily practices into liters and in turn into monetary value.

Beyond the large-scale advertising campaigns that could be seen all over Soweto, Johannesburg Water also organized events that had an explicitly pedagogical purpose. "Tappie Roadshow," a traveling educational program involving "Tappie," a furry human tap, explained to school children what they could do to help save water—from closing the tap while brushing their teeth to not letting the water run unnecessarily. A "Water Festival" held annually at Zoo Lake in the northern suburbs of Johannesburg also saw scores of township schoolchildren bussed into the wealthy, historically white northern suburbs to learn about water. Another event I attended, the Johannesburg Water Car Wash, took place in Soweto's Thokoza Park and was designed to teach residents how to wash their cars with a bucket of ten liters rather than a hose. While the vast majority of Sowetans in attendance did not in fact have a car to wash, many had used the opportunity to have picnics in the park, or to listen to the entertainment program on stage, which was hosted by YFM, Johannesburg's hip youth radio station, while car owners were soaping their cars on the side streets helped by utility employees. Despite a few interruptions—such as the open mic session, which was used by several residents to complain about the prepaid water system—this form of "edutainment" was hailed by Johannesburg Water as

25   Johannesburg Water, Operation Gcin'amanzi Pamphlet, no date, obtained in 2005.

a great success. Many such events and campaigns sought to render water saving tangible and to produce the kinds of affective and sensory modes of valuation that would render the numbers meaningful. In the process, practices of measurement and calculation also became tied to a notion of virtuous citizenship and a nationalist narrative of conservationism that presented water as a "national asset."

And yet, despite such efforts of resignification, many residents held on to the idea that they should not have to pay for water, seeing in it a common resource "from God" or "nature." This, indeed, was how Joyce saw it. She was active in her church and viewed water as something God-given that should not be "for sale." It turned out then that the problem was not simply that residents didn't value water; rather, at issue here was a clash between multiple, competing modalities of valuation (Appadurai 1986; Guyer 2004). Water was linked to distinct imaginaries in which the public—or, indeed humankind—owned water as a collectivity.

For utility officials, this way of understanding water's value—a water fetishism of sorts—was particularly annoying, since it seemed to disregard the intricacies of water provision and the efforts expended in the process. As one city council member suggested tersely to me, when you have a leak in a pipe, "you don't call the local priest." To address this problem and in yet another effort at requalification, the utility began circulating PR material that described water as a *produced* substance whose social life went through several stages to arrive in residents' taps. Following this logic, most brochures distributed by the utility included a pictorial description of the water distribution cycle, detailing the necessary steps and efforts expended at each juncture: water was captured by a dam, purified in plants, tested in labs, reticulated via pipes that needed to be laid and maintained, and removed via sewage systems. Such brochures and pamphlets often included glossy photos of workers digging trenches, operating large machinery, and repairing massive pipes. Water, it was shown, required *work*. In an ironic reversal of the Marxian story of commodification, it was thus necessary to divest residents of their fetishism ("water is from God") and to instead introduce a folk labor theory of value that could show water to be a product of concrete labor and machinery.

In order to work as subjectivating devices, much work was required to render numbers semiotically stable, for example, by drawing clear connections between numbers and the properties they referred to. And yet, looked at from within the household and its infrastructures, this semiotic stability could never quite be achieved, most importantly because the numbers were read by residents in sometimes dramatically different ways: for clearly, the numbers transmitted by the meter were not in fact price signals. They did not provide the precondition for rational choice in a market place; there were no fluctuations in price, goods or sellers, because there was no "market" in water, a problem often glossed as the "missing market" in microeconomics. Indeed, water, given its singular materiality is an "uncooperative commodity;"[26] when delivered through mains and taps, it can only flow from the same provider, via rigid pipes to one consumer. Rather than seeing the meters as enabling them to calculate their budgets, residents often experienced the limitations introduced by the meter and its numbers as yet another monetary constraint in an already insecure situation. If many residents welcomed the prospect of having their arrears written off at last and thus of freeing themselves from the burden of debt, their experience of living with the meter—of living prepaid—also came with a new temporality, one that in certain respects mapped onto a larger experience of precarity that has become the norm rather than the exception in South Africa (Barchiesi 2011; Ferguson 2015).

LIVING PREPAID

> Everything is now prepaid. We prepay for the phone, for
> electricity, and now we prepay for water. Who knows, tomorrow,
> we'll have to prepay for the sun to be switched on and off![27]

After months of protests, refusals, court cases against "vandalizing" activists, the prototype project in Phiri was finally completed. There were still a handful of residents who persisted in refusing the installation of the meters, but most had, in the absence of any water connection, finally agreed to having the meter installed. Johannesburg Water proudly pronounced Operation Gcin'amanzi's prototype project in Phiri a "great success" and presented surveys that indicated a 98 percent satisfaction rate, another numerical claim that would later be challenged.[28] Most residents, the utility argued, were buying water for about R20 a month, and many managed to budget to remain within the free basic water amount. This "success" of the project in Phiri meant that Operation Gcin'amanzi would now be rolled out to the rest of Soweto. A multimillion rand loan for the completion of

26   The term "uncooperative commodity" is Karen Bakker's (2003b) and refers primarily to piped water. Bottled or provided in tankers, that is, prepacked in specific units rather than in a continuous flow, water can be branded and circulated in a market (Kaplan 2007; Wilk 2006).

27   Comment by a protester from Soweto during a demonstration against prepaid meters outside the Johannesburg Civic Centre in November 2004.

28   Ninety-eight percent, it was later found, was the "acceptance rate of prepaid meters," that is, the figure indicated how many residents had signed for a prepaid meter. Given that the alternative to "accepting" was a downgrading in service, presenting the high acceptance rate as "satisfaction," activists argued, was deceptive. Indeed, another City survey showed 30 percent of residents thought the meter had been forced on them and 45 percent felt they had had no choice but to accept the meter (see Makoatsane Affidavit 2007).

the project had been received from a French donor agency, which, activists pointed out, locked the program in place, as it was now dependent on loan repayment. Many residents in Phiri continued to be angry at the lack of consultation, but had increasingly come to accept the inevitability of the project. Getting used to the meter and the changes it brought about, however, was another matter.

As science studies scholars have argued, technologies like the prepaid meter are "stabilized" through accommodation within a network of heterogeneous relations.[29] As I suggested in the previous chapter, prepaid meters, like most technologies, are co-constructed with their users, that is, both are produced and adapted in the process. And yet, while technologies are usually adapted with the aim of serving the consumer better—to make them user-friendly, for example—in the case of prepaid meters, and infrastructure technology more broadly, the consumer and the buyer are two different actors, whose interests and needs diverged at times, and were directly at cross-purposes at others (cf. Akrich 1992). The Johannesburg Water officials, who tendered for and bought large batches of meters from the meter manufacturers, needed a device that would be easy to maintain, reliable, and cheap; it also needed to be secure. And yet the *users* of the meters were the residents of Phiri, whose needs often diverged from those of the utility. Thus, in this process of innovation, the users were always represented and mediated by the buyer, that is, by the utility.

The prepaid water meters deployed in Phiri had gone through numerous innovations and transformations throughout their development. Since Operation Gcin'amanzi was the first large-scale deployment of prepaid water meters in the world, there were no precedents to draw on, and the Phiri prototype project had been an experiment from the start.[30] As Jan van der Merve, the CEO of one of the water meter manufacturers told me in his Pretoria office, while normally they wouldn't put a product on the market until it was fully developed, in the case of Phiri's prepaid water meters this was impossible; because the meters were "so closely linked with the user" the developers were dependent on constant feedback. Pausing for a moment, he added, "It was like a laboratory almost." Indeed, unlike with other technologies his company produced, the design of the meters used in Phiri had never been "frozen" for production, but remained open to transformation and experimentation throughout, precisely in order to

29   As Bijker and Law suggest, "a technology is stabilized if and only if the heterogeneous relations in which it is implicated, and of which it forms a part, are themselves stabilized. In general, then, if technologies are stabilized, this is because the network of relations in which they are involved, ... together with the various strategies that drive and give shape to the network—reach some kind of accommodation" (Bijker and Law 1992: 10).

30   Before Operation Gcin'amanzi began, the utility had already tested the meters in a trial run in the informal settlement Orange Farm (cf. Coalition against Water Privatisation 2004).

accommodate unforeseen effects, such as malfunctioning hardware and other complaints, but also to enable the addition of security features should Soweto residents begin to bypass their meters. And yet there were clear limits to the flexibility of the technology; the central mechanism—to automatically regulate and, if necessary, curtail residents' water supply—was never in question, and the onus was on residents to accommodate themselves to the cutoff mechanism.

Thus, from the perspective of the utility, initially the meter did indeed function well for the most part—it limited supply and ensured payment. It also made water supply measurable and leaks detectable. And yet in each household, how the meter worked, how "accommodation" was reached, and what transformations this effected widely diverged. In other words, the network of relations into which the meter entered and that it transformed took numerous shapes. If the utility envisioned a responsibly budgeting household, most of the time, this did not quite take the form idealized in brochures and pamphlets. How the money was come up with, who was responsible for managing water usage, and what kinds of relations that required was not settled in advance. In Phiri, accommodation happened in a myriad of often haphazard ways, always dependent on the kinds of relations and the kind of household into which the meter was introduced and into which it intervened.

When Joyce was explaining her water calculations to me and how they could be used against the city, her sister Teboho was doing the laundry in the back, carefully balancing two large plastic dishes underneath the tap in the yard, washing the clothes in one and rinsing them in the other. She made sure to keep the used laundry water for other purposes. Rinsing the clothes under running water, as she had done before the meter arrived, was now a luxury best avoided. Joyce's brother, who ran an informal mechanic shop in the backyard, also needed to stop using water to clean up the cars on which he worked. Although Joyce's household was relatively small, which meant that the free basic allowance would last longer, the meter had introduced many changes in how her and her family used water. Joyce had not originally agreed to the meter when the utility contract worker came by to ask for a signature of consent. But her father, a pensioner and not one to start arguing with the utility or the council, had had enough of quarreling with his daughter over the meter and, one day, had single-handedly gone to the Johannesburg Water office to sign for it. As the title-deed and account holder of the house, this was his prerogative, Joyce conceded, but she continued to be angry about it. Her father passed away not long thereafter from gangrene in his foot.

Operation Gcin'amanzi produced a myriad of such negotiations and ways of "making do," always dependent on the kinds of households the meter entered into and how they could accommodate themselves to the new restrictions on consumption.[31] Not far from Joyce's house, Tshepo handed a bucket of water over the fence to his neighbor Xoliswa. Xoliswa smiled and took the bucket into her yard. Tshepo, like Joyce a member of Phiri Concerned Residents Forum affiliated with the Anti-Privatisation Forum (APF), had refused to sign authorization for the prepaid meter, and, as a result, his house was the only one in his street whose water was not metered or subject to cutoff, leaving him with a standpipe in the yard. This meant that while his household still had unlimited access to water, it was no longer possible to flush his toilet or to clean dishes in the kitchen as internal plumbing had been cut in the process. Everyone on his plot was now tied to the same standpipe in the backyard. Because water was still in unlimited supply, however, he could give some to his neighbor whose water was now prepaid. In another area of Phiri, an elderly man sat on top of a big upside-down bucket. Since the prepaid meters were installed he'd been charging two rand for taking buckets to a neighboring area, where water was still unmetered, and fetching water for households cut off in the process. In another house, where the meter had been installed more recently, Sibongile and Tumi, two sisters in their early forties whose families shared her mother's plot, now pooled together their washing on Saturdays to save water. They did so grudgingly, teasing each other about who did most of the work. Phyllis, a pensioner who lived nearby, said she rarely went beyond the free basic water amount. Above all, she was happy that her debt had been written off and that she would no longer be running up any further debts. "With the prepaid," she added, "it's your own baby." Like Teboho, she developed new routines in how she washed dishes and clothes, and she also taught her grandchildren not to let the water run or play with it.

On another plot, Mpho, who has two shacks in her backyard which she rented out, was managing the relations between the three households. Since the meter arrived, she charged each of the tenants higher flat rates per month in order to buy water credits. "Ten rand, ten rand, ten rand, and more rounds if we run out" she said, pointing to each of the structures on her plot. The tenants later quietly complained that she overcharges them, given they had no plumbing inside their shacks. In Phiri's Block C, Mathews was annoyed, because, he said, his sister who had a baby kept using up the water because she needed to wash so many nappies, sometimes leaving him unwashed in the morning before going to work at 5:00 am when the water pay point was still closed.

---

31   See also Ahmed Veriava's analysis of Operation Gcin'amanzi and his theorization of "life strategies" (Veriava 2007). On the multiplicity of informal economic practices through which lives are sustained in Soweto and other townships, see Bähre 2007; James 2014; Krige 2011.

If the prepaid meter was designed to produce budgeting households and new forms of calculating water consumption, such calculations took a multiplicity of forms, few of which looked like the idealized civic water-saving practices projected in Johannesburg Water's brochures and publicity events. Similarly, rather than flattening relations, as many accounts of commodification suggest, they produced new relations and intensified existing ones. Some were hierarchical, as in landlord-tenant or family relationships, others were defined by new forms of solidarity or reluctant cooperation. While the program did indeed succeed in creating water-budgeting households, these were households that needed to rearrange themselves in ways that would allow them to pay. Produced here were not so much virtuously calculating citizens, but rather people making do somehow, always dependent on the particular constellations of their households. While smaller households usually were relatively unaffected by the meter, because the basic water amount would last longer, on plots with many residents, those that, for example, had backyard structures or larger families, the meter often produced dramatic transformations.

As Thembi, a teenage girl from Phiri who lived on a plot with over fifteen people, had once put it, with the agreement of her friends, the prepaid "is killing our grandmothers." Like many families in Phiri, most of the girls' families relied on the elders' pensions and on child grants as the primary stable incomes. In many instances, the prototypical Phiri *homo economicus* thus turned out to be older women, who were often also the title deed holders of the houses. Thus, they were responsible for managing the accounts and often bore responsibility for catering to daily needs and doing the kinds of accounting labor required to remain connected to infrastructures on a daily basis.

Many residents in Phiri described the changes after the installation as the need for new "routines" and new "rules." Previously taken for granted, and thus habitual, daily actions, like flushing the toilet or doing the laundry, now often became an explicit object of deliberation and calculation. The close linking of thought and bodily practices this produced was clearly recognized by Thembi, who suggested that, with the prepaid meter, "You will think about using that water, think about using that electricity." When making tea, she went on, one would now just fill the kettle with enough water for a cup, rather than fill the whole kettle. "So they want you to think, be disciplined, use yourself, you will learn something about that. You will learn how to use your money. It's more like, you need to make a budget!" The other girls agreed; it was "all about budget." Once the prepaid meter was installed, a new set of habits were required. Simultaneously, it was, as Thembi suggested, *through* these practices that such calculation is produced; calculation here came to hinge on a shift in embodied practices. Indeed, another resident likened the new economy introduced by the meter to "a pill you have to remember to swallow every day." If calculation is commonly associated with disembodied reasoning and abstraction, here, the production of calculability was achieved via a diversity of practices, not least of which were the transformation of bodily techniques and their insertion within a socio-technical network constructed by infrastructures and the new constraints they imposed.

There were also less visible sensory transformations that were brought about by this new economy of water. For example, because it was no longer possible to rinse laundry under running water, blankets and clothes often continued to smell like soap. Indeed, the soapy smell was a ubiquitous complaint in Phiri. Similarly, flushing the toilet was now limited and ideally done with previously used laundry water, which tended to leave them smelly. Yards, which often either had a bit of lawn or a dirt floor, which residents might periodically sprinkle with a bit of water to keep it from raising clouds of dust, now often had to remain dusty. Given the dryness of Johannesburg's climate, especially in the winter, this meant that dust could rise up and into eyes and throats more easily. Thus, the new water routines were also sensed and felt in a diversity of ways.[32]

If prepaid meters were installed with the intention to enforce a particular budgetary rationality, there was an apparent slippage in the concept of budgeting as it moved from the utility's projections to residents' homes. While utility officials presented the meters as an empowering mechanism that would "enable" residents to calculate consumption and thus to better manage their budgets, this conception of budgeting hinged on the availability of a stable income, often implicitly assumed to be a monthly wage.[33] Similarly, rather than floating "price signals" to enable choice, from the point of view of residents, the numbers *repeatedly counted down* credit toward the moment of cutoff rather than counting continuously upwards, as would a regular credit meter. "Counting down" (or as the editor had put it, seeing the numbers "ticking down") also often introduced a particular temporal sensibility. Thus, in many instances, the numbers and the new temporality they introduced were simply experienced as penalizing.

At the same time, "living prepaid" with an always precarious connection to services in certain respects mirrored the precariousness of life after what Mbembe and Roitman (1995) have called the "end of the salary." If salaries, just as bills, relied on a regular and cyclical temporality, in which a

---

32   See here also Catherine Fennell's theorization of a "sensory politics" in her analysis of Chicago public housing reform (Fennell 2011).

33   As Franco Barchiesi (2011) has shown, despite overwhelming unemployment and informal, intermittent forms of income, the wage continues to structure the ideals of citizenship. The "end of the salary" (Mbembe and Roitman 1995) in South Africa, then, does not mean the end of the wage as the *aspirational logic* of citizenship and, in turn, the imaginaries through which state projects such as Operation Gcin'amanzi are often conceived.

recurring monthly income could be used to pay equally recurring monthly expenses, in a context of increasingly persistent unemployment—in Phiri about 50 to 70 percent, depending on who calculates and how—and intermittent, insecure incomes, the prepaid meter can be seen as a technology of precarity that gives up on such temporal regularity (Allison 2013). Indeed, because many Phiri residents rely on informal and often irregular forms of income, there often simply is no stable budget to manage, as residents often pointed out to me during conversations.[34] My questions about how it was possible to "budget" as the utility suggested were sometimes simply laughed off with the suggestion that budgeting requires something to budget with. Residents often described the moment when the free water would run out—anywhere from a week into the month to just before the end of the month—as a frantic search for a few rands to keep the water running. As Zozo, one of Joyce's neighbors, once put it to me when we discussed the "emergency" allowance that was about to be introduced by the utility, "Eish, emergencies! We have emergencies here every month!" Indeed, water disconnections, which used to be an exceptional measure experienced by very few residents before, were now potential events every month that were built into the very technology of the meters. Moreover, because basic foodstuffs, like maize, had become much more expensive, many poorer households already had difficulties making meager incomes last. As Zanele, a member of the Phiri Concerned Residents Forum and the daughter of Lindiwe Mazibuko, the main complainant in the legal case, suggested in exasperation, after explaining that they could no longer buy maize and sugar in bulk because basic supplies had gotten so expensive, "Where's the budget in that!?"

Budgeting, enforced and translated through the meter, therefore often meant weighing one necessary expense against another. Here, then economics became quite literally *oiko-nomia*, affecting each household, however wrongly identified by the planners. What was projected from one side of the meter as "empowering" often meant an enforced weighing of basic daily priorities, on the other. While the utility measured success by the amount of "signage" it had gathered or "buy-in" achieved by its local workers, inside the household, that is, on the other side of the meter, "success" meant a diversity of outcomes, most of which entailed a reliance on new relations or the deepening of others. And although the precise effects of the meters were infinitely variable depending on the household in which they entered, the prepaid meter ultimately *enforced* drastic changes in how daily priorities needed to be weighed.

34   In the mid-2000s, 51 percent of Phiri households had an income below R1600, while 18.5 percent reported no income at all.

In many instances, as with Thembi's grandmother, it was elderly women who came to take on the tasks of such calculations, managing the household's income, maximizing their small pensions or child or disability grants, and any other income that might come their way. Their tasks simultaneously often included affective labor—they needed to exhort, encourage, tell off, remind, punish, negotiate, and so forth.[35] Given the prevalence of backyard structures and informal living arrangements in Soweto, in many instances their role also included that of the landlord, managing relations between several households, and sometimes abusing their power over the residents housed informally in the backyard.[36] Considering the vast numbers of backyard structures in Soweto, this internal politics of payment often de facto concerned many more people than the official account holders who were the only explicit targets of Johannesburg Water and municipal policies more generally. For the residents of informal backyard structures, the prepaid meter often meant a higher, more or less fairly calculated flat rate imposed by the landlord which they were not always in a position to negotiate or contest.

How calculation was delegated within the household was a matter of complex negotiations, which in turn often produced a particular household politics. Although in many instances, the prepaid water meter simply meant an intensification of prior relations—one more item on the list of priorities—often it prompted the introduction of new ways of prioritizing needs and wants (whether to water the garden or not, how and when to pool washing dishes or the laundry) and, by extension, new ways of understanding the "necessary" and the "unnecessary."

Such calculations did not always remain at the level of the household, but at times became the subject of explicit debate and deliberation. One day in Phiri, Bongi—a fellow member of the APF Research Subcommittee—and I became involved in a debate over such calculations on our way to a meeting. When we passed a man in his mid-twenties washing his car, Bongi, always wont to teasing people, shouted mockingly: "My brother, you're wasting water!" The man looked up with an air of slight irritation at first, but, realizing the smile around Bongi's eyes, started laughing. "No, I'm

35   On the concept "affective labor," see Michael Hardt (1999) and Muehlebach (2011).

36   Backyard structures (often called "backyard shacks") are informal forms of housing (sometimes shacks made of corrugated iron or other informal materials, but also more sturdily built "rooms") set up on plots of formal houses. They are rented from the owners or residents of the formal houses, who are also usually the account holders. There are thus a large number of "informal" living arrangements within otherwise "formal" townships (cf. Crankshaw, Gilbert, and Morris 2000). Often several households are living on one stand, but are connected to one official account. Residents of backyard structures are thus often not accounted for by the state. In the case of the allocation of Free Basic Water, for example, backyard structures were initially not part of the calculation, which was based only on an eight-person household.

using the bucket, man. It's only five or ten liters. And I've stopped washing it from the inside." We stopped and chatted for a while. Clearly, the car, an old Toyota, indicated a level of income not matched by many residents in Phiri, though as it turned out, the other members of the household, like many if not most in Phiri, were unemployed. After a few minutes of debating the advantages and disadvantages of the meters and a few of his friends and neighbors joining in, a friendly but serious debate developed. Up until this point, everyone had joined in the lists of complaints about the prepaids that Bongi and I had heard frequently before—from the difficulty of watering gardens to arguments over who in the family used the most water, to the ever-present troubles with washing blankets and soapy smells.

One man, who had introduced himself as Lazarus, but not said much up until then, spoke up and said that, actually, he was quite happy with the meter. He recounted that he ran a shebeen and the meter was working fine. It cost him R50 every month, and they did have to reduce their water usage, but that was fine as the water was now both cheaper and cleaner.[37] This elicited some grumblings and dry laughter from the other guys. Undeterred, Lazarus continued, "But most people who say that they are struggling to buy water and electricity, it is easy for them to go and buy alcohol. You will find them carrying boxes of alcohol, but at the end of the day they will tell you that they don't have money [to pay for water]." Most of the guys now broke out in derisive laughter, clearly implying that he was rehashing a morality tale often told by Johannesburg Water's local outreach staff. Lazarus now slightly louder affirmed that "This is a true story! You will find them drinking the whole month." Bongi, always quick with responses, countered "Is it not just that they want to have fun? Like maybe today, I and my friend, we like drinking a beer?" Of course, this did not answer Lazarus' complaint at all; in fact, it inverted the entire logic by which the conversation had unfolded up until this point (what is "necessary" and what is more than necessary, surplus, or luxury). By elevating "having fun" onto the same moral plane as satisfying "basic water needs," Bongi had disregarded Lazarus's point entirely. Lazarus, noting this of course, suggested, "Okay, fine, so you must think to yourself: 'Before I have fun, let me put this money aside and do this thing [paying the prepaid] first. If I can take R15 or R20 then I can have fun with the change.'" Bongi's temporary destabilization of the boundary between "need" and "surplus" was thus quickly resurrected, much to the amusement of the other guys who, again, broke out in loud laughter at their friend's calculations.

---

37   This was contrary to frequent complaints that the water was now "brown" and "hot," due to the shallow pipes just beneath the pavement, which meant that water would be heated up by the sun.

Lazarus was not the only resident in Phiri who said he was happy with the meter. As I pointed out in the previous chapter, many residents expressed relief at no longer being burdened by debt and about being able to stay out of a debt relation to the city. In Soweto's wealthier areas, some residents were even actively campaigning for the rollout of the project, since they no longer wanted to pay the larger flat rate and their households were often smaller.

What this conversation threw into sharp relief, then, was the question of how—through what moral calculations—to determine "basic needs." What makes a need "basic"? Is it a basic need to flush the toilet every time, or to water the garden? Is it a basic need to rinse clothing properly or to sprinkle the floor against the dust? Can having a beer with a friend now and then be counted as a basic need? In Phiri, the conversation, and the laughter with which Lazarus's analysis was met, also showed that the terms of "costs" and "benefits" were not established, but fundamentally undetermined and always subject to negotiation. If the question of alcohol made the calculations seem morally simple, similar conversations and conflicts over such calculations often revolved around how to determine what kinds of expenses were critically important and which ones could be dispensed with. Of course, such questions were not asked only in Soweto, but were subject to debate within the council and amongst experts of various kinds, in particular since much of South Africa's current social policies revolve around the provision of a "basic minimum" or "lifeline" (cf. Ferguson 2015; Naidoo 2007). Indeed, determining the limits of "basic needs" would also become a central juridical and political question in the constitutional case against Operation Gcin'amanzi.

If commodification is often presented as producing a flattening of social relations—what Maurer (2006) terms the "acid theory of money"—in Phiri the new metrologies of water introduced by Operation Gcin'amanzi (re)produced hierarchies, kinship, and gender relations, binding households together in new and old ways. This process did not create cold-blooded utility maximizers, but rather relations of coercion, affect, and interdependencies based on kinship, neighborly solidarity, or unequal tenant-landlord relations. Hence Thembi's *gogo*, (grandmother) and the labor of caring and disciplining she performs and the constraints she is put under, becomes readable as a central figure in the socio-technical assemblage of calculation introduced by corporatization. Similarly, the affects and disciplines thus mobilized are central to its "success."

It is in this sense, then, that we should see corporatization as a particular technique to make spaces of calculability through a heterogeneous complex of material and nonmaterial practices and devices. In the process, tasks became redistributed, and epistemic agencies were delegated to ever-smaller spheres, including, in the last instance, the manager of the household. This happened through an iterative process of "ring-fencing": The water utility, previously an integral part of the city, became an independent company. Soweto was delimited within the wider water flows of Johannesburg; in turn, Phiri and the prototype project were ring-fenced within Soweto. Phiri was internally divided up into "superblocks" through which progress could be measured. The smallest ring-fenced unit was the individual household, which, like the other spaces could be rendered visible through numbers. In the process, the labors of calculation were decentralized one by one and ultimately came to rest on the household as the most important location within which calculations would occur and to which metrological practices could be *delegated*. Thus, urban restructuring, and the fetish of efficiency that animates it, came to operate via a series of delegations that ultimately shifted the burden of calculative action onto individual households and, indeed, onto people like Thembi's granny.

Households have of course always been spaces of calculability, and women have often been at the center doing the labor of such calculation: budgeting, caring, and disciplining.[38] New here, then, is not calculation per se, but rather the ways in which such practices became integrated within a broader state project that tied each household to the larger reform of the city. Households thus became the capillary ends of a larger set of reforms concerned with both efficiency and with rehabituating residents to regular payment. The calculating household thus produced also ultimately depended on pre-existing social relations, capacities, and habits, which often were repurposed for new goals. This form of affective labor—the labor of caring, exhorting, penalizing, coaxing, or teaching—is central to the ways in which projects such as Operation Gcin'amanzi come to work.

COUNTERMEASURES

The metrological reforms introduced by Operation Gcin'amanzi were often articulated as projects to introduce new subjectivities and dispositions—from an ethos of budgeting to a new environmental sensibility. It is also at this register that many of the protests unfolded. In the course of Operation Gcin'amanzi's implementation, Phiri saw many, sometimes violent, confrontations, most of which involved the infrastructure for the project. Residents dug out the freshly laid pipes at night, a few times traffic was

---

38 Feminist scholarship has long argued that housework and related forms of reproductive labor should be seen as integral to capitalist relations (Federici 2012). It is important to note, though, that in a very different way such relations became central to neoliberal thinking at roughly the same time, most famously in Gary Becker's theorization of the family (Becker 1981).

stopped with burning tires on the main road, and protesters ripped out meters and paraded them in front of the local council office. Many of these protests were organized by the Phiri Concerned Residents Forum, sometimes with help from activists of the Anti-Privatisation Forum (APF). Few of these protests acquired the spectacular notoriety and public soul searching produced by the Diepsloot protest with which this book began, but the media periodically reported about the ongoing conflicts in Phiri, often in similar terms.

One such protest began with a small gathering mostly made up of women which soon turned into a march of a couple of hundred people. Walking down Koma Road, the main artery leading to Phiri, the marchers began to chant. As they marched, they passed a banner overhead with a smiling Thabo Mbeki promising A BETTER LIFE FOR ALL and encouraging them to VOTE ANC! A few steps further another banner, this time courtesy of Johannesburg Water, displayed two smiling children, one white one black, exhorting residents to save water. Cheering as they walked past the placards, the marchers made their way to the local council office, which also housed the local Johannesburg Water pay point, where residents would usually go to buy water credits for their meters. The police had been alerted, and the office yard was already filled with a line of police in riot gear. Mostly locked out from the office yard by a metal fence, the protesters began *toyi-toying*, chanting, and stumping their feet. Despite the threat projected by the presence of the police, it was a cheerful, almost carnivalesque atmosphere. Many chants, often adapted from antiapartheid songs, ridiculed the local councilor, who, as often in such situations, was nowhere to be found.

After about an hour outside the council, the crowd having doubled in size in the meantime, Zodwa, a woman known to be at the center of such protests, stepped into the middle of the yard and began shaking and circling her hips, and mocking whichever local official would dare to peek around the office doors. She had brought with her one of the plastic measuring buckets the utility had provided with the meter, filled with an as yet unidentifiable substance. Placing it on the dusty ground outside the gates, she halfway lifted her skirt and pretended to relieve herself, all the while continuing to shake and circle her hips. The crowd around her cheered. She then emptied the half-filled bucket into the council yard. The riot police, only superficially unfazed by this graphic display, took a step back. Several other women emerged from the crowd with sewage-filled buckets and followed her example, the police now getting visibly more uncomfortable. A brief standoff ensued, but the presence of a camera led to a peaceful resolution.

Looked at from afar, or through the lenses of the media, which had arrived halfway into the protest, this was yet another example of residents unschooled in or unappreciative of the norms of civic engagement in a democracy. Viewed from within the context of Operation Gcin'amanzi outlined above, however, Zodwa had performed a satirical operation that quite literally turned the logic of measuring consumption upside down. By displaying and measuring her own excrement and, as she put it to me later, by "throwing it back at them," she confronted not just the techno-political interventions of Operation Gcin'amanzi, but also the modalities of subjectivation such interventions sought to promote. By turning her body into a site of protest, she made visible and indeed subverted the logic of calculating basic needs that had come to structure Phiri residents' daily lives. Her graphic protest outside the council office also reconnected the domain of formal political representation with a display of the administrative and infrastructural forms of state power that usually remained invisibly located in each resident's household.

If such public rituals of rejection were one way in which protest against the project unfolded, there were other ways in which Operation Gcin'amanzi was opposed. Many of them made the numbers introduced by the project and transmitted by the meter do a different kind of work. Here, I want to return to Joyce's activist accounting with which I began this chapter. In the course of the opposition to the metering project, residents had formed the Phiri Concerned Residents Forum, which in turn had joined the Anti-Privatisation Forum (APF). Amongst the various activities the group engaged in, much emphasis was placed on research, and a special committee—the Research Subcommittee—had been formed for this purpose. The committee brought together academics, activists, and concerned residents to carry out research that would provide evidence for the residents' multiple complaints about the meters. The group coordinated the collective research effort and ran workshops on writing and research methods. In turn, Phiri activists collected data: running surveys, administering questionnaires, and conducting interviews. Thus they collected an array of numbers, each with specific targets and epistemological groundings that together produced a form of "countermetrology," which mapped Phiri and rendered calculable its water supply in a different way.

The numbers collected by activists and residents took a diversity of forms. Some sought to dispute the city's claims; in regularly measuring and recording her water consumption, Joyce was, at one level, simply checking the accuracy of the City's calculations (Is the meter dispensing the right amount of water? Do the City's estimates of average water consumption in Soweto add up?) Here, the mobilization of numbers became central to a particular "politics of accuracy" that challenged the City and Johannesburg Water on its own numerical terrain (Rose 1999: 199). But activists also collected numbers to summon collectivities, to make claims on being counted and accounted for by governmental care. For example, they ran surveys charting the average household size in Phiri to prove that households were larger than the City's calculations allowed for, and thus required more free water than the City currently supplied.[39] Here, numbers were enrolled in a claim for recognition and care from the state—a type of cadastral politics of number that mobilized moral-political demands through demographic data and articulated claims of citizenship in the language of "population."[40]

But Joyce's measurements also pointed to a third, more performative form of mobilizing numbers that was specifically directed at their subjectivating properties. In this form of making numerical claims, disagreement was not necessarily with *what* is counted, nor primarily with accuracy, but rather with *how* counting is done, the effects it is designed to produce and the kinds of persons it is to shape. This was a form of opposition that did not contest the numbers on the same terrain; instead, it disrupted the subjectivating properties and goals of such forms of enumeration. Joyce, while using the same numbers and engaging in the same practices of calculation promoted by the utility, was deliberately engaged in a project to generate numbers that could contest the City's project as a whole. She produced what could be called "insurgent numbers," in large part by making numbers do a different kind of work and, in the process, investing measurement with new affective value.[41]

When Joyce sat down to read her meter, she not only collected numbers against the City, she also redirected the very forms of subjectivation such numbers were designed to propel. Rather than using the numbers to budget her household's water use, she turned the private, individualized numbers projected by the meter into public numbers that could represent and make a larger claim about the lives of Phiri residents and how they had been affected by Operation Gcin'amanzi. Similarly, while the budgetary practices of calculation encouraged by the utility worked in a logic of "countdown," Joyce's counting involved checking for regularity and thus *witnessing* numbers. The subjectivity and affect enabled and generated by counting was not budgetary; rather, it was animated by the understanding that the individual numbers she collected represented many of her neighbors' and thus could be used toward a larger end: namely, testifying to the effects of the metrological regime now operational in Phiri. In this performative politics of number, the practices of measurement and, indeed, the numbers themselves were resignified and invested with new meanings.

39   For example, such research suggested that the number of residents living on one stand in Soweto was double the City's estimates (16 rather than 8 residents), with residents often living in informal structures in the backyard (Coalition against Water Privatisation 2005).

40   For other accounts of activist practices of self-enumeration, see Appadurai (2001, 2012) and Chatterjee (2004) on India, and Robins (2014) and Storey (2014) on similar activism in Cape Town. Appadurai (1996) uses the notion of "cadastral politics" in his discussion of the colonial politics of numbers.

41   I am using "insurgent" here in a non-normative way similar to James Holston (2009: 34).

The numbers collected by Joyce and other activists also had different effects in the world. Once collected Joyce's numbers were fed into a larger claim against the City, a demand to account for and make visible Sowetans' plight, a demand that would—hopefully—change not just how the City provided water, but also the metrologies through which citizenship was being refashioned. While the utility used the numbers collected from residents as a way to account for water usage in Soweto (and thus as part of the effort to render Sowetans' consumption legible), the numbers collected by Joyce and others would add up to make a different claim. With help from the Research Subcommittee, they became part of activist-produced research reports, which were presented at community meetings and press conferences, and submitted to officials. The public launches of such research reports were also sites of demonstration with hundreds of residents filling a community hall and many getting up and giving individual testimonies. The reports also were translated into multilingual "popular booklets" designed as mobilization tools for distribution amongst fellow Soweto residents. And finally, and perhaps most dramatically, the numbers became part of a constitutional court case against Operation Gcin'amanzi brought by activists against the City of Johannesburg. In several ways, then, activists developed a numerical language with which to engage fellow Sowetans, local government officials, and, via the media, larger public debates.

The numbers collected by activists had an immediate instrumental value—they could be used in the court case to prove that her family did not have enough water, they could show the miscalculations of the city, and they could be used to demand concrete changes in policy. However, these numbers were also crucially important in the way in which they challenged the subjectivating processes involved in the metering project. Apart from turning people into experts, such countermeasures became "technologies of the self," fashioning activist subjectivities counter to the habits and dispositions the utility sought to produce (Foucault 1988). Here, a politics of numbers emerged that worked more by subtle resignification than by radical subversion. Instead of entirely disrupting the numerical language game of the metrological project, Joyce began from the existing measure of things and, via a process of resignification, deployed the numbers to new ends. Indeed, Joyce's practices of countermeasurement, despite her refusal of the budgetary rationality, rendered her an active, calculating citizen, if not of the kind envisaged by the utility. Thus, the ways in which numbers are mediated and can be rendered semiotically unstable became a central resource that activists drew on.

Both in their refusals and in the performative acts of enumeration, the activists showed measurement to be a political act—what is to be measured, how it is to be measured, by whom and with what desired effect. Importantly, this was not simply a refusal of measurement tout court—it was not based on an argument against quantification per se. Neither, however, was it simply a claim for more "accurate" numbers. Rather, it was a disagreement about the epistemology of measurement and the ontological politics bound up with it. It was precisely the understanding that how something is measured shapes the realities available to make political claims.

CONCLUSION

Over two decades ago, François Ewald (1991: 160) suggested provocatively that we might study social modernity via its techniques of measurement. This chapter has taken measurement as both a vantage point and an object of ethnographic inquiry to explore the ways in which political languages have shifted and taken on new forms in a context of postapartheid reform. Measurement, I have suggested, transforms the very terrain of politics; as such, it is often a political, and not merely a technical act. It is precisely this techno-politics of measurement that activists point to as they "countermeasure." Understanding this metrological terrain and how numbers become politically efficacious requires paying close attention to how numbers are generated and materially transmitted, what grounds their epistemological hold and their semiotic stability.

While the postapartheid state often continues to rely on apartheid forms of producing and using knowledge, numbers today also work toward different ends and perform different tasks. Instead of being solely designed to objectify and intervene, today numbers increasingly also come to take on subjectivating properties that seek to construct the *frames* within which certain agencies can be enabled and encouraged. Such numbers and the socio-technical process by which they are produced and transmitted are indicative of new modes of delegating the labors of counting to smaller entities, with the "household" as their most capillary frame. Such new numerical logics also include novel forms of accounting for "basic needs" and neoliberal welfare policies that don't quite as easily map onto the more familiar trope of entrepreneurialism that is usually associated with neoliberalism. "Living Prepaid," apart from transforming the temporal rhythms of everyday life, also forces residents to engage in novel forms of calculations produced by technologies like the prepaid meter. It is this redistribution of epistemic capacities and tasks that in part marks the contemporary proliferation of numbers as distinct from the "mania of measurement" of grand-apartheid-era bureaucrats.

Simultaneously, in a context of democracy in which the apartheid state's racialized measures increasingly recede, so too does the resonance of the kinds of political languages that enabled countermeasures during the antiapartheid struggle. The shift from the racial-bureaucratic "mania for measurement" to the contemporary liberal-democratic practices of enumeration has also transformed the political terrain in which numbers and countermeasures become strategically efficacious. In its place, new countermeasures emerge that take different representational forms, that perform new tasks and that, in turn, are bound up with different affective investments

Finally, we might then also return to Joyce and her notebook. In a context in which numbers increasingly come to matter in constituting households and shaping subjectivities, it is perhaps not surprising that activists "countermeasure," in the process making the numbers produced by projects like Operation Gcin'amanzi do a different kind of work. Such metrological projects, and the numbers through which they work, become the terrain for ongoing negotiation and expressions of disagreement, and, as such, should be seen as profoundly political. This is so not merely because corporatization has been subject to protest and dissent at all junctures, but perhaps more importantly because reframing spaces of calculability simultaneously reframes what counts as political. Such countermeasures—alongside numerous other forms of battles on a technical terrain—are thus also bound up with much larger questions of civic virtue, democracy, and visions for the future, albeit in different material and discursive forms.

Chapter 6

PERFORMING DIGNITY

Human Rights and the Legal Politics of Water

Water is Life, Sanitation is Dignity.

—TITLE OF THE STRATEGIC FRAMEWORK OF WATER SERVICES
(DEPARTMENT OF WATER AFFAIRS AND FORESTRY 2003).

Social and economic rights by their very nature [involve] rationing.
Such rationing should not be considered a restriction of or a
limitation . . . , but the very condition for [their] proper exercise.

—CONSTITUTIONAL COURT JUSTICE ALBIE SACHS (2005)

In May 2011, shortly before the nationwide local elections, South African newspapers announced the "The Toilet Election."[1] The announcement—transmitted via headlines posted alongside roads and displayed on front pages—came in the aftermath of a drawn-out dispute in the Western Cape province between the locally ruling Democratic Alliance (DA) and the opposition African National Congress (ANC). For weeks, the ANC had accused the DA-controlled City of Cape Town of building toilets without enclosures in the township of Khayelitsha. This was part of a larger "site and service" scheme in which residents were provided with a plot of land and infrastructure connections, but were expected to build their own housing. The toilet walls were to be added by residents themselves. In articles illustrated by photographs of the exposed toilets in the midst of empty plots, political commentators lamented the "image of a woman sitting on a toilet without an enclosure" as an unimaginable indignity demonstrating

1 "The Toilet Election," *Mail & Guardian* (Johannesburg), May 13, 2011.

the "lack of compassion" in postapartheid South Africa.[2] Shortly thereafter, the Cape Town High Court ruled that the City had violated the residents' constitutional right to have their dignity protected and ordered officials to build enclosures for the toilets. Grudgingly accepting the judgment, DA leader Helen Zille argued in defense that "it was precisely because we believe communal toilets impinge on the dignity of people that the city sought to extend sanitation services to every household within available budgets."[3]

Commentators would later describe the open toilet debacle as an "election stunt," especially since it turned out that unenclosed toilets had also been installed in ANC-ruled municipalities. Yet the public spectacle and the moral anxieties it prompted ultimately pointed to larger questions; here, in the language of rights, dignity, and populist electoral gamble, a woman exposed on an open toilet became a symbol for the disappointments of the postapartheid condition. Indeed, the toilet debate and the way in which it was framed by the courts and the media demonstrated with particular clarity how central moral-legal languages of human dignity had become not only as a repertoire for making claims on the state, but also as a form of rationalizing and articulating citizenship and its entitlements. For, political differences aside, human dignity was a value no party to the debate could afford not to lay claim to.

Of course, many other ways could have been found to express discontent with the toilet situation; the politics of infrastructure in South Africa comes in many shapes and forms. Most obviously, perhaps, the altercation took place in a context of widespread, and at times violent, "service delivery protests" all over the country—of the kind that, in the past, had rarely received a similarly sympathetic coverage or public support. Shortly after the toilet debate, Cape Town would also witness the rise of the "poo wars" during which residents of informal settlements protested by spilling sewage at central locations. Moreover, the controversy transpired amid persistent concern about the inability of communities to participate in decision making regarding housing or basic service provision, and, more broadly, a pervasive disappointment with the speed of postapartheid transformation. Yet, as in many instances before, a moral-legal language of human dignity framed the ensuing public debate around state obligation.

In this chapter, I track the ambivalent consequences of this contemporary prominence of moral-legal forms of claiming and adjudicating state duty by following Operation Gcin'amanzi and the prepaid meter to court.

2   Fienie Grobler and Molaole Montsho, "Open Toilets Symbolize 'Lack of Delivery,'" SAPA, May 13, 2011.
3   "City of Cape Town Loses Toilet Battle," *Mail & Guardian* (Johannesburg), May 29, 2011.

I explore how the fight against the project came to be articulated in a judicial language when five Phiri residents brought a case against the City and Johannesburg Water in a constitutional challenge that many perceived as precedent setting. In *Lindiwe Mazibuko and Others v. City of Johannesburg, Johannesburg Water Pty. Limited and the Department of Water Affairs and Forestry* (2009),[4] the residents with the help of a legal NGO, argued that the City of Johannesburg had violated their right to water as enshrined in the constitution. While *Mazibuko* has been of particular interest to legal scholars, here, I use the case, and the epistemologies and evidentiary practices on which it was built, as a lens to explore "what human rights do" *in relation to* citizenship and the political terrain.[5] The case is significant not only because it demonstrates the translation of the politics of infrastructure into a juridico-political language, but also because it enables an exploration of the larger questions of citizenship and state obligation that were elicited by the struggles around Operation Gcin'amanzi. Building on anthropological work that has examined the centrality and limits of law- and rights-based politics in South Africa (Comaroff and Comaroff 2006a; Robins 2006), I explore how conceptions, techniques, and practices of citizenship have been reconfigured in a moment in which languages of humanity come to frame not just state obligations but citizenship itself.

As I showed in previous chapters, postapartheid techno-politics often took fiscal and infrastructural forms with close ties to and continuities with the late-apartheid period. Here, I investigate a techno-politics that took shape at the judicial level and that was in part a result of wider global processes that accompanied the "transition," in particular the circulation of globalized human rights norms and expertise. I investigate how the multiple complaints and demands surrounding Operation Gcin'amanzi were turned into a specific form of "lawfare" (Comaroff and Comaroff 2006a) and how the residents' diverse complaints were re-articulated as legal-technical claims.

Following the legal techno-politics that came to define the case, and the debates and protests it sparked, I ask: How were the particular discontents produced by Operation Gcin'amanzi narrativized as a moral-legal problem and as a violation of "human dignity"? What meanings does "human dignity" take on as it travels between different contexts, and what are its performative effects? How do globally circulating norms intervene in historically specific political arguments, and how are they appropriated and transformed? What new formations of citizenship emerge in this context?

---

4   Mazibuko and Others v City of Johannesburg and Others 2008 (4) All SA 471 (W).
5   Talal Asad (2000) uses the phrase "what human rights do" to point to the performative effects of languages of rights in relation to politics.

THE "HUMAN" AS A POLITICAL TERRAIN

Beginning with Burke and Marx, the distinction between man and citizen, first articulated in the Declaration of the Rights of Man and Citizen, has often functioned as both target and heuristic for the critique of human rights. In one of the most searing commentaries, Hannah Arendt argued that human rights were hollow without citizenship: "Man had hardly appeared as a completely emancipated, completely isolated being that carried his dignity within himself . . . , when he disappeared again into a member of a people" (Arendt 2004 [1951]: 369). Appeals to the "human," she argued, were at best meaningless without membership in a political community where such rights could be claimed, recognized, and protected.[6] Recent anthropological scholarship has critically explored the implications of Arendt's argument in relation to new and emergent questions regarding the state and citizenship. There is by now a large literature documenting the ambivalent ethico-political consequences of humanitarianism and human rights as new governmental grammars, and, importantly, also as languages to stake political claims. This scholarship has focused largely on populations outside normative modern structures of accountability, such as refugees, undocumented migrants, the stateless, or populations unprotected by state institutions (see, e.g., Feldman 2007; Malkki 1996; McKay 2012; Redfield 2013; Ticktin 2011).

Although this focus on "exceptional" populations has been extremely productive, less attention has been paid to how citizenship itself has been transformed in the context of this global prominence of languages of humanity.[7] Indeed, critical discussions of human rights and humanitarianism at times implicitly hinge on the modernist figure of the citizen as a normative foil. In this chapter, I explore how the case against Operation Gcin'amanzi brought to the fore a peculiar contemporary reversal of Arendt's problematic. To make effective claims on the state, Phiri's residents needed to use the language of human rights in order to be "heard." Rather than being trumped by and subordinate to citizenship as Arendt argued, in the contemporary moment human rights become a specific mode of articulating citizenship and its entitlements. Thus, this chapter analytically follows the activists who mobilize notions of human dignity on the streets and in the courts, along with the experts, lawyers, and judges

6   And yet, Arendt's institutionalist vision of the political blinded her to the possibilities of a politics outside state structures and led her to relegate the "merely human" to the status of the prepolitical (Arendt 1982; cf. Rancière 2004).

7   But see Didier Fassin's analysis of "humanitarian reason" in relation to French social policy (Fassin 2012) and Joao Biehl and Adriana Petryna's exploration of the judicialization of the right to health in Brazil (Biehl 2013; Biehl and Petryna 2011).

who adjudicate, measure, and attempt to fill the concept with content. In analyzing the specific modalities through which "human dignity" is performed and the publics it addresses and brings into being, I trace the transformation of a political terrain shaped by the modernist languages of liberation, solidarity, and social citizenship of the antiapartheid struggle and its articulation with more minimalist idioms of individual rights and the satisfaction of "basic needs."

These transformations take shape against the larger backdrop of a seemingly paradoxical post–Cold War moment of widespread neoliberal reforms, on the one hand, and the rise to prominence of economic and social rights (ESR), as an extension of global human rights frameworks, on the other. While many activists and legal scholars view economic and social rights as a counterpoint to neoliberal reforms, in the following, I explore some of the more complex and less obvious links between the two.

Much scholarship has pointed to the contemporaneity and conceptual kinship between human rights and neoliberalism (see, e.g., Asad 2003: 157; Barnett and Weiss 2008; Comaroff and Comaroff 2006a); here, I make a more concrete argument about their conceptual association. As I elaborate below, human rights-based forms of rationalizing social provisions can be seen as one way in which modernist forms of social citizenship—with its logics of equality, solidarity, and interdependence—are being rethought and re-articulated in a context of neoliberal reform. While neoliberalism has often been associated primarily with the destruction of welfare mechanisms or the celebration of entrepreneurialism, recent analyses suggest that neoliberal reforms do not simply curtail state provisions. Rather, social provisions come to be authorized in different terms and actualized through different techniques, thus producing specific modalities of care and subjects of need (Collier 2011; Muehlebach 2012). The increasing recasting of social provisioning in the language of human rights can be seen as one way in which state care is being reconceived. If human rights and humanitarianism abandon the utopian *telos* of total transformation in favor of short-term relief and a "minimal biopolitics" (Redfield 2013: 18ff; see also Moyn 2010), the neoliberal imagination "evacuates" the near future in strikingly similar ways (Guyer 2007). Social provisions are no longer necessarily authorized by a modernist utopian horizon and temporality of dramatic societal transformation, but are frequently aimed at providing more immediate relief and satisfying "basic needs," often remaining agnostic about the longer term goals of state assistance (Ferguson 2015).[8]

Bringing these conceptual associations into ethnographic focus, I explore the transformations of techniques and practices of the political in

---

8   See here also Thushara Hewage's reflections on the "temporality of the social" (Hewage 2014).

a postapartheid moment in which languages of citizenship and humanity come to be related in novel ways. As activists mobilize "human dignity" to make claims on the state, and legal experts try to measure and adjudicate the precise contents of the human and its needs, the courts and the law itself emerge as yet another terrain on which disagreements and claims on citizenship and democracy are often resolved. By "political terrain," I mean both the discursive and the semiotic-material modalities in which certain political languages are rendered legible and come to resonate, whereas others cannot. My interest here is in what structures possible actions and conditions intelligibility, what "makes up" political agents and, in turn, what forecloses other forms of political imagination as modernist hopes and expectations appear to recede from view. In South Africa, where the political terrain was for generations defined by modernist idioms of popular sovereignty and utopian horizons of collective freedom, this turn toward moral-legal languages of the "human" is particularly striking. Against this backdrop, languages of humanity simultaneously open up space for new ways of making political claims and narrow the space for others—in the process recombining familiar modernist tropes with novel forms of articulating disagreement. Neither simply apparatus of domination nor unproblematic language of resistance, and at once enabling and obliging, here, the human itself becomes a terrain of political action.

MAZIBUKO V. CITY OF JOHANNESBURG AND THE LOCATIONS OF THE POLITICAL

In 2007, following on the heels of intense, at times violent protests, five residents from Phiri, took legal action against the City of Johannesburg on the basis of their constitutionally guaranteed "right to access to water."[9] Taking legal action had been discussed for a long time amongst APF activists in Soweto and Johannesburg, including in our weekly Research Subcommittee meetings, but it had not been an easy endeavor. Creating a promising case—a judicial assemblage of sorts that required representative residents, skilled lawyers, funding, institutional support, and specific forms of evidence—was a very time-consuming and obstacle-ridden process.

Despite the complexity and multiplicity of objections to Operation Gcin'amanzi, many of which I outlined in the previous chapter, the case needed to focus primarily on the complaints that could be rendered

9   Although there had been several important socio-economic rights cases before, *Mazibuko* was the first to mobilize the right to water. For discussions of *Mazibuko*, see Bond and Dugard (2008) and Dugard (2010).

judicially legible and compelling. The applicants, all five of them members of the Phiri Concerned Residents Forum, charged that the meters cut them off without fair notice and that the limited lifeline of free water they received per month was "insufficient for a dignified human existence."[10] The ensuing cutoffs from water supply, their affidavits argued, violated their right to access to sufficient water, and also discriminated against them on the basis of race, given that the imposition of the meters was limited to the historically black townships.

After years of preparation and then months of waiting, in April 2008 the residents won the case in the Johannesburg High Court. In an unprecedented ruling and with a clear sense of outrage, the presiding judge, Moroa Tsoka, held that the enforced installation of prepayment meters in Soweto residents' yards and the resultant disconnections from water supply had been unlawful and unconstitutional. In strong language, Tsoka maintained that the utility had shown an apartheid-style "patronization" of poor township residents, that the project had indeed engaged in "discrimination solely based on colour," and that water prepayment technology was unconstitutional. What made the ruling particularly satisfying to the Phiri activists involved in the case was Justice Tsoka's palpable sense of outrage at the City of Johannesburg, his suggestion that Johannesburg Water's actions had not merely been misguided, but were purposefully deceitful and disingenuous, and that its measures were defined by a disdain for the poor. He argued that prepaid water meters had been "approved for and not by the residents of Phiri" and that, hence, what the City termed a "consultative process" should in fact be seen as merely a "publicity drive" after the fact (Tsoka Judgment 2008: para 122). Moreover, he clearly linked the city's policies with legacies of apartheid. As he put it,

> To argue, as the respondents do, that the applicants will not be able to afford water on credit and therefore it is "good" for the applicants to go on prepayment meters is patronising. That patronisation sustained apartheid: its foundational basis was discrimination based on colour and decisions taken on behalf of the majority of the people of the country as "big brother felt it was good for them." This is subtle discrimination solely on the basis of colour. Discrimination based on colour is impermissible in the terms of the Constitution. It is outlawed. It is unlawful.
>
> The underlying basis for the introduction of the prepayment meters, seems to me, to be credit control. If this is true, I am unable to understand why this credit control measure is only suitable in the historically poor black areas and not the historically rich white areas. Bad payers cannot be described in terms

10 *Lindiwe Mazibuko and Others v. City of Johannesburg, Johannesburg Water Pty. Limited, and the Department of Water Affairs and Forestry* (2009).

of colour or geographical areas. There may be as many bad customers in the historically rich white areas as there are in the historically poor black areas. Bad debt is a human problem not a racial problem (ibid.: para 153–54).

Importantly, particularly for my purposes here, he ruled that the free life-line of six kiloliters of water per household per month was insufficient to satisfy basic needs. Drawing on international human rights norms advocating a specific "minimum core" of economic and social rights authorized by the WHO, Tsoka mandated the city to double the monthly water lifeline from twenty-five to fifty liters per person per day to comply with the constitution. In a relatively unusual move, he thus not only overruled existing government policy, but also replaced it with specific directives that drew on international human rights norms and globally circulating standards of "basic needs."[11]

Justice Tsoka's emphatic and wide-ranging ruling was celebrated by water rights activists globally as a precedent-setting outcome and a confirmation of the emancipatory possibilities of judicial activism. Indeed, transnational water rights listservs and websites, as well as activist publications, were brimming with excitement at this resounding success, which activists hoped would be replicable elsewhere. For the Soweto activists gathered inside and outside the High Court in downtown Johannesburg, the unexpected judgment finally gave official recognition to their long-standing complaints, which the City had dismissed for years. To them, Tsoka's ruling was a *political* as much as a legal victory.

From a different perspective, this was also the assessment of Johannesburg's mayor, Amos Masondo, who, clearly furious, suggested in a press conference that the ruling was "distorted" and that Judge Tsoka "should not interfere with the government."[12] In a striking choice of words, he announced that the City would appeal the judgment: "Judges are not above the law. We cannot have a situation where a judge wants to take over the role of government. Judges must limit their role to what they are supposed to do. If they want to run the country they must join political parties and contest elections."[13]

Mayor Masondo's angry outburst, much criticized by activists and the media for its disrespect for the judiciary, crystallized a paradox at the heart of the "judicialization of politics" in South Africa and elsewhere (Comaroff and Comaroff 2006a). While many activists took Masondo's statement to be symptomatic of a pervasive elite arrogance amongst government officials that effectively prevented the poor from participating in the political

11 For a discussion of "minimum core," see Danchin (2010) and Young (2008).
12 Kingdom Mabuza, "Union to Challenge Mayor over Appeal," *Sowetan*, May 16, 2008.
13 Kingdom Mabuza, "Jozi to Contest Ruling on Water," *Sowetan*, May 15, 2008.

process, Masondo apparently saw himself as defending postapartheid democratic sovereignty against intervention by unaccountable judges and decontextualized references to international human rights norms. This quarrel was not merely about the details of a legal judgment; it was a more fundamental disagreement about the proper location of politics, including different conceptions of democracy, sovereignty and justice.

A year later, the Constitutional Court justices sided with Masondo when, ruling on an appeal, they unanimously overturned the judgment of the lower courts and dismissed the case, arguing that the constitution does not require "courts to take over the tasks that in a democracy should properly be reserved for the democratic arms of government."[14] This outcome was an immense disappointment to the activists and lawyers who had worked on the case, many of whom suggested that the ruling followed a pattern of implicit judicial endorsements of the government's neoliberal policies, in this instance the harsh enforcement of cost recovery via prepaid water meters. Here again, while the activists saw in human rights a political language to challenge what they perceived as the neoliberal antipolitics of an otherwise tone-deaf state, the mayor and the judges viewed this use of human rights as interference with popular sovereignty guaranteed by the electoral process. In the following, I suggest that one way to disentangle these divergent interpretations is to think anew about the relationship between citizenship, human rights, and neoliberalism.

FROM THE SOCIAL TO THE HUMAN?

One of the defining pillars of social rights as they emerged in the late nineteenth and into the twentieth century was a universalist account of social citizenship often animated by utopian ideas of equality, interdependence, and solidarity (cf. Donzelot 1988; Marshall 1992). This universalist quality distinguished social rights from the earlier "poor relief," which was primarily residualist and "disaggregated" from citizenship.[15] Viewed from this longer historical perspective, the contemporary moment appears paradoxical. In many parts of the world, there has been a noted hollowing of social citizenship in a context of neoliberal reforms, as state services are cut,

14   *Mazibuko* (2009), Judgment.
15   Esping-Anderson distinguishes between marginalist forms of welfare based on a notion of collective solidarity, and institutionalist forms that are targeted towards the "human residual that is incapable of self-help" (Esping-Andersen and Kopi 1987: 40). If the poor laws were defined by their de facto expulsion of the poor from citizenship, today's measures, though clearly not formally outside citizenship, still produce a particular form of "disaggregated citizenship" (Benhabib 2005).

privatized, or made contingent on specific conditions. Yet, at the same time, there is also an increasing focus on economic and social rights (ESR), both internationally and locally, often via the inclusion of such rights within constitutions and international documents.[16] Thus, while social citizenship appears to be in decline substantively, *formally* it is stronger than ever before, as human rights have been expanded to cover new ground including, for example, rights to water, food, or health, and such rights are now increasingly recognized as justiciable within national constitutions.

Unlike social citizenship in the twentieth century, contemporary economic and social rights are not usually tethered to national welfare traditions, but are part of a broader, international move toward human rights in the aftermath of the Cold War.[17] Thus, they are often not anchored in a solidaristic notion of the body-politic or universal civic entitlement, but instead are frequently based on a minimalist conception of absolute basic needs without a necessary utopian *telos*.[18] By extension, the recipient of social provisions is often no longer the universal citizen and part of a larger, interdependent collective, but rather an individual subject of needs, a figure that in the liberal imagination has often functioned as the constitutive outside to the autonomous, rights-bearing citizen (Brown 1995). In South Africa, this increasing recoding of the social via the human is visible in the shift in language and content from the 1955 Freedom Charter to the 1996 constitution. While the Freedom Charter deployed a modernist idiom of "the people" and called for large-scale economic redistribution and a program of public services, the constitution is distinct in both content and tone.

The constitution, often hailed as one of the most progressive in the world, was an important pillar of the compromise that ended apartheid. While the constitution's property clause pre-empted radical redistribution, the inclusion of socio-economic rights was viewed by many as a way to balance the sanctity of property with a more transformative agenda (Huchzermeyer 2003; Sachs 2005). At the same time, the establishment of the constitution also coincided with the Growth, Employment and Redistribution (GEAR) strategy, the neoliberal reform program that had rendered unfeasible many of the more wide-ranging redistributive reforms originally envisioned by the liberation movement and, more broadly, with the globalization of a particular liberal vision of democracy in the aftermath of the

16   A good example is the explicit recognition of the right to water by the UN in 2011.

17   First recognized in the UN Declaration of Human Rights, it was only with the establishment of the Committee on Economic, Social and Cultural Rights (CESCR) in 1985 that economic and social rights became a focus within international human rights.

18   This resonates with the larger shift in development thinking since the mid-1970s from utopian ideals of modernization theory or socialist-inspired development toward a focus on "basic needs" and "poverty alleviation." This form of development seeks to ameliorate misery, but gives up on the idea of its complete supersession.

Cold War.[19] This paradoxical context of liberation and liberalization in part accounts for the prominence of human rights language in South Africa and has shaped it in specific ways.

The constitution recognizes a justiciable right to access to housing, health care, food, water, social security, and education, closely following the International Covenant on Economic, Social and Cultural Rights (ICESCR). Crucially, the state does not have to fulfill these rights immediately (which it might be financially unable to do); rather, it is charged with the "progressive realization" of socio-economic rights by taking "reasonable" measures toward their fulfillment. As will become clear below, "reasonableness" and the measurement of "basic needs" sufficient for human dignity became the crux in *Mazibuko*. In turn, much hinged on the precise definition of human dignity.

Human rights claims often rely on a Kantian definition of human dignity as an ontological realm of individual worth outside of commensuration or monetary valuation.[20] Lori Allen (2009) has compellingly analyzed the specific "politics of immediation" at work in the mobilization of such claims through which human rights gain performative power by appearing to be free from mediation. Thus mobilized, human dignity appears as a presocial and prepolitical value that universally *grounds* claims to human rights. Yet, when mobilized in a legal argument, human dignity can no longer remain an unmediated floating signifier, but needs to be delimited and defined (Riley 2008). Indeed, as I argue below, rather than grounding human rights law, the precise meaning of human dignity is ultimately often *produced* in court.

Traveling concepts work in much the same way as technical devices. Akin to the prepaid meter which can be enrolled in various ethical regimes

19   Between 1989 and 1999, more than a third of UN member states adopted new constitutions, including constitutional review, and a quarter of them introduced bills of rights (Klug 2000: 12). Many perceived the increasingly hegemonic normativity of human rights and their incorporation within a justiciable national framework as a progressive move against the backdrop of a history state of authoritarianism. And yet, this "new constitutionalism" also needs to be seen as an integral part of a globalizing liberal consensus, with a unitary vision of the means and ends of democratic transformation and a penchant towards transferring difficult political questions to the legal realm. The "global constitutionalism," as it came to be called, thus managed to suture otherwise potentially incommensurate positions of antiapartheid activists and neoliberal reformers on the basis of a shared stance against state authoritarianism (cf. Klug 2000).

20   "In the kingdom of ends everything has either a price or a dignity. If it has a price, something else can be put in its place as an equivalent; if it is exalted above all price and so admits of no equivalent, then it has a dignity" (Kant 1964: 102; as cited in Asad 2003: 137n). Constitutional court justice Albie Sachs draws on such a conception in his distinction between the utilitarian concerns of government and the more qualitative concerns invoked by human dignity (Sachs 2005).

and political projects, traveling concepts like "human dignity" gain performative force only in distinct assemblages. Thus, what a concept "does," which projects it is enrolled into, and with what targets, is dependent both on the ethico-political horizon within which it intervenes and on the specific modes of authorization that propel it. While in South Africa, "human dignity" has often been seen as part of a transformative jurisprudence, rather than simply a tool for the protection of individual rights (Liebenberg 2005), *Mazibuko* showed both the possibilities and the limits of that promise.

A LEGAL TECHNO-POLITICS: PERFORMING DIGNITY IN COURT

Preparations for the case began in the fraught context of ongoing protest against Operation Gcin'amanzi in Soweto and increasing arrests of activists engaging in direct action. The litigation emerged from collaboration between a legal NGO—the Centre for Applied Legal Studies (CALS) at the University of the Witwatersrand—and activists of the Coalition Against Water Privatisation, including most centrally the APF and the Phiri Concerned Residents Forum. This collaboration itself was not without its ambivalences, especially since there had previously been disagreements between members of the social movements and the legal professionals and academics. While the activists' political goals were diverse, the lawyers, though similarly animated by the political and ethical stakes of the case, also needed to find pragmatic solutions to a legal problem delimited by the ambit of the constitution. This need was reflected in the substance and style of the affidavits, which, while raising a much broader set of ethical and political questions, were organized around a number of very specific legal arguments. Indeed, one of the lawyers involved in the case described their task to me as that of a "translation machine" that would rearticulate the residents' discontents in a legally convincing narrative.

Apart from charges of discrimination and unfair administrative action, the case against Operation Gcin'amanzi came to rest on the amount of water dispensed for free each month. In their affidavits, the applicants argued that the free basic lifeline of 6,000 liters was insufficient for Soweto's large households. This limit, they argued, "subjects the applicants and others who live in conditions of extreme poverty to living conditions that violate our human dignity and amounts to inhuman treatment."[21] Given this identification of the problem, a primary task was to establish *how much*

---

21   *Mazibuko v. City of Johannesburg*, Founding Affidavit, 2007, para 145.

water would be required to sustain a "dignified existence." Of course, this demand entailed a paradox. While human dignity is often defined as a value *beyond* measure or price, the law by definition commensurates, determining specific punishments for specific crimes or, in this instance, adjudicating and delimiting the precise content of "human dignity." The court's paradoxical task, in other words, was to measure a value commonly defined by its immeasurability and singularity.

As much scholarship has shown, the law is dependent on knowledges and epistemologies outside what might be popularly understood by "legal knowledge" (Latour 2010; Pottage and Mundy 2004; Sarat, Douglas, and Umphrey 2007; Valverde and Levi 2008). In a context in which the law is called on to adjudicate ever more complex ethical and political questions, such "outside" knowledges—often, but not always, provided by expert testimony—gain in increasing importance. Such expertise does not merely guide the court's decisions, but takes on a definitional, performative labor, setting up the parameters of the problem that the court then sets out to adjudicate. How research is presented, by which experts, and through which modes authorization thus becomes crucial. Often this produces what one might call a *legal techno-politics* through which political questions are turned into legal-technical ones, and, conversely, legal-technical questions are turned into political problems or produce political effects. While legal evidentiary practices have been of interest to legal anthropologists (Good 2008; Wilson 2011), I explore them here as both constitutive of a specific political terrain and, more broadly, as a window onto formations of citizenship in contemporary South Africa.

LEGAL EPISTEMOLOGY I: EMBODYING INDIGNITY

Shortly before the case went to court, I visited Sophia Malekutu, a pensioner and the oldest applicant in the case. A few months earlier, Sophia had volunteered to provide a statement on her difficulties with repeated disconnections from water supply due to a faulty meter. Although Sophia was usually very talkative and wont to tell jokes, that day her mood was somber. As we pondered the impending proceedings sitting in her small, darkened living room, Sophia said she was a bit anxious about having to appear in court. She wondered aloud about why she had been chosen to be part of the case—she was old, she said, and her memory sometimes failed her. Why had the lawyers not asked younger, more knowledgeable members of the residents' group, who could explain the problem with the prepaid meters in a more articulate fashion? Why her? I tried to reassure her by explaining that she would not need to stand up and speak in court and that the statement she had given to the researchers had been sufficient.

Later, it became clear to me that Sophia had put her finger on the peculiar evidentiary protocols and modes of authorization of this legal quest to prove suffering. Indeed, Sophia's expertise *did not* take the form of objective or scientific corroboration; rather, her expertise—the specialized knowledge that made her an authoritative witness—was *experience*, that is, her ability to authentically embody a particular *type* of suffering, in this instance the struggles of a poor elderly woman trying to manage and live with the consequences of a malfunctioning prepaid water meter.[22] As I suggest below, this legal epistemology of experience, and the conception of human needs thus mobilized, produced a specific target of social provisioning by the state and thus a particular way of understanding, rationalizing, and claiming citizenship *qua* subject of needs.

The five Phiri residents that had been selected to become part of the case were to represent Phiri as a place inhabited by a particular "class of people" and thus as a "disadvantaged community."[23] Each applicant was chosen on the basis of individual predicaments, and each thus represented a particular type of suffering and had a specific function within the larger legal argument. For example, Lindiwe Mazibuko's "household" included over twenty people—the several households living on her plot—demonstrating the miscalculations of the City and the resulting inadequate water provision.[24] On Vusimuzi Paki's stand, a fire in an informal backyard structure had killed two children, because the water credit had run out and there was no water left to extinguish the fire. Another resident, Grace Munyai, told of her struggles to care for her niece, who was suffering from AIDS and needed to be washed several times a day. In this way, each applicant represented a particular experience of "indignity" incurred by the lack of water.

Apart from filling certain functional points in the legal argument, each affidavit was also phrased in order to demonstrate particular forms of suffering. For example, in order to prove the violations of dignity and the government's failure to treat "poor and vulnerable households" with "compassion,"[25] the affidavits established the residents' living conditions in

---

22   In his genealogy of witnessing, Didier Fassin points to the increasing focus on witnessing as a representation of experience over forms of witnessing as third-person observation. It is this authority of "the subjective truth of experience" that was at stake here (Fassin 2008: 539).

23   *Mazibuko*, Makoatsane, Replying Affidavit, 2008.

24   As I discussed in the last chapter, the term "household" used by the City was problematic, as many infrastructure connections de facto service several households, often one formal building and one or two structures in the backyard. Although the City revised its terminology to refer to "consumer units," this did not end the problem of how to count and account for residents and their needs.

25   *Mazibuko*, Makoatsane, Replying Affidavit, 2008, para. 57.

great detail.[26] As I elaborate below, this near-ethnographic quality of the affidavits was in part a product of the logic through which the constitutional challenge operated.

The primary applicant, Lindiwe Mazibuko, had been a prominent activist in the protests against the installation of the meters. In Lindiwe's affidavit, establishing her identity required naming and detailing her suffering in precise terms. In her statement, Lindiwe was asked to give a detailed account of her living circumstances, her "facts of life." She listed the expenses of her family, including medical and school fees. She documented the size of her "household," the twenty persons living on her stand and their ages and the relations between them. She detailed the illnesses some of them endured, the income derived solely from child support grants and a pension, as all members of the household were unemployed. Her life was laid bare. In turn, her affidavit presented her household's poverty as part of a wider condition:

> The people of Phiri are very poor. They are all black. There are many people who live in households with even more people than I do. Many of them are women who take care of children, elderly members of their family, or other members of the community who are ill. Many of the people in my community are HIV positive or have AIDS.[27]

The founding affidavit thus established Lindiwe as exemplary of a wider condition of poverty, identified with race, gender, and HIV status. Similarly, many of the affidavits were defined by a focus on bodily existence. Grace Munyai, for example, detailed how her niece's worsening AIDS had led to her continuous "soiling of the bed" such that more water was required to wash her and to clean her clothes and blankets. The installation of prepaid water meters had dramatically affected her life and that of her niece, who passed away before the case came to court. In Jennifer Makoatsane's affidavit the exposed body and its needs were similarly essential to the narrative:

> I feel that my rights to water and human dignity have been violated. Sometimes I share a bath with my niece and nephew to save water. This becomes even more inconvenient when I menstruate. During this time, I have to flush the toilet without having to at least wait for the second person to use it in order to save water. Otherwise I would feel very embarrassed should a male person (even my brother for that matter) use an unflushed toilet behind me.[28]

26   Indeed, *Mazibuko* was praised by legal commentators as being "remarkable for the detailed analysis of the lived realities of poor communities in South Africa" (Liebenberg 2008).

27   *Mazibuko*, Founding Affidavit, 2007, para 77.

28   *Mazibuko*, Makoatsane, Replying Affidavit, 2008.

In the course of such narratives of suffering, a specific notion of human dignity was produced that hinged on minimalist conceptions of bodily injury and shame.[29] Human dignity thus came to be defined *inversely* by showing it "in breach." Rather than liberal subjects able to transcend and keep private their bodies, Phiri's residents—and women in particular— were shown as vulnerable beings and particular subjects of needs. At stake was the production of what Lynn Festa has called a "sentimental humanity," that is, a humanity not defined by a Kantian focus on reason and autonomy, but rather a humanity in "minimal form, carrying with it no prerogative, except to suffer" (Festa 2010: 13). Indeed, a member of the legal team later suggested to me that, in her estimation, part of the reason that the legal challenge was ultimately unsuccessful was because Soweto, given its status as a formal township, did not comport with the justices' "romantic notion of poverty," that is, the common association of poverty with the externally visible destitution of informal settlements. Ironically, it was the residents' access to formal infrastructures—brick houses with water and electricity connections—that, in the eyes of the judges, signaled their relative wealth. Less visibly, as I showed in the previous chapter, this access was often only precariously available, particularly for backyard dwellers, and unemployment rates were often as high as in informal settlements.

Similarly, the residents could not convince the judges that they were "merely" suffering victims, "without prerogative." Indeed, the lawyers suggested that the fact that all applicants were members of the Anti-Privatisation Forum (APF), which had been the most militant opponent of Operation Gcin'amanzi, had worked against the image of pure, disinterested victims in need of assistance. From this perspective, then, the justices were not merely a legal audience, but also a sentimental one, whose empathy needed to be mobilized by emphasizing particular forms of injury and mobilizing specific suffering subjects—a bare humanity without affiliation or special interests.[30] It was in part on this basis that the case failed.

This privileging of *experiences* of suffering is in part the answer to Sophia's puzzlement about why she had been chosen to be an applicant in the court case. She was asked to testify not because of her knowledge, eloquence, or activist commitment (each of which she did in fact possess), but because she was emblematic of a particular type of injury that she had experienced first-hand. This was a moral-legal politics that had to mobilize Phiri residents as vulnerable, needy beings, in contrast to other popularly available forms of representing and claiming injustice, such as the figure of the wronged citizen who performatively hands over a memorandum of

29   As has been observed by many scholars, a secular preoccupation with bodily suffering and integrity often runs through humanitarian narratives (Laqueur 1989; see also Asad 2003).
30   On the "mobilization of empathy," see Wilson and Brown (2011).

demands to public officials at the end of a demonstration, or of the angry resident *toyi-toying* and chanting outside local government offices. As will become clear below, outside the courts, these modalities of expressing discontents often blurred (cf. Fassin 2008).

If the performance of indignity became a device to articulate and document the legal problem at hand, its resolution required a positive definition of dignity to establish *how much* water would be required to enable a dignified existence. This in turn necessitated a different form of evidence and a different legal epistemology, one that would make dignity measurable.

Legal Epistemology II: Metrologies of Dignity

As Latour (2010) has argued, the mundane materiality of files is central to the ways in which the law is produced and judgments are reached. The law is crucially dependent on particular modes of authorization that frame certain statements as relevant and others as irrelevant to the judicial gaze (see Valverde and Levi 2008: 818). Thus, certain documents become legal knowledge via a process of authorization. In *Mazibuko*, this mode of authorization was a central advantage for the City. Able to fund and access expertise and data on any aspect of the case, the City responded to the legal application with piles of studies, expert testimonies, and other evidence. This mass of documentation proved to be an enormous logistical obstacle for the much less funded legal NGO working on the case and took its staff months to work through. Indeed, one member of the legal team described the City's response to me as a form of "deliberate sabotage." The applicants' replying affidavit itself suggested only slightly less explicitly that the City and Johannesburg Water had "attempted to frustrate our application simply by flooding us with reams of unnecessary paper which would make it difficult for us to respond."[31] Yet, it was in part these reams of paper that would authorize and render stable the legal argument. Beyond the simple logistical obstacle posed by the mass of files, the case would also ultimately come to hinge on the authority of research reports and statements from experts, pitting international versus local standards, one set of numbers against another set of numbers, and, most importantly, one measure against another measure of dignity.

The residents' affidavits were supported by a number of expert statements, including one by Peter Gleick, an internationally recognized expert on water policy and head of a large NGO in the United States. Gleick began his statement by outlining the international legal context of the right to water and calculations of water needs by international organizations such as the World Health Organization (WHO). Given a situation of competing

31   *Mazibuko*, Makoatsane, Replying Affidavit, 2008, para. 4–5.

fiscal demands in Johannesburg, the important question would be to determine *how much* water would be necessary to satisfy basic needs. Gleick argued that "based on substantial international comparative research" the minimum requirement for the fulfillment of human water needs would be 50 liters per person per day, the targeted amount demanded by the legal challenge.[32] He then proceeded to outline in more detail how his global framework would relate to the specific case at hand:

> In the hot, dry, climate of Soweto, a 70-kilogram human will sweat between four and six liters per day, meaning a minimum drinking water requirement of 5 lpcd. [litres per capita per day] A basic requirement for sanitation of 20 lpcd would be the minimum to ensure healthy living conditions in a densely populated area like Phiri. If the houses are connected with inefficient conventional sewerage systems such as is common in South African townships, the minimum water requirement for sanitation increases to more than 75 lpcd.[33]

While Gleick spent much of his affidavit on such calculations, throughout he did not explicitly address the question of "dignity"; he was primarily concerned with understanding and computing "basic needs."

In its response, the City rejected Gleick's argument and responded with its own expert witness drawn from the Palmer Development Group (PDG), a well-funded local consultancy known for its neoliberal bent. On the basis of extensive research that he had compiled in a report, Ian Palmer himself provided the statement supporting the City's larger claim that Operation Gcin'amanzi had been "reasonable" given practical and fiscal constraints. He argued that Gleick's affidavit was a "theoretical piece"[34] with little or no bearing on the situation in South Africa. Given Gleick's lack of familiarity with the specific situation in South Africa, Palmer argued, he "completely misunderstands the water use patterns of Soweto residents [and] Phiri in particular."[35] Thus, for Palmer, the authority of Gleick's expert status was undermined by a lack of contextual detail and local knowledge; what was missing, in other words, was thick description. For example, Palmer suggested, calculating water on the basis of individual usage was "unreasonable," since research had shown that water usage within households was often communal, rather than individual. Unlike individual forms of water consumption, such as drinking water, practices like washing clothes or watering a garden were shared forms of consumption, and hence, would only increase slightly or not at all with a larger household size. To demonstrate this calculation, Palmer had produced an extensive research report,

32   *Mazibuko*, Gleick affidavit, 2008, para 18.
33   Ibid., para 22.1–4.
34   *Mazibuko*, Palmer Affidavit, 2008, para 9.
35   Ibid., para 12.3.

which was attached to his affidavit alongside transcripts of focus groups, survey results, and other research-related documents. Here, a particular form of local knowledge—of residents' habits, consumption practices, and intrahousehold relations—was of central epistemological value and was deployed against Gleick, whose positionality was thus implicitly shifted from ally of the poor to U.S. academic interfering with domestic policy issues that he was not competent to judge.[36]

Palmer also introduced a new typology of water needs that gradually transformed the notion of human dignity. His affidavit differentiated between water consumption with a public benefit and consumption with a private benefit and a homologous argument about the difference between water as a social good versus water as an economic good:

> At a certain level of consumption water is a social good but beyond that it is an economic good. Using water for a swimming pool, for example, cannot be considered socially important and this water should be paid for at a price which is sufficient to cover the cost, taking the externalities which occur due to the impact on the environment and ability of others to access water into consideration.[37]

The swimming-pool, perennial metonym for white privilege and apartheid-era inequalities, gave Palmer's statement an ethical obviousness and logical simplicity not borne out by what followed. It was precisely because it was unclear *where* one should draw the line between the social and the economic, the necessary and the unnecessary, that the court looked to Palmer as an expert witness.

Palmer's affidavit explicitly raised the difficulties of measuring human dignity and translating it into numbers. Indeed, a subheading of his affidavit—"Quantifying the amount of water needed for health (and human dignity)"—heralded the elision that marked the rest of his statement. As Palmer put it:

> The health benefits associated with access to water are clearly important. But what of "human dignity"? This is a very difficult concept to define. . . . Perhaps it can be used in relation to having one's clothes and dwelling clean, although there are some health benefits to these conditions as well. Beyond this, it is difficult to define how the use of water can contribute to 'human dignity'? I assume that a person who has enough water to drink, to prepare food, wash themselves,

---

36   It is here that the particular *modes* of legal authorization mattered. Importantly, it is no longer obvious that "universal" knowledge automatically trumps "local knowledge." While ethnographic, contextual data used to be the primary mode of argument by subaltern litigants, today such "local knowledge" has become a central resource of those who have historically often spoken in the name of universality (Choy 2011; Riles 2006).

37   *Mazibuko*, Palmer Affidavit, 2008, para 8.3.3.

wash their clothes, and keep their dwelling clean has sufficient water for health and human dignity.[38]

Thus, Palmer conflated health and human dignity under the rubric of basic needs. Again, the ethnographic summoning of Phiri residents' daily habits and practices was central to the argument and to the research report on which it drew. Palmer suggested that Gleick had wildly overestimated the water needs of Phiri residents, and had not mustered any evidence for his numbers. The figure of 75 liters per day for sanitation, he suggested, "implies 7 to 8 flushes per day per person which is both grossly wasteful and almost impossible practically." Indeed, flushing the toilet, he argued, was largely a "question of aesthetics" that

> relates strongly to personal habits. It is in fact only essential to flush after defecation which takes place once for a healthy adult. . . . A full flush after each urinating event may be quite commonly practiced, but is wasteful and does not promote improved health.[39]

Thus, drawing on his research in Soweto, he proposed that "1.5 flushes per day is a reasonable provision."

Such statements brought to the fore with exceptional clarity how the case came to rely on the quantification of bodily needs, in the process conjuring particular notions of humanity. These affidavits, and the calculations and research through which they were authorized, ultimately became a central axis of the legal battle, setting the residents' experts against the City's experts and one set of numbers against another set of numbers. Indeed, the Supreme Court of Appeal, ruling on an appeal by the City, made the question of quantification central to its judgment, which relied heavily on the two expert statements.

While the Supreme Court upheld the High Court judgment, it did so on different grounds. In sober language, the court rejected the claim by the Phiri residents that Palmer had mistakenly conflated public and private benefit with the questions of needs and dignity:

> It is clear from his evidence that [Palmer] realised that *what he had to determine was the quantity of water required for dignified human existence* and that that was what he attempted to do. His quantification is specifically done under the heading "Quantifying the amount of water needed for health (and human dignity)." . . .
>
> The only real difference between the evidence of Gleick and Palmer is that Palmer is of the opinion that 15 litres of water would suffice for waterborne

38   Ibid., para 8.3.4.
39   Ibid., para 8.13.6.

sanitation whereas Gleick is of the opinion that 20 litres are required. There is no basis upon which the evidence of Gleick can on the papers be preferred to that of Palmer. . . . For these reasons I am of the view, on the evidence presented, that 42 litres water per person per day would constitute sufficient water.[40]

Thus, over the course of the case, "human dignity" was gradually conflated with a notion of basic needs. In the process, the case narrowed down to a contest between two different forms of needs calculation. By extension, the judges' decision came to hinge on which of the expert testimonies they found more authoritative.

While the legal team working on behalf of the residents had explicitly tried to forgo a narrowly construed legal argument and had included a much broader set of ethical and political questions in the original affidavits, these larger questions were not ultimately considered within the circumscribed nature of the case. Instead, the Supreme Court's focus was on the facts produced by experts such as Gleick and Palmer and the "bodily facts" produced by the residents' affidavits. The line separating a dignified from an undignified life thus was drawn at forty-two liters. Here, the attempt at using the law to stake political claims was met with legal techno-politics that reframed the residents' complaints as questions of "indignity" and "basic needs" to be delimited by competing forms of expertise.

Rather than grounding the law, then, specific notions of human dignity were produced in the course of the case via the mobilization of two epistemologies; an ethnographic depiction of Soweto residents as embodying dignity "in breach," and expert testimonies that numerically demarcated a dignified from an undignified life. Legally mediated, "human dignity" could not exist as a singular, immeasurable value; instead, it became a quantifiable condition and central to a particular mode of comparative accounting. Thus, human dignity emerges neither as a prepolitical given, nor as by definition hollow, but rather as always already shaped by the ethical and political context within which it is deployed, always dependent on particular modes of authorization and the summoning of particular publics and political subjects.

THE AMBIVALENCES OF HUMAN DIGNITY

Many scholars have observed the paradoxical situation of subaltern litigants, who on the one hand are "given voice" to make claims on the state, yet have to do so in a juridical language that shapes how their demands

---

40   *Mazibuko*, Supreme Court Judgment, 2009, para 23–24 (my emphasis).

can be expressed (Brown and Halley 2002; Povinelli 2002). In this sense, the law is also performative, conjuring specific modalities of humanity and justice that "help to shape political actors" (Asad 2003: 140; Esmeir 2012). To speak the legal language of human rights effectively, the residents' affidavits had to express injustice in terms of basic needs that, in turn, hinged on a particular mediation of dignity and indignity. This requirement to render residents' complaints legible to the court and, more so, the way in which they were selectively taken up by the court could not always capture the multiplicity of discontents that residents had with the water project. Judicially mediated, the language of "human dignity" tended to recode and overwrite the residents' diverse objections, but it also at times produced new languages of justice. This ambivalence became apparent when activists took up the language of dignity outside the courtroom, in an act of double translation, in which the legal battle came to be translated back into activist practice. Here, the multiple publics addressed by activists (the judges, the media, fellow Soweto residents, utility officials, or city council politicians) and the specific modalities of addressing them (affidavits, meter bypasses, protests, leaflets, research reports, banners, or memoranda) at times blurred.

Shortly before the Supreme Court of Appeal heard the case in February 2009, a group of about sixty women marched through downtown Johannesburg in support of the legal challenge. The protest was organized as part of the Coalition Against Water Privatisation's "Women and Water Campaign" launched to support and raise awareness about the case. Women of all ages had gathered, some wearing T-shirts reading,

I AM SICK AND TIRED OF BEING SICK AND TIRED.

Another read:

STOP THE WAR ON WOMEN'S BODIES.

A banner suggested more elliptically:

SANITATION = WATER IS DIGNITY FOR WOMEN.

Most symbolically charged, many of the women wore soiled and red-stained underwear on top of their trousers and skirts, which they proceeded to drop at the feet of the riot police who stood outside the local government building. When interviewed by reporters, one of the women declared: "We are marching because we are dirty." The coordinator of the campaign, Petunia Nkhasi, responded more elaborately: "Women without water and sanitation are as good as dead and have no dignity. With the prepaid meters our ability to access water will be denied and inability to access water denies human beings the right to life and more with women the right to dignity."[41] Despite the somberness of such statements, most of the women laughed as they took off their mock underwear giving the protest a carnivalesque air.

While the formal legal submission implicitly defined "indignity" as the subjection to the urgency and shame of bodily needs, in this instance, activists mobilized this notion outside the court room. In performing themselves as needy, embodied, and sexed (not only gendered) beings, the women dramatically reduced themselves to bare life, albeit in a decidedly ironic, Rabelaisian way. The protest was thus reminiscent of previous activist mobilizations that had resignified and politicized "bare life" (Comaroff 2007; Robins 2006, 2009), but it also brought to the fore some of the ambivalences of political subjectivation, as modes of subordination were at once subverted and repeated. In this instance, the residents' performance of "indignity" appeared not merely as a display of opposition against the water project, but also as an ironic commentary on the legal application; it was an explicit, if ambivalent dramatization of the legal argument before the court.

In my conversations with the applicants, most of whom I had known for a few years before they became part of the litigation, some of these ambivalences became apparent. While the activists—unlike many ordinary Phiri residents—at times adopted a language of dignity to make their case, in conversation, it became clear that their notions of dignity frequently differed from the notion of dignity produced in court. They often identified dignity with relational concepts, such as respect or obligation, rather than with intrinsic values or basic needs. Jennifer, the applicant I had known longest, expressed some of this ambivalence when I sat down with her to interview her more formally about the case:

> **Q**: So if you were to be given 50 liters per person per day [as asked for in the legal application], would that be fine?
> **J**: The way they are saying and according to the WHO that would be fine, that would be fine.
> **Q**: But what do *you* think?
> **J**: [It is] not for them to tell us. Because [even if] you're living [with] three in the family, they don't know our extra needs and . . . emergencies that come by, like a funeral, a wedding. Worst of all a funeral, because it doesn't tell when it's gonna come to the house. That's where people use a lot of water.

---

41   Dieketseng Maleke and Zandile Mbabela, "Women Protest Water Metres," *Times* (Johannesburg), February 12, 2009.

In referencing the WHO, Jennifer partly stepped back into her role as an applicant in the case. And yet, in suggesting that it was "not for them to tell us" and "they don't know our extra needs," Jennifer implicitly challenged the very basis of the case—that is, the possibility of objectively adjudicating "basic needs." Similarly, the example of an unforeseeable event such as a funeral suggested a logic outside of the calculable predictability the case sought to establish, rendering "need" unpredictable. And yet, crucially, this was not an objection to calculation *per se*—as I elaborated in the previous chapter, residents were used to having to calculate limited budgets on a regular basis, and Soweto activists regularly mobilized numbers and calculations in arguments against Operation Gcin'amanzi. Instead, this was an objection to *who* did these calculations and *how*. In other words, for many residents, such calculations were not merely an administrative matter, but were bound up with ethical and political questions.

Indeed, Jennifer raised what in Phiri regularly emerged as one of the main complaints against Operation Gcin'amanzi: the pervasive feeling of being treated as objects by the state, of feeling managed, of being subjected to what Judge Tsoka would later describe as the "patronizing" attitude of the City. She expressed this more explicitly when I asked her what dignity meant to her.

> Dignity means how we are able to carry on with our culture. And how we are supposed to show respect and do our rituals in a right way, without having to think. . . .
>
> [H]aving to go and expose ourselves and say, "yes, we are indigent." We hate that. What's that? [Even] the apartheid regime didn't say that all those who are poor have to come in front and tell the whole world that we are poor.

Although Jennifer's reference to being "able to carry on with our culture" was part of the affidavit in which she detailed how the ritual events and hosting of relatives during her father's funeral had been difficult because of the limited water supply, most of the other opinions she expressed in the course of our conversation were not part of the formal legal argument. Again, dignity is here construed as the ability to live life "without having to think," that is, without the constant pressure to compute water supplies in order to avoid being automatically disconnected by the meter. Similarly, Jennifer's objections are directed against having to expose herself as "indigent" or as a "special case."[42] Throughout my conversations with Phiri residents, this was a recurrent complaint. As city officials acknowledged, relatively few people

---

42   Both "indigents" and "special cases" are official terms for populations targeted in policies of social assistance in South Africa. See Prishani Naidoo's (2007) analysis of the "indigent" category.

had registered as indigent, in part because of the stigma attached to it. Yet it is precisely this issue that the case did not, and, indeed, *could not*, address. On the contrary, the case ultimately *required* the residents to present themselves as a particular circumscribed community and to make demands for a targeted approach. As Jennifer's own affidavit had put it, her claim was made on behalf of a particular disadvantaged "class of people"—"the poor."[43] In contrast to the many protests and activist memoranda preceding the case, which were defined by a diversity of objections—from mundane complaints to principled expressions of disagreement with the postapartheid reforms— residents were here assigned and indeed *had to assign themselves*, a collective identity of marginality. This legal techno-politics thus also introduced a different temporality of political claim-making, one that moved away from the expressions of broader, more diverse concerns about postapartheid transformation and toward a more short-term and limited problematic of satisfying "basic needs."

Another striking aspect of my conversations with the residents was that their discontents with the water project were often of an entirely different order from those that emerged in the legal case. For many, a crucial point of contention was that they had not been involved in decision making, and that the utility had implemented the project in a technocratic fashion. As one elderly man in Phiri had explained to me a couple of years earlier, residents never got the chance to "sit down and discuss" the project. Instead utility officials "simply come and dig here [to install pipes] . . . without asking us about what we want." The postapartheid democracy, while granting them the right to vote, increasingly appeared to many residents to be defined by such technocratic interventions in their daily lives. Similarly, the operation of government often seemed opaque and mysterious. For example, on one of my visits, Lindiwe Mazibuko's eighteen-year-old daughter, who had recently finished matric, but had been unable to find a job, wondered aloud about whether Thabo Mbeki was responsible for the meter policy or if the utility had started Operation Gcin'amanzi "behind his back." Despite the arrival of democracy and a liberation movement in government, in residents' daily interactions with local bureaucrats and the utility, the state often continued to operate in an eerily familiar technocratic and often mystifying manner. Although such disagreements, concerned with everyday experiences of citizenship, belonging, and democracy had been included in the residents' affidavits, as the case wended its way to the Constitutional Court, these questions increasingly disappeared from view.

It can, of course, be convincingly argued that judging the case on how well it represented residents' grievances, that is, on something it did not set out to do, is missing the point. Indeed, the lawyers and many of the activists

---

43 *Mazibuko*, Makoatsane, Replying Affidavit, para 138.

were well aware of the inherent limitations of the litigation, and most regarded it as just one among a number of other tactics. Moreover, the lawyers' focus on including as many ethical and political questions as possible and, indeed, Judge Tsoka's wide-ranging ruling showed the extent of flexibility within the law and the potential to express larger political visions even within juridical constraints, especially when accompanied by social movement mobilizations. The litigation had also been partially successful even as the case was ultimately dismissed by the Constitutional Court—over the course of the proceedings, the City voluntarily increased the free basic water allowance to 10,000 liters per household per month.[44] This allowance, however, was specifically targeted toward "indigent" households. To be eligible for the increase, residents were required to file an application with the City to be officially categorized as indigent, something that, city officials acknowledged, relatively few people had done in the past, in part because of the attached stigma. Thus, they were officially re-affirmed as indigent subjects in their relation with the state.

CONCLUSION

In several ways, *Mazibuko* demonstrated some of the paradoxes of using the law to make claims on the state. Much like the image of the woman sitting on an exposed toilet mobilized during the "toilet election" with which I began this chapter, throughout the case, the "impaired" humanity of Phiri residents became the constitutive outside to the aspirational economy of postapartheid citizenship. In turn, the bodies of Phiri residents came to exemplify a particular notion of suffering and a corresponding form of redress identified as the satisfaction of basic needs. Human dignity and the legal techno-politics through which it was adjudicated and filled with content produced a specific accounting of injuries and calculus of provisioning, and, by extension, more narrowly conceived notions of justice and, indeed, humanity.

As a mode of narrativizing a disagreement over state obligations, *Mazibuko* also enables a wider exploration of how citizenship and its entitlements are understood and rationalized in contemporary South Africa. Here, social citizenship is not simply given up, as many critics of neoliberalism have argued; rather, state obligations are rationalized in different terms and calculated and administered via different socio-technical forms. Unlike the modernist techniques of social citizenship that were based on universalist logics of solidarity and interdependence, rights-based forms of

---

44 Many of these arguments are convincingly advanced by activists (cf. Dugard 2010).

articulating state obligation provided the grounds for a rethinking of social provisions in individualized and targeted terms, primarily designed to satisfy a minimum of "basic needs" required for a "dignified existence." Thus, while socio-economic rights provided a repertoire of arguments against neoliberal reforms, they also and at the same time proved to be eminently compatible with neoliberal modes of rethinking social provisions and subjects of need. And yet, despite the strong influence of neoliberal reform prescriptions in the early 2000s when Operation Gcin'amanzi was first conceived, de facto multiple, and at times competing, modalities and traditions of social provisioning continue to be at work in South Africa, vitiating any shorthand conclusions and demonstrating the ways in which neoliberal reforms always already take shape in relation to existing formations.[45]

If appeals to human dignity gain performative power precisely because they appear to reference universal, prepolitical values, ethnographically following specific mediations of dignity and the diverse publics they interpellate enables a more complex picture of the performative force that languages of "humanity" compel. Whether in the legal techno-politics in the courts or in the performances of indignity outside government offices, languages of citizenship and humanity now often come to coincide in a multiplicity of ways, thus reshaping a political terrain previously primarily defined by older modernist traditions.

The specific South African context also illuminates conceptual questions with a longer historical arc in relation to the distinction between "man" and "citizen." If modernist notions of citizenship have often provided a normative foil for the critique of human rights and humanitarianism, their stability is today increasingly in question, with important consequences for the political terrain and the activist imagination it affords. Indeed, the shift toward moral discourses of suffering and indignity also affects the conditions of intelligibility of political claims; how claims on the state can be expressed, what claims are "heard" by the state, and what kinds of political actors they shape. Of course, languages of the human are not the only way to express discontents in contemporary South Africa; indeed, the dramatic rise in so-called service delivery protests over the past decade is only the most visible testimony to the diversity of forms claims on the state can take. As the media spectacle surrounding the "toilet election" showed, however, while certain *forms* of political expression become legible or, indeed, hypervisible, others are rendered illegible and often illegitimate.

---

45 Indeed, neoliberal modes of "reprogramming" often encounter various modernist obstacles, at times re-enforcing at other times running up against them, foremost amongst them the intransigence of apartheid infrastructures (cf. Collier 2011). See Ferguson (2010) and Hart (2008) for a discussion on the usefulness of the concept of neoliberalism in South Africa.

While Soweto activists politicized "bare life" and indeed thrived on its carnivalesque performance, they also, and often in the same moment, identified the ambivalences of this postapartheid political terrain, which at once affords and frames novel languages of opposition, whilst at times foreclosing or overwriting others. The judicialization of politics, then, is also symptomatic of a present in which modernist futures and hopes, and the political terrain shaped by them, have been significantly revised. Indeed, if the hegemony of moral-political languages of humanity—and what Habermas (2010) termed the "realistic utopia" of human rights—signals the end of the modernist *telos* and romantic temporality of "total revolution," *Mazibuko* and the debates and protests surrounding it showed both the promise and the limits of this emergent politics of "man and citizen."[46]

46 For the modernist, anticolonial romantic emplotment of postcolonial politics, see David Scott (2004).

CONCLUSION

Infrastructure, Democracy, and the Postapartheid Political Terrain

In a speech given in July 2013, Julius Malema, controversial former ANC Youth League president and founder of a new opposition party, the Economic Freedom Fighters (EFF), toilets took center stage. In the widely publicized speech, Malema decried the fact that twenty years after the end of apartheid, many residents of townships and informal settlements still lacked access to proper sanitation. "You fail to deliver toilets and you think we can take you seriously," he said addressing the ANC-led government. "We need toilets, you must never be ashamed. If there is a need for a toilet revolution we must engage in a toilet revolution. Let them say we are a toilet organisation."[1] Malema's statement was only the latest in a series of debates and demonstrations in which toilets had become the center of attention. In the months leading up to his speech, residents of informal settlements around Cape Town had repeatedly emptied buckets of sewage at central locations in what came to be known as the "poo wars" in protest of the temporary toilets that the municipality had set up.

In the populist language of Malema and the Rabelaisian politics of the "poo wars," infrastructure yet again became both medium and object of discontents. The renewed protests and the more recent rise of the EFF provoked ambivalent responses. While much public commentary was sympathetic to the protesters and the larger situation of continued inequality that their protests had dramatically made visible, many established political commentators viewed these events as indicative of a broader, and largely worrisome, populist turn. There was broad agreement that although the toilet situation was indeed dire, the ways in which it had monopolized and banalized public debate in the country was a sign of worse to come.

---

1   Genevieve Quintal and Pendell Dlamini "Malema Blasts ANC for Lack of Housing and Toilets" *Mail & Guardian* (Johannesburg), July 27, 2013.

Throughout the commentary, an image thus emerged of democracy under threat from ruthless populists whose strategy of spectacle and emotive sloganeering ultimately degraded a cleaner, more sober and deliberative ideal of democracy, a democracy for which South Africa had moreover been globally celebrated.[2]

Shortly thereafter, a different piece of infrastructure took hold of the public imagination. In November 2014, South Africa's powerful electricity parastatal Eskom introduced "load shedding"—planned rolling blackouts—to deal with a strained electricity grid and to avoid unplanned and potentially devastating national power outages. Unlike the temporary toilets, the effects of which were only felt by the residents of informal settlements, load shedding appeared to be a somewhat more democratic experience, one that most residents of South Africa would encounter firsthand at some point. And yet, as people shuffled in the dark to look for candles or torches, as generator noises could be heard echoing through the wealthier suburbs and people with cars left for areas that had light, the effects again turned out to be unevenly distributed. The debates on load shedding and Eskom, which preoccupied call-in radio shows and news headlines for weeks, again showed seemingly technical matters to be bound up with much larger political questions. Amidst accusations of corruption, lack of capacity and transparency, the apparently frail and unreliable electricity grid became a metaphor for deeper failures—yet another example of the ways in which South Africa had failed in the project to become a proper liberal democracy, an "ordinary country" like any other in the world.

These concerns about corruption, lack of capacity, and populism have only intensified in recent years in a context in which the gains of liberal democracy are seen as under threat from multiple directions, both inside and outside of the ANC. And yet, such debates also risked missing what was most dramatically exposed by the "poo wars" and the many so-called service delivery protests that had preceded them. Much like the events in Diepsloot ten years earlier with which this book began, they rendered apparent the sharp disjunctures at the heart of the postapartheid democracy, between the celebrated public sphere, its progressive constitution, and its consistently free and fair elections, on the one hand, and the often dramatically distinct local and lived experiences of democracy, on the other. These everyday experiences of democracy—that are often mediated by local bureaucracies, technical procedures and infrastructures—are shaped by both

2   See here, for example, Laclau's analysis of populism and its link to "dangerous excess which puts the clear-cut moulds of a rational community in question" (Laclau 2005: x). With a more specific focus on South Africa, see Deborah Posel's analysis of Malema's populism (Posel 2014) and Jean Comaroff's reflections on populism's relation to late liberalism (Comaroff 2011).

apartheid's less visible, material legacies and new forms of techno-political intervention that increasingly recast central political questions of the anti-apartheid struggle as administrative problems. This split between the po-litical and the administrative domain is not exceptional, but an ordinary feature of liberal democracy, that needs to be continuously performed. In South Africa, where the terrain of infrastructure and administration had for decades been a central political arena in which much of the urban struggle unfolded, producing liberal democracy, including the constitutive splits be-tween the public and the private and the political and the administrative, became a central task of the postapartheid state, one that has always been prone to failure and contestation from multiple directions.

This book has outlined the contours of this techno-political terrain beginning in the late-apartheid period when infrastructure and action on the administrative terrain became a central feature of the antiapartheid struggle. To explore this terrain, this book has traced connections between infrastructure and democracy of a less spectacular kind and, in turn, a less public mode of politics. Infrastructures here emerge as more than neutral tools for more substantive ends. As Brian Larkin (2013: 375) reminds us, infrastructures work at numerous levels at the same time. They are func-tional, in that they enable, constrain, and shape the circulation of goods, people, or ideas, but they can also become signs and symbols; they make us do things and elicit affect, and they can work via the spectacular and the sublime as much as the mundane and the banal. They can also become ethical objects, conduits of power, or be wielded as tools to express discon-tents. It is this multilayeredness and multivalence that makes them not only productive objects of ethnographic inquiry, but also enables them to be-come "political matter" in a diversity of ways (Braun and Whatmore 2010).

At one level, then, infrastructures are simply good to think with. And yet, the mobilization of infrastructure in scholarly inquiry just as in politi-cal demands is always strategic and contingent. The conceptual or political work infrastructure can do, cannot be guaranteed in advance, but is con-stituted always in relation to specific ethical and political problem spaces and historically constituted fields of intervention (cf. Scott 1999). Thus, the value of infrastructure qua empirical object only emerges against the backdrop of specific historical formations and present concerns. In many contexts, infrastructures may indeed be as "boring" as common sense has it (Star 1999). It is thus crucial to ask in what precise moments infrastructure makes a difference in our thinking and to probe the specific critical inter-ventions infrastructure may—or may not—enable.

Infrastructure has made its appearance in several forms in this book—as an empirical object, an epistemological vantage point and as a metaphor. First, and most tangibly, it has been my object of study, from the intri-cacies of metering devices and water pipes, to the bureaucratic expertise that supports them through calculations, certifications, and routine administrative procedures. I have also tracked the ways in which infrastructure became an object and medium of activist mobilization, in a variety of forms—from countermeasures and bypasses, to protest and legal action. Taking infrastructure as an ethnographic object in the specific context of postapartheid South Africa thus opens up conceptual space for an account of political engagement that is attuned to material, counterpublic, and indeed nonpublic modalities of political engagement.

Beyond ethnographic object, then, infrastructure has also provided an epistemological vantage point, a perspective from which to think differently about South Africa's "transition." Indeed, throughout these chapters, I have suggested that infrastructure as a vantage point forces us to consider the multiplicity of experiences of the state, in particular in South Africa where national and urban citizenship has historically been split and where local bureaucracies often continue to function in an undemocratic fashion that, to many residents, is reminiscent of apartheid (cf. Jolobe 2014). It is in this sense that infrastructure helps us excavate the diverse ways in which the late-apartheid period inhabits the present. Exploring these more oblique transformations of governing urban areas thus also points us to the manner in which administrative-governmental and juridico-political change is often out of joint. From this perspective, while the first general election in 1994 marks the beginning of democracy in South Africa, the continuities and discontinuities with the late-apartheid era often unfold at different speeds and in distinct registers. The infrastructural, against this specific political horizon, provides a perspective onto these constitutive disjunctures of democracy, to account for and render legible apartheid's less visible legacies and their material and affective durability.

In the postapartheid period, many of the questions that animated the liberation struggle are often continually being negotiated and re-articulated in a variety of spaces. In lieu of the larger political antagonism in which apartheid defined the constitutive outside of the struggle, there are now a myriad of dispersed and often less evident locations of negotiation, accommodation, and disagreement. Many of the questions that were central to the antiapartheid movement—questions concerning the precise shape of democracy and citizenship, which the "transition" at times hastily overwrote, but in many instances could not solve—continue to be raised in a multiplicity of sites. It is in such sites that the work of making liberal democracy continues to unfold in less linear and often uneven ways.

These spaces—in which concerns and desires are expressed at a variety of material, symbolic, and affective registers—are also locations where political subjectivities are fashioned and refashioned, where struggles over citizenship and local democracy unfold, and where the concepts and techniques of the liberation struggle are resignified. Such spaces are often defined by protracted, low-intensity battles that may take shape on terrains not immediately apprehensible as political. If the protest in Diepsloot—and the many protests that followed in places like Harrismith, Khutsong, or, most dramatically, Marikana—catapulted them vividly to the surface, such expressions of disagreement take shape in diverse ways and in often less visible sites, including as I outlined here, inside and outside court-rooms, in residents' yards, in the negotiation of payment and debt, in the "bridging" of meters, and in domains of "technical" expertise. Partly for this reason, the late-apartheid moment also lives on in the often micro-political ways in which people relate to the state, in the attitude of bureau-crats and in strained relationships with the local state. Local experiences of the state often appear eerily reminiscent of the late-apartheid period, rekindling embodied memories of its administrative modalities of power and associated bureaucratic practices.

To be sure, the poo wars, and the many protests that preceded them, are in many respects an indictment of the continued and indeed increased inequality and abjection that continue to follow the racial lines laid by colonialism and apartheid. As such, they are demands for a "decent" life aimed at holding the state responsible for its failed promise of transform-ing deeply embedded forms of structural discrimination.

But the protests also point to the often unaccountable ways in which the local state continues to operate, in particular in a context of the rise of reforms inspired by "new public management" that often de facto pro-mote and deepen such relations at the local level (Chipkin 2011). In this sense, they are also a reflection of the ways in which apartheid continues to resonate in the present not merely in the continuities of racial inequal-ity, but also in more mundane everyday relationships and uneven experi-ence of state power that are embodied in modalities of installing toilets and standpipes, in the reach and effect of power grids, or in the mediation performed by technical devices like the prepaid meter. This is a politics in which liberal norms do not necessarily govern, that doesn't always circulate freely, and that may appear encumbered and constrained; here, the admin-istrative, the technical, and the infrastructural become both sites and forms of ethical and political negotiations.

In this specific moment, the perspective of infrastructure enables a view of the less visible grounds and experiences of citizenship after apartheid; they show democracy to be disjunctive, fragmented, and experienced un-evenly. But this administrative register also enables us to think differently about liberal democracy in a moment in which it has become both the normative political paradigm globally and in which, simultaneously, ac-cess to its formal institutions and procedures is always de facto limited. If the protracted work of transition and the postapartheid present renders these dynamics particularly visible, they are not limited to South Africa, but take shape in various ways in many places in the world. This focus on the more oblique political mediations thus also unsettles normative liberal-secular accounts of politics with their imaginaries of the public as a disembodied sphere of deliberation and their fantasies of "free" circulation and global modularity. Beyond ethnographic object and epistemological vantage point, infrastructure thus also emerges as a metaphor for the many techno-political relationships and administrative connections to the state that unfold below democracy's normative horizons. In the politics of meters, pipes, and wires, in the mobilization of numbers, metrological knowledge, or legal expertise, a different kind of politics takes shape that at once grounds, mediates, and challenges democracy.

REFERENCES

Abelin, Mireille. "'Entrenched in the BMW': Argentine Elites and the Terror of Fiscal Obligation." *Public Culture* 24, no. 2 67: (2012): 329–56.

Adas, Michael. *Machines as the Measure of Men: Science, Technology, and Ideologies of Western Dominance.* Ithaca, NY: Cornell University Press, 1990.

Adler, Glenn, and Jonny Steinberg. *From Comrades to Citizens: The South African Civics Movement and the Transition to Democracy.* Basingstoke and London: Macmillan, 2000.

Agamben, Giorgio. *Means without End: Notes on Politics.* Theory out of Bounds. Minneapolis: University of Minnesota Press, 2000.

Ajulu, Rok. *Wiehahn and Riekert: New Mechanism for Control and Oppression of Black Labour and Trade Unions.* Maseru: National University of Lesotho, Institute of Labour Studies, 1981.

Akrich, Madeleine. "The De-Scription of Technical Objects." In *Shaping Technology/ Building Society: Studies in Sociotechnical Change*, edited by Wiebe Bijker and John Law, 205–24. Cambridge: MIT Press, 1992.

Alexander, Neville. *An Ordinary Country: Issues in the Transition from Apartheid to Democracy in South Africa.* Essen: Berghahn Books, 2002.

Alexander, Peter. "Rebellion of the Poor: South Africa's Service Delivery Protests–a Preliminary Analysis." *Review of African Political Economy* 37, no. 123 (2010): 25–40.

Allen, Lori A. "Martyr Bodies in the Media: Human Rights, Aesthetics, and the Politics of Immediation in the Palestinian Intifada." *American Ethnologist* 36, no. 1 (2009): 161–80.

Allison, Anne. *Precarious Japan.* Durham, NC: Duke University Press, 2013.

Althusser, Louis. "Ideology and Ideological State Apparatus (Notes Towards an Investigation)." In *Lenin and Philosophy and Other Essays*, 127–86. New York: Monthly Review Press, 1971.

Anand, Nikhil. "Pressure: The Politechnics of Water Supply in Mumbai." *Cultural Anthropology* 26, no. 4 (2012): 542–64.

Appadurai, Arjun. *Modernity At Large: Cultural Dimensions of Globalization.* Minneapolis: University of Minnesota Press, 1996.

Appadurai, Arjun. "Deep Democracy: Urban Governmentality and the Horizon of Politics." *Environment and Urbanization* 13, no. 2 (2001): 23.

Appadurai, Arjun. "Why Enumeration Counts." *Environment and Urbanization* 24, no. 2 (2012): 639–41.

Appadurai, Arjun, ed. *The Social Life of Things: Commodities in Cultural Perspective.* Cambridge, New York: Cambridge University Press, 1986.

Appel, Hannah. "Walls and White Elephants: Oil Extraction, Responsibility, and Infrastructural Violence in Equatorial Guinea." *Ethnography* 13, no. 4 (2012): 439–65.

Arendt, Hannah. *The Human Condition.* Chicago: University of Chicago Press, 1958.

Arendt, Hannah. *On Revolution.* Westport, CT: Greenwood Press, 1982.

Arendt, Hannah. *The Origins of Totalitarianism.* New York: Harcourt, 1951.

Asad, Talal. *Formations of the Secular: Christianity, Islam, Modernity.* Stanford, CA: Stanford University Press, 2003.

Asad, Talal. "What Do Human Rights Do? An Anthropological Enquiry." *Theory & Event* 4, no. 4 (2000).

Ashforth, Adam. "Down the Old Potch Road and to Lekoka Street: Of State Power and Social Space in Soweto." *Architectural Theory Review* 1, no. 2 (1996): 60–78.

Ashforth, Adam. *The Politics of Official Discourse in Twentieth-Century South Africa.* Oxford, New York: Oxford University Press, 1990.

Ashforth, Adam. "Reflections on Spiritual Insecurity in a Modern African City (Soweto)." *African Studies Review* 41, no. 3 (1998): 39–67.

Ashforth, Adam. *Witchcraft, Violence, and Democracy in the New South Africa.* Chicago: University of Chicago Press, 2005.

Atkinson, Doreen. "Municipal Governance and Service Delivery: Case Studies from the Free State." In *State of the Nation: South Africa 2007*, edited by Sakhela Buhlungu, John Daniel, Roger Southall, and Jessica Lutchman. Pretoria: HSRC, 2007a.

Atkinson, Doreen. "Taking to the Streets: Has Developmental Local Government Failed in South Africa?" *State of the Nation: South Africa* 2007 (2007b): 53–77.

Bähre, Erik. "Reluctant Solidarity Death, Urban Poverty and Neighbourly Assistance in South Africa." *Ethnography* 8, no. 1 (2007): 33–59.

Bakker, Karen. "Archipelagos and Networks: Urbanization and Water Privatization in the South." *The Geographical Journal* 169, no. 4 (2003a): 328–41.

Bakker, Karen. *An Uncooperative Commodity: Privatizing Water in England and Wales.* Oxford; New York: Oxford University Press, 2003b.

Ballard, Richard, Adam Habib, and Imraan Valodia. *Voices of Protest: Social Movements in Post-Apartheid South Africa.* Durban: University of KwaZulu-Natal Press, 2006.

Ballestero, Andrea. "Transparency Short-Circuited: Laughter and Numbers in Costa Rican Water Politics." *PoLAR: Political and Legal Anthropology Review* 35, no. 2 (2012): 223–41.

Barchiesi, Franco. *Precarious Liberation: Workers, the State, and Contested Social Citizenship in Postapartheid South Africa*. Buffalo, NY: SUNY Press, 2011.

Barchiesi, Franco. "Privatization and the Historical Trajectory of 'Social Movement Unionism': A Case Study of Municipal Workers in Johannesburg, South Africa." *International Labor and Working-Class History* 71, no. 1 (2007): 50–69.

Barnett, Michael Nathan, and Thomas George Weiss. *Humanitarianism in Question: Politics, Power, Ethics*. Ithaca, NY: Cornell University Press, 2008.

Barry, Andrew. "The Anti-Political Economy." *Economy and Society* 31, no. 2 (2002): 268–84.

Barry, Andrew. *Material Politics: Disputes Along the Pipeline*. Oxford: Wiley-Blackwell, 2013.

Barry, Andrew. *Political Machines: Governing a Technological Society*. London; New York: Athlone Press, 2001.

Barry, Andrew. "Technological Zones." *European Journal of Social Theory* 9, no. 2 (2006): 239–53.

Beall, Jo, Owen Crankshaw, and Sue Parnell. *Uniting a Divided City: Governance and Social Exclusion in Johannesburg*. London; Sterling, VA: Earthscan Publications, 2002.

Beall, Jo, Owen Crankshaw, and Sue Parnell. "Victims, Villains and Fixers: The Urban Environment and Johannesburg's Poor." *Journal of Southern African Studies* 26, no. 4 (2000): 833–55.

Bear, Laura. *Lines of the Nation: Indian Railway Workers, Bureaucracy, and the Intimate Historical Self*. New York: Columbia University Press, 2007.

Beavon, Keith Sidney Orrock. *Johannesburg: The Making and Shaping of the City*. Pretoria: Unisa Press, 2004.

Becker, Gary. *The Economics of Discrimination*. Chicago: University of Chicago Press, 1957.

Becker, Gary. *A Treatise on the Family*. Cambridge: Harvard University Press, 1981.

Beinart, William, and Colin Bundy. *Hidden Struggles in Rural South Africa: Politics & Popular Movements in the Transkei & Eastern Cape, 1890–1930*. Berkeley: University of California Press, 1987.

Benhabib, Seyla. "Disaggregation of Citizenship Rights." *Parallax* 11, no. 1 (2005): 10–18.

Benjamin, Walter. *The Arcades Project*. Cambridge: Harvard University Press, 1999.

Bennett, Jane. *Vibrant Matter: A Political Ecology of Things*. Durham, NC: Duke University Press, 2009.

Biehl, João. "The Judicialization of Biopolitics: Claiming the Right to Pharmaceuticals in Brazilian Courts." *American Ethnologist* 40, no. 3 (2013): 419–36.

Biehl, João, and Adriana Petryna. "Bodies of Rights and Therapeutic Markets." *Social Research* 78, no. 2 (2011): 359–86.

Bijker, Wiebe, Thomas P. Hughes, and Trevor Pinch, eds. *The Social Construction of Technological Systems: New Directions in the Sociology and History of Technology*. Cambridge: MIT Press, 1987.

Bijker, Wiebe, and John Law, eds. *Shaping Technology/Building Society: Studies in Sociotechnical Change*. Cambridge: MIT press, 1992.

Bjorkman, Lisa. *Pipe Politics, Contested Waters: Embedded Infrastructures of Millennial Mumbai*. Durham, NC: Duke University Press, 2015.

Boellstorff, Tom. *Coming of Age in Second Life: An Anthropologist Explores the Virtually Human*. Princeton: Princeton University Press, 2008.

Bond, Patrick. *Elite Transition: From Apartheid to Neoliberalism in South Africa*. London: Pluto Press, 2000.

Bond, Patrick. *Unsustainable South Africa: Environment, Development and Social Protest*. London, Pietermaritzburg: Merlin Press, University of Natal Press, 2002.

Bond, Patrick, George Dor, and Greg Ruiters. "Transformation in Infrastructure Policy from Apartheid to Democracy." *Municipal Services Project*. Occasional Papers Series (1999).

Bond, Patrick, and Jackie Dugard. "The Case of Johannesburg Water: What Really Happened at the Pre-Paid 'Parish Pump'." *Law, Democracy & Development* 12, no. 1 (2008): 1–28.

Bonner, Philip, and Lauren Segal. *Soweto: A History*. Cape Town: Maskew Miller Longman, 1998.

Booysen, Susan. "With the Ballot and the Brick: The Politics of Attaining Service Delivery." *Progress in Development Studies* 7, no. 1 (2007): 21.

Boraine, Andrew. "Security Management Upgrading in the Black Townships." *Transformation* 8 (1989): 47–63.

Bourdieu, Pierre. *In Other Words: Essays Towards a Reflexive Sociology*. Stanford, CA: Stanford University Press, 1990.

Bowker, Geoffrey C, and Susan Leigh Star. *Sorting Things Out: Classification and Its Consequences*. Cambridge: MIT Press, 2000.

Braun, Bruce, and Susan Whatmore, eds. *Political Matter: Technoscience, Democracy, and Public Life*. Minneapolis: University of Minnesota Press, 2010.

Breckenridge, Keith. *Biometric State: The Global Politics of Identification and Surveillance in South Africa, 1850 to the Present*. Cambridge: Cambridge University Press, 2014.

Breckenridge, Keith. "The World's First Biometric Money: Ghana's E-Zwich and the Contemporary Influence of South African Biometrics." *Africa* 80, no. 4 (2010): 642–62.

Bremner, Lindsay. *Johannesburg: One City Colliding Worlds*. Johannesburg: STE, 2004.

Brenner, Neil, and Nikolas Theodore, eds. *Spaces of Neoliberalism: Urban Restructuring in North America and Western Europe*. Oxford: Blackwell, 2002.

Brown, Wendy. *States of Injury: Power and Freedom in Late Modernity*. Princeton: Princeton University Press, 1995.

Brown, Wendy, and Janet E. Halley, eds. *Left Legalism/Left Critique*. Durham, NC: Duke University Press, 2002.

Burawoy, Michael, and Katherine Verdery, eds. *Uncertain Transition: Ethnographies of Change in the Postsocialist World*. London: Rowman & Littlefield Pub Inc., 1999.

Burchell, David. "The Attributes of Citizens: Virtue, Manners and the Activity of Citizenship." *Economy and Society* 24, no. 4 (1995): 540–58.

Buur, Lars. "The South African Truth and Reconciliation Commission: A Technique of Nation-State Formation." In *States of Imagination: Ethnographic Explorations of the Postcolonial State*, edited by Thomas Blom Hansen and Finn Stepputat, 149–181. Durham, NC: Duke University Press, 2001.

Çalışkan, Koray, and Michel Callon. "Economization, Part 1: Shifting Attention from the Economy Towards Processes of Economization." *Economy and Society* 38, no. 3 (2009): 369–98.

Callon, Michel. *Acting in an Uncertain World: An Essay on Technical Democracy.* Cambridge: MIT Press, 2009.

Callon, Michel, ed. *The Laws of the Markets.* Oxford; Malden: Blackwell Publishers/ The Sociological Review, 1998.

Callon, Michel. "Society in the Making: The Study of Technology as a Tool for Sociological Analysis." In *The Social Construction of Technological System: New Directions in the Sociology and History of Technology*, edited by Wiebe Bijker, Thomas P. Hughes and Trevor Pinch, 81–103. Cambridge: MIT Press, 1987.

Callon, Michel. "Some Elements of a Sociology of Translation: Domestication of the Scallops and the Fishermen of St. Brieu Bay." In *Power, Action and Belief: A New Sociology of Knowledge*, edited by John Law, 196–233. London: Routledge, 1986.

Callon, Michel. "What Does It Mean to Say That Economics Is Performative?" In *Do Economists Make Markets? On the Performativity of Economics*, edited by Donald A. MacKenzie, Fabian Muniesa and Lucia Siu, 311–57. Princeton: Princeton University Press, 2007.

Callon, Michel, Cecile Méadel, and Vololona Rabeharisoa. "The Economy of Qualities." *Economy and Society* 31, no. 2 (2002): 194–217.

Callon, Michel, Yuval Millo, and Fabian Muniesa, eds. *Market Devices.* Malden; Oxford: Blackwell/The Sociological Review, 2007.

Carr, Will J. P. *Soweto: Its Creation, Life, and Decline.* Johannesburg: South African Institute of Race Relations, 1990.

Carse, Ashley. *Beyond the Big Ditch: Politics, Ecology, and Infrastructure at the Panama Canal.* Cambridge: MIT Press, 2014.

Castells, Manuel. *The City and the Grassroots: A Cross-Cultural Theory of Urban Social Movements.* Berkeley: University of California Press, 1983.

Chadwick, Edwin. *Report on the Sanitary Condition of the Labouring Population of Great Britain.* London: Clowes and Sons, 1842.

Chalfin, Brenda. *Neoliberal Frontiers: An Ethnography of Sovereignty in West Africa.* Chicago: University of Chicago Press, 2010.

Chalfin, Brenda. "Public Things, Excremental Politics, and the Infrastructure of Bare Life in Ghana's City of Tema." *American Ethnologist* 41, no. 1 (2014): 92–109.

Chanock, Martin. *The Making of South African Legal Culture 1902–1936: Fear, Favour and Prejudice.* Cambridge: Cambridge University Press, 2001.

Chari, Sharad. "The Antinomies of Political Evidence in Post-Apartheid Durban, South Africa." *Journal of the Royal Anthropological Institute* 14, no. s1 (2008): S61–S76.

Chari, Sharad. "Detritus in Durban: Polluted Environs and Biopolitics of Refusal." In *Imperial Debris: On Ruins and Ruination*, edited by Ann Laura Stoler, 131–61. Durham, NC: Duke University Press, 2013.

Chari, Sharad. "An 'Indian Commons' in Durban? Limits to Mutuality, or the City to Come." *Anthropology Southern Africa* 37, no. 3–4 (2014): 149–59.

Charney, Craig. "Class Conflict and the National Party Split." *Journal of Southern African Studies* 10, no. 2 (1984): 269–82.

Chaskalson, Michael, Karen Jochelson, and Jeremy Seekings. "Rent Boycotts, the State, and the Transformation of the Urban Political Economy in South Africa." *Review of African Political Economy* 14, no. 40 (1987): 47–64.

Chatterjee, Partha. *Lineages of Political Society: Studies in Postcolonial Democracy.* New York: Columbia University Press, 2011.

Chatterjee, Partha. *The Nation and Its Fragments: Colonial and Postcolonial Histories.* Princeton: Princeton University Press, 1993.

Chatterjee, Partha. *The Politics of the Governed: Reflections on Popular Politics in Most of the World.* New York: Columbia University Press, 2004.

Chipkin, Ivor. "Citizenry and Local Government: A New Political Subject?" *Indicator South Africa* 13 (1995): 37–40.

Chipkin, Ivor. *Do South Africans Exist?: Nationalism, Democracy and the Identity of "the People."* Johannesburg: Witwatersrand University Press, 2007.

Chipkin, Ivor. "'Functional' and 'Dysfunctional' Communities: The Making of National Citizens." *Journal of Southern African Studies* 29, no. 1 (2003): 63–82.

Chipkin, Ivor. "Transcending Bureaucracy: State Transformation in the Age of the Manager." *Transformation: Critical Perspectives on Southern Africa* 77, no. 1 (2011): 31–51.

Chipkin, Ivor. "Whither the State? Corruption, Institutions and State-Building in South Africa." *Politikon* 40, no. 2 (2013): 211–31.

Choy, Timothy K. *Ecologies of Comparison: An Ethnography of Endangerment in Hong Kong.* Durham, NC: Duke University Press, 2011.

Christie, Renfrew. *Electricity, Industry, and Class in South Africa.* London: Macmillan, 1984.

Chu, Julie. "When Infrastructures Attack: The Workings of Disrepair in China." *American Ethnologist* 41, no. 2 (2014): 351–67.

Clark, Nancy L. *Manufacturing Apartheid: State Corporations in South Africa.* New Haven: Yale University Press, 1994.

Clarno, Andy. "Rescaling White Space in Post-Apartheid Johannesburg." *Antipode* 45, no. 5 (2013): 1190–212.

Clendinning, Anne. *Demons of Domesticity: Women and the English Gas Industry, 1889–1939.* Aldershot; Burlington: Ashgate, 2004.

Cobbett, William. "Turning the Meters Back to Zero: Electricity Distribution and Local Government in Urban Areas." Paper presented at the Proceedings of the African National Congress National Meeting on Electrification. Cape Town, 1992.

Cock, Jacklyn, and Laurie Nathan. *War and Society: The Militarisation of South Africa*. Cape Town: David Philip, 1989.

Coalition Against Water Privatisation. "'Nothing for Mahala': The Forced Installation of Prepaid Water Meters in Stretford, Extension 4, Orange Farm, Johannesburg, South Africa." Durban: Centre for Civil Society Research Report, 2004.

Coalition Against Water Privatisation. "The Struggle against Silent Disconnections: Prepaid Meters and the Struggle for Life in Soweto." Johannesburg, 2005.

Cole, Josette. *Crossroads: The Politics of Reform and Repression, 1976–1986*. Johannesburg: Ravan Press, 1987.

Coleman, E. Gabriella. *Coding Freedom: The Ethics and Aesthetics of Hacking*. Princeton: Princeton University Press, 2012.

Collier, Stephen J. *Post-Soviet Social: Neoliberalism, Social Modernity, Biopolitics*. Princeton: Princeton University Press, 2011.

Collier, Stephen J., and Aihwa Ong. "Global Assemblages, Anthropological Problems." In *Global Assemblages: Technology, Politics, and Ethics as Anthropological Problems*, edited by Stephen J. Collier and Aihwa Ong, 3–21. Malden, MA: Blackwell, 2005.

Comaroff, Jean. "Beyond Bare Life: AIDS, (Bio) Politics, and the Neoliberal Order." *Public Culture* 19, no. 1 (2007): 197.

Comaroff, Jean. "Populism and Late Liberalism: A Special Affinity?" *Annals of the American Academy of Political and Social Science* 637, no. 1 (2011): 99–111.

Comaroff, Jean, and John Comaroff. *Millennial Capitalism and the Culture of Neoliberalism*. Durham, NC: Duke University Press, 2001.

Comaroff, Jean, and John Comaroff. "Figuring Crime: Quantifacts and the Production of the Un/Real." *Public Culture* 18, no. 1 (2006b): 209–46.

Comaroff, Jean, and John Comaroff. *Theory from the South: Or, How Euro-America Is Evolving toward Africa*. Boulder, CO: Paradigm Publishers, 2012.

Comaroff, Jean, and John Comaroff, eds. *Law and Disorder in the Postcolony*. Chicago: University of Chicago Press, 2006a.

Connolly, William E. *Neuropolitics: Thinking, Culture, Speed*. Minneapolis: University of Minnesota Press, 2002.

Cooper, Frederick. *Africa since 1940: The Past of the Present*. Cambridge: Cambridge University Press, 2002.

Corrigan, Terence. *Beyond the Boycotts: Financing Local Government in the Postapartheid Era*. South African Institute of Race Relations, 1998.

Cowen, Deborah. *The Deadly Life of Logistics: Mapping Violence in Global Trade.* Minneapolis: University of Minnesota Press, 2014.

Crankshaw, Owen, Alan Gilbert, and Alan Morris. "Backyard Soweto." *International Journal of Urban and Regional Research* 24, no. 4 (2000): 841–57.

Cross, Jamie. "The 100th Object: Solar Lighting Technology and Humanitarian Good." *Journal of Material Culture* 18 (2013): 367–87.

Cruikshank, Barbara. *The Will to Empower: Democratic Citizens and Other Subjects.* Ithaca, NY: Cornell University Press, 1999.

Danchin, Peter G. "A Human Right to Water? The South African Constitutional Court's Decision in the Mazibuko Case." *EJI Talk* (January 2010). http://www.ejiltalk.org/a-human-right-to-water-the-south-african-constitutional-court%E2%80%99s-decision-in-the-mazibuko-case/.

Das, Veena, and Deborah Poole, eds. 2004 *Anthropology in the Margins of the State.* Santa Fe: SAR Press.

Daston, Lorraine, and Peter Galison. *Objectivity.* New York; Cambridge, Mass.: Zone Books/MIT Press, 2007.

Daunton, Michael J. *House and Home in the Victorian City: Working Class Housing, 1850–1914.* London; Baltimore: E. Arnold, 1983.

Davie, Grace. "Strength in Numbers: The Durban Student Wages Commission, Dockworkers and the Poverty Datum Line, 1971–1973." *Journal of Southern African Studies* 33, no. 2 (2007): 401–20.

Dawson, Marcelle. "The Cost of Belonging: Exploring Class and Citizenship in Soweto's Water War." *Citizenship Studies* 14, no. 4 (2010): 381–94.

Dawson, Marcelle C., and Luke Sinwell, eds. *Contesting Transformation: Popular Resistance in Twenty-First Century South Africa.* London: Pluto Press, 2012.

De Laet, Marianne, and Annemarie Mol. "The Zimbabwe Bush Pump Mechanics of a Fluid Technology." *Social Studies of Science* 30, no. 2 (2000): 225–63.

Decoteau, Claire Laurier. *Ancestors and Antiretrovirals: The Biopolitics of HIV/AIDS in Post-Apartheid South Africa.* Chicago: University of Chicago Press, 2013.

Deleuze, Gilles. *Foucault.* Minneapolis: University of Minnesota Press, 1988.

Department of Water Affairs and Forestry. "Water Supply and Sanitation Policy White Paper," Pretoria: DWAF, 1994.

Department of Water Affairs and Forestry. "Strategic Framework for Water Services: Water Is Life, Sanitation Is Dignity." Pretoria: DWAF, 2003.

Desai, Ashwin. *We Are the Poors: Community Struggles in Post-Apartheid South Africa.* New York: Monthly Review Press, 2002.

Dlamini, Jacob. *Native Nostalgia.* Johannesburg: Jacana Media, 2009.

Donovan, Kevin. "The Biometric Imaginary: Bureaucratic Technopolitics in Post-Apartheid Welfare." *Journal of Southern African Studies* 41, no. 4 (2015): 815–33.

Donzelot, Jacques. "The Promotion of the Social." *Economy and Society* 17, no. 3 (1988): 395–427.

Dow Schüll, Natasha. *Addiction by Design: Machine Gambling in Las Vegas.* Princeton: Princeton University Press, 2012.

Dubbeld, Bernard. "Envisioning Governance: Expectations and Estrangements of Transformed Rule in Glendale, South Africa." *Africa* 83, no. 03 (2013): 492–512.

Dubow, Saul. "Liberalism and Segregation Revisited." Collected Seminar Papers. Institute of Commonwealth Studies, 1990.

Dubow, Saul. *Racial Segregation and the Origins of Apartheid in South Africa, 1919–36*. New York: St. Martin's Press, 1989.

Dubow, Saul. *Scientific Racism in Modern South Africa*. Cambridge: Cambridge University Press, 1995.

Dugard, Jackie. "Civic Action and Legal Mobilisation: The Phiri Water Meters Case." In *Mobilising Social Justice: Perspectives from Researchers and Practitioners*, edited by Jeff Berkhout and Remko Handmaker, Pretoria: Pretoria University Law Press, 2010, 71–101.

Ecoplan. "Development Guidance System for Soweto Council, Diepmeadow Council." Pretoria: Ecoplan Consortium, 1979.

Edwards, Paul. "Infrastructure and Modernity: Force, Time, and Social Organization in the History of Sociotechnical Systems." In *Modernity and Technology*, edited by Thomas Misa, Philip Brey, and Andrew Feenberg, 185–225. Cambridge: MIT Press, 2003.

Edwards, Paul N., and Gabrielle Hecht. "History and the Technopolitics of Identity: The Case of Apartheid South Africa." *Journal of Southern African Studies* 36, no. 3 (2010): 619–39.

Egan, Anthony, and Alex Wafer. "The Soweto Electricity Crisis Committee." 1–26. Durban: Center for Civil Society, 2004.

Eichelberger, Laura. "SARS and New York's Chinatown: The Politics of Risk and Blame During an Epidemic of Fear." *Social Science & Medicine* 65, no. 6 (2007): 1284–95.

Elias, Norbert. *The Civilizing Process*. New York: Pantheon Books, 1982.

Elyachar, Julia. *Markets of Dispossession: NGOs, Economic Development, and the State in Cairo*. Durham, NC: Duke University Press, 2005.

Elyachar, Julia. "Next Practices: Knowledge, Infrastructure, and Public Goods at the Bottom of the Pyramid." *Public Culture* 24, no. 1 66 (2012): 109–29.

Elyachar, Julia. "Phatic Labor, Infrastructure, and the Question of Empowerment in Cairo." *American Ethnologist* 37, no. 3 (2010): 452–64.

Esmeir, Samera. *Juridical Humanity: A Colonial History*. Stanford, CA: Stanford University Press, 2012.

Espeland, Wendy, and Mitchell L. Stevens. "Commensuration as a Social Process." *Annual Review of Sociology* 24, no. 1 (1998): 313–43.

Esping-Andersen, Gosta, and Walter Korpi. "From Poor Relief to Institutional Welfare States: The Development of Scandinavian Social Policy." In *The Scandinavian Model: Welfare States and Welfare Research*, edited by Robert Erikson, Erik Hansen, Stein Ringen, and Hanno Uusitalo, 39–74. Armonk, NY: M. E. Sharpe, 1987.

Evans, Ivan Thomas. *Bureaucracy and Race: Native Administration in South Africa*. Berkeley: University of California Press, 1997.

Ewald, François. "Insurance and Risk." In *The Foucault Effect: Studies in Governmentality*, edited by Graham Burchell, Colin Gordon, and Peter Miller, 197–210. Chicago: Chicago University Press, 1991.

Fassin, Didier. *When Bodies Remember: Experiences and Politics of AIDS in South Africa*. Berkeley: University of California Press, 2007.

Fassin, Didier. "The Humanitarian Politics of Testimony: Subjectification through Trauma in the Israeli–Palestinian Conflict." *Cultural Anthropology* 23, no. 3 (2008): 531–58.

Fassin, Didier. *Humanitarian Reason: A Moral History of the Present*. Berkeley: University of California Press, 2012.

Fassin, Didier. "Policing Borders, Producing Boundaries: The Governmentality of Immigration in Dark Times." *Annual Review of Anthropology* 40, no. 1 (2011).

Federici, Silvia. *Revolution at Point Zero: Housework, Reproduction, and Feminist Struggle*. PM Press, 2012.

Feldman, Ilana. "Difficult Distinctions: Refugee Law, Humanitarian Practice, and Political Identification in Gaza." *Cultural Anthropology* 22, no. 1 (2007): 129–69.

Fennell, Catherine. *Last Project Standing: Civics and Sympathy in Post-Welfare Chicago*. Minneapolis: University of Minnesota Press, 2015.

Fennell, Catherine. "'Project Heat' and Sensory Politics in Redeveloping Chicago Public Housing." *Ethnography* 12, no. 1 (2011): 40–64.

Ferguson, James. *The Anti-Politics Machine: "Development," Depoliticization, and Bureaucratic Power in Lesotho*. Minneapolis: University of Minnesota Press, 1990.

Ferguson, James. *Expectations of Modernity: Myths and Meanings of Urban Life on the Zambian Copperbelt*. Berkeley: University of California Press, 1999.

Ferguson, James. "Formalities of Poverty: Thinking About Social Assistance in Neoliberal South Africa." *African Studies Review* 50, no. 2 (2007): 71–86.

Ferguson, James. *Give a Man a Fish: Reflections on the New Politics of Distribution*. Durham, NC: Duke University Press, 2015.

Ferguson, James. *Global Shadows: Africa in the Neoliberal World Order*. Durham, NC: Duke University Press, 2006.

Ferguson, James. "The Uses of Neoliberalism." *Antipode* 41, no. s1 (2010): 166–84.

Festa, Lynn. "Humanity without Feathers." *Humanity: An International Journal of Human Rights, Humanitarianism, and Development* 1, no. 1 (2010): 3–27.

Fiil-Flynn, Maj. "The Electricity Crisis in Soweto." *Municipal Services Project Occasional Papers Series* 4 (2001).

Fine, Ben. "Privatisation and the RDP: A Critical Assessment." *Transformation*, no. 27 (1995).

First, Ruth. "The Bus Boycott." *Africa South* 1, no. 4 (1957): 55–64.

Fischer, Claude. *America Calling: A Social History of the Telephone to 1940*. Berkeley: University of California Press, 1994.

Foucault, Michel. *The Birth of Biopolitics: Lectures at the Collège de France, 1978–79.* Basingstoke; New York: Palgrave Macmillan, 2008.

Foucault, Michel. *Discipline and Punish: The Birth of the Prison.* 1st American ed. New York: Pantheon Books, 1977.

Foucault, Michel. "Governmentality." In *The Foucault Effect: Studies in Governmentality* edited by Graham Burchell, Colin Gordon and Peter Miller, 87–104. Chicago: University of Chicago Press, 1991.

Foucault, Michel. *The History of Sexuality.* Volume 1, *An Introduction.* New York: Random House, 1978.

Foucault, Michel. "Polemics, Politics and Problematizations." In *The Essential Works of Foucault,* edited by Paul Rabinow, 111–120. New York: The New Press, 1998.

Foucault, Michel. "The Subject and Power." In *Power—the Essential Works of Michel Foucault, 1954–1984,* vol. 3, edited by James Faubion, 326–48. New York: The New Press, 1997.

Foucault, Michel. "Technologies of the Self." In *Technologies of the Self: A Seminar with Michel Foucault,* edited by Luther H Martin, Huck Gutman and Patrick H. Hutton. Amherst: University of Massachusetts Press, 1988.

Frankel, Philip. "Municipal Transformation in Soweto: Race, Politics, and Maladministration in Black Johannesburg." *African Studies Review* 22, no. 02 (1979): 49–63.

Fraser, Nancy. "Rethinking the Public Sphere: A Contribution to the Critique of Actually Existing Democracy." *Social Text* 25/26 (1990): 56–80.

Fredericks, Rosalind. "Vital Infrastructures of Trash in Dakar." *Comparative Studies of South Asia, Africa and the Middle East* 34, no. 3 (2014): 532–48.

Gandy, Matthew. "Rethinking Urban Metabolism: Water, Space and the Modern City." *City* 8, no. 3 (2004): 363–79.

Gaule, Sally, and Noor Nieftagodien. *Orlando West, Soweto: An Illustrated History.* Johannesburg: Wits University Press, 2012.

Geertz, Clifford. *The Interpretation of Cultures.* New York: Basic Books, 1973.

Gelb, Stephen. *South Africa's Economic Crisis.* Cape Town: D. Philip, 1991.

Gelb, Stephen, and Duncan Innes. "Economic Crisis in South Africa: Monetarism's Double Bind." *Work in Progress* 36 (1985): 31–39.

Gibson-Graham, Julie Katherine. *"The" End of Capitalism (as We Knew It): A Feminist Critique of Political Economy.* Minneapolis: University of Minnesota Press, 1996.

Giliomee, Hermann. *The Parting of the Ways: South African Politics 1976–1982.* Cape Town: David Philip, 1982.

Giliomee, Hermann. "Apartheid, Verligtheid, and Liberalism." In *Democratic Liberalism in South Africa: Its History and Prospect,* edited by Jeffrey Butler, Richard Elphick, and David Welsh, 363–83. Middletown, CT: Wesleyan University Press, 1987.

Gillespie, Kelly. "Moralizing Security: 'Corrections' and the Post-Apartheid Prison." *Race/Ethnicity: Multidisciplinary Global Contexts* 2, no. 1 (2008): 69–87.

GJMC. *Igoli 2002: Making the City Work–It Cannot Be Business as Usual.* Johannesburg: Metropolitan Corporate Services, 1999.

Good, Anthony. "Cultural Evidence in Courts of Law." *Journal of the Royal Anthropological Institute* 14, no. s1 (2008): S47–S60.

Gooday, Graeme. *The Morals of Measurement: Accuracy, Irony, and Trust in Late Victorian Electrical Practice.* Cambridge; New York: Cambridge University Press, 2004.

Gordon, Colin. "Governmental Rationality: An Introduction." In *The Foucault Effect: Studies in Governmentality*, edited by Graham Burchell, Colin Gordon, and Peter Miller, 1–51. Chicago: University of Chicago Press, 1991.

Goswami, Manu. *Producing India: From Colonial Economy to National Space.* Chicago: Chicago University Press, 2004.

Graham, Stephen, and Simon Marvin. *Splintering Urbanism: Networked Infrastructures, Technological Mobilities and the Urban Condition.* London; New York: Routledge, 2001.

Gray, John. *Hayek on Liberty.* 3rd ed. London; New York: Routledge, 1998.

Greenberg, Stanley B. *Legitimating the Illegitimate: State, Markets, and Resistance in South Africa.* Berkeley: University of California Press, 1987.

Grinker, David. *Inside Soweto: The Inside Story of the Background to the Unrest.* Johannesburg: Eastern Enterprises, 1986.

Gupta, Akhil. *Red Tape: Bureaucracy, Structural Violence, and Poverty in India.* Durham, NC: Duke University Press, 2012.

Guy, Simon, and Stephen Graham. "Pathways to "Smarter" Utility Meters: The Socio-Technical Shaping of New Metering Technologies." *Electronic Working Paper* 23, (1995): 1–41.

Guyer, Jane I. *Marginal Gains: Monetary Transactions in Atlantic Africa.* The Lewis Henry Morgan Lectures. Chicago: University of Chicago Press, 2004.

Guyer, Jane I. "Percentages and Perchance: Archaic Forms in the Twenty-First Century." *Distinktion: Scandinavian Journal of Social Theory* 15, no. 2 (2014): 155–73.

Guyer, Jane I. "Prophecy and the Near Future: Thoughts on Macroeconomic, Evangelical, and Punctuated Time." *American Ethnologist* 34, no. 3 (2007): 409–21.

Guyer, Jane I, Naveeda Khan, and Juan Obarrio. "Introduction: Number as Inventive Frontier." *Anthropological Theory* 10, no. 1–2 (2010): 36–61.

Habermas, Jürgen. *Toward a Rational Society: Student Protest, Science, and Politics.* Boston: Beacon Press, 1971.

Habermas, Jürgen. *The Structural Transformation of the Public Sphere: An Inquiry into a Category of Bourgeois Society.* Cambridge: MIT Press, 1989.

Habermas, Jürgen. "The Concept of Human Dignity and the Realistic Utopia of Human Rights." *Metaphilosophy* 41, no. 4 (2010): 464–80.

Habib, Adam, and Vishnu Padayachee. "Economic Policy and Power Relations in South Africa's Transition to Democracy." *World Development* 28, no. 2 (2000): 245–63.

Hacking, Ian. *The Taming of Chance*. Cambridge; New York: Cambridge University Press, 1990.

Hansen, Thomas Blom. *Melancholia of Freedom: Social Life in an Indian Township in South Africa*. Princeton: Princeton University Press, 2012.

Hardt, Michael. "Affective Labor." *Boundary* 2 (1999): 89–100.

Hart, Gillian. *Disabling Globalization: Places of Power in Post-Apartheid South Africa*. Berkeley: University of California Press, 2002.

Hart, Gillian. "Post-Apartheid Developments in Historical and Comparative Perspective." In *The Development Decade? Economic and Social Change in South Africa, 1994–2004*, edited by Vishnu Padayachee, 13–32. Cape Town: HSRC Press, 2006.

Hart, Gillian. "The Provocations of Neoliberalism: Contesting the Nation and Liberation after Apartheid." *Antipode* 40, no. 4 (2008): 678–705.

Harvey, Ebrahim. "Managing the Poor by Remote Control: Johannesburg's Experiments with Prepaid Water Meters." In *The Age of Commodity: Water Privatization in Southern Africa*, edited by David A. McDonald and Greg Ruiters, 120–27. London: Earthscan, 2005.

Harvey, Penny, and Hannah Knox. *Roads: An Anthropology of Infrastructure and Expertise*. Ithaca, NY: Cornell University Press, 2015.

Hayek, Friedrich. *The Road to Serfdom*. Chicago: University of Chicago Press, 1944.

Hayek, Friedrich. "The Use of Knowledge in Society." *American Economic Review* 35 (1945): 519–30.

Hayek, Friedrich. *The Sensory Order: An Inquiry into the Foundations of Theoretical Psychology*. Chicago: University of Chicago Press, 1952.

Hayek, Friedrich. *The Constitution of Liberty*. Phoenix edition. ed. Chicago: University of Chicago Press, 1960.

Hayek, Friedrich. *Law, Legislation and Liberty: A New Statement of the Liberal Principles of Justice and Political Economy*. Phoenix ed. 3 vols Chicago: University of Chicago Press, 1978a.

Hayek, Friedrich. "The Errors of Constructivism." In *New Studies in Philosophy, Politics, Economics, and the History of Ideas*. London: Routledge and K. Paul, 1978b.

Hecht, Gabrielle. *The Radiance of France: Nuclear Power and National Identity after World War II*. Cambridge: MIT Press, 2009.

Hecht, Gabrielle. *Being Nuclear: Africans and the Global Uranium Trade*. Cambridge: MIT Press, 2012.

Martin, Heidegger. "The Question Concerning Technology." In *The Question Concerning Technology, and Other Essays*, edited by William Lovitt, 3–35. New York: Harper & Row, 1977.

Heiman, Rachel. *Driving after Class: Anxious Times in an American Suburb*. Berkeley: University of California Press, 2015.

Helmreich, Stefan. "An Anthropologist Underwater: Immersive Soundscapes, Submarine Cyborgs, and Transductive Ethnography." *American Ethnologist* 34, no. 4 (2007): 621–41.

Hetherington, Kregg. *Guerrilla Auditors: The Politics of Transparency in Neoliberal Paraguay*. Durham, NC: Duke University Press, 2011.

Hetherington, Kregg. "Waiting for the Surveyor: Development Promises and the Temporality of Infrastructure." *Journal of Latin American and Caribbean Anthropology* 19, no. 2 (2014): 195–211.

Hewage, Thushara. "Rethinking Postcolonial Emergency Constitutional Revolution and the Temporality of the Social in Sri Lanka." *Comparative Studies of South Asia, Africa and the Middle East* 34, no. 2 (2014): 243–59.

Hindson, Doug. "The Role of the Labour Bureaux in South Africa: A Critique of the Riekert Commission Report." In *Working Papers in Southern African Studies*, edited by Doug Hindson. Johannesburg: Ravan Press, 1983.

Hindson, Doug. *Pass Controls and the Urban African Proletariat in South Africa.* Johannesburg: Ravan Press 1987a.

Hindson, Doug. "Orderly Urbanisation and Influx Control: From Territorial Apartheid to Regional Spatial Ordering in South Africa." In *Regional Restructuring under Apartheid: Urban and Regional Policies in Contemporary South Africa*, edited by Richard Tomlinson and Mark Addleson, 74–105. Johannesburg: Ravan Press, 1987b.

Hirschkind, Charles. "Civic Virtue and Religious Reason: An Islamic Counterpublic." *Cultural Anthropology* 16, no. 1 (2001): 3–34.

Hoag, Colin. "The Magic of the Populace: An Ethnography of Illegibility in the South African Immigration Bureaucracy." *PoLAR: Political and Legal Anthropology Review* 33, no. 1 (2010): 6–25.

Hoernlé, Reinhold Friedrich Alfred. *South African Native Policy and the Liberal Spirit.* The Phelps-Stokes Lectures, Delivered before the University of Cape Town, May, 1939. Cape Town: Phelps-Stokes Fund/University of Cape Town Press, 1939.

Holston, James. *Insurgent Citizenship: Disjunctions of Democracy and Modernity in Brazil.* Princeton: Princeton University Press, 2008.

Holston, James. "Insurgent Citizenship in an Era of Global Urban Peripheries." *City & Society* 21, no. 2 (2009): 245–67.

Horkheimer, Max, and Theodor W. Adorno. *Dialectic of Enlightenment: Philosophical Fragments.* Stanford, CA: Stanford University Press, 2002.

Hornberger, Julia. *Policing and Human Rights: The Meaning of Violence and Justice in the Everyday Policing of Johannesburg.* London: Routledge, 2011.

Horwitz, Ralph. *The Political Economy of South Africa.* New York: Praeger, 1967.

Huchzermeyer, Marie. "Housing Rights in South Africa: Invasions, Evictions, the Media, and the Courts in the Cases of Grootboom, Alexandra, and Bredell." *Urban Forum* 14, no. 1 (2003): 80–107.

Hughes, Thomas P. *Networks of Power: Electrification in Western Society, 1880–1930.* Baltimore: Johns Hopkins University Press, 1999.

Hull, Matthew S. 2012. *Government of Paper: The Materiality of Bureaucracy in Urban Pakistan.* Berkeley: University of California Press.

Hunter, Jane. "Israel: South Africa's Springboard to World Markets." *The Washington Report on Middle East Affairs (1982–1989)*, no. 4 (1986): 1.

Hutt, William H. *The Economics of the Colour Bar: A Study of the Economic Origins and Consequences of Racial Segregation in South Africa*. London: Institute of Economic Affairs, 1964.

Hutt, William H. "South Africa's Salvation in Classic Liberalism." *Il Politico* 30, no. 4 (1965): 782–95.

Innes, Duncan. "Privatisation: The Solution?" *South African Review* 4 (1987): 551–567.

Isin, Engin. *Being Political: Genealogies of Citizenship*. Minneapolis: University of Minnesota Press, 2002.

James, Deborah. *Money from Nothing: Indebtedness and Aspiration in South Africa*. Stanford, CA: Stanford University Press, 2014.

Jensen, Steffen. *Gangs, Politics & Dignity in Cape Town*. James Currey Ltd, 2008.

Jerome, Jerome K. "Automatic Machines." *The Idler* (1892).

Jessop, Bob. "Liberalism, Neoliberalism, and Urban Governance: A State-Theoretical Perspective." *Antipode* 34, no. 3 (2002): 452–72.

Jochelson, Karen. "Reform, Repression and Resistance in South Africa: A Case Study of Alexandra Township, 1979–1989." *Journal of Southern African Studies* 16, no. 1 (1990): 1–32.

Johnson, R. W. *Not So Close to Their Hearts: An Investigation into the Non-Payment of Rents, Rates and Service Charges in South Africa's Towns and Cities*. Johannesburg: The Helen Suzman Foundation, 1999.

Johnstone, Frederick A. "White Prosperity and White Supremacy in South Africa Today." *African Affairs* 69, no. 275 (1970): 124–40.

Jolobe, Zwelethu. "The Crisis of Democratic Representation in Local Government." WISER, University of the Witwatersrand, 2014.

Joyce, Patrick. *The Rule of Freedom: Liberalism and the Modern City*. London: Verso, 2003.

Judin, Hilton, and Ivan Vladislavić, eds. *Blank—: Architecture, Apartheid and After*. Rotterdam: NAI Publishers, 1998.

Kane-Berman, John Stuart. *Soweto: Black Revolt, White Reaction*. Johannesburg: Raven Press, 1978.

Kant, Immanuel. *Groundwork of the Metaphysic of Morals*, Trans. H. J. Paton. New York: Harper Torchbook, 1964.

Kaplan, Martha. "Fijian Water in Fiji and New York: Local Politics and a Global Commodity." *Cultural Anthropology* 22, no. 4 (2007): 685–706.

Keane, Webb. "Semiotics and the Social Analysis of Material Things." *Language and Communication* 23, no. 3–4 (2003): 409–25.

Keane, Webb. "Market, Materiality and Moral Metalanguage." *Anthropological Theory* 8, no. 1 (2008): 27–42.

Kelty, Christopher M. *Two Bits: The Cultural Significance of Free Software*. Durham, NC: Duke University Press, 2008.

Khunou, Grace. ""Massive Cut-Offs": Cost Recovery and Electricity Services in Diepkloof, Soweto." In *Cost Recovery and the Crisis of Service*, edited by David A. McDonald and John Pape. London, New York: Zed Books, 2002.

Kipnis, Andrew B. "Audit Cultures: Neoliberal Governmentality, Socialist Legacy, or Technologies of Governing?" *American Ethnologist* 35, no. 2 (2008): 275–89.

Kistner, Ulrike. *Commissioning and Contesting Post-Apartheid's Human Rights: HIV/AIDS, Racism, Truth, and Reconciliation*. Münster: LIT Verlag 2003.

Klug, Heinz. *Constituting Democracy: Law, Globalism and South Africa's Political Reconstruction*. Cambridge: Cambridge University Press, 2000.

Kockelman, Paul. "Enemies, Parasites, and Noise: How to Take up Residence in a System without Becoming a Term in It." *Journal of Linguistic Anthropology* 20, no. 2 (2010): 406–21.

Kockelman, Paul. "The Anthropology of an Equation: Sieves, Spam Filters, Agentive Algorithms, and Ontologies of Transformation." *HAU: Journal of Ethnographic Theory* 3, no. 3 (2013): 33–61.

Krige, Detlev. "Power, Identity and Agency at Work in the Popular Economies of Soweto and Black Johannesburg." PhD Thesis. University of the Witwatersrand, 2011.

Laclau, Ernesto. *On Populist Reason*. London: Verso, 2005.

Lakoff, Andrew, and Stephen J. Collier. "Ethics and the Anthropology of Modern Reason." *Anthropological Theory* 4, no. 4 (2004): 419–434.

Lalu, Premesh. *A Subaltern Studies for South Africa*. University of the Western Cape, Department of History, 2007.

Lalu, Premesh. *The Deaths of Hintsa: Postapartheid South Africa and the Shape of Recurring Pasts*. Pretoria: Human Sciences Research Council, 2009.

Lalu, Premesh. "The Absent Centre: Human Capital, Nationalism and the Postcolonial Critique of Apartheid." Unpublished manuscript, 2013.

Lampland, Martha. "False Numbers as Formalizing Practices." *Social Studies of Science* 40, no. 3 (2010): 377–404.

Lampland, Martha, and Susan Leigh Star. *Standards and Their Stories: How Quantifying, Classifying, and Formalizing Practices Shape Everyday Life*. Ithaca, NY: Cornell University Press, 2009.

Laqueur, Thomas. "Bodies, Details, and the Humanitarian Narrative." In *The New Cultural History*, edited by Lynn Hunt, 176–204. Berkeley: University of California Press, 1989.

Larkin, Brian. *Signal and Noise: Media, Infrastructure, and Urban Culture in Nigeria*. Durham, NC: Duke University Press, 2008.

Larkin, Brian. "The Politics and Poetics of Infrastructure." *Annual Review of Anthropology* 42, no. 1 (2013): 327–343.

Latour, Bruno. "Where Are the Missing Masses? The Sociology of a Few Mundane Artifacts." In *Shaping Technology/Building Society: Studies in Sociotechnical Change*, edited by Wiebe Bijker and John Law, 225–58. Cambridge: MIT Press, 1992.

Latour, Bruno. "Why Has Critique Run out of Steam? From Matters of Fact to Matters of Concern." *Critical Inquiry* 30, no. 2 (2004): 225–48.

Latour, Bruno. *Reassembling the Social: An Introduction to Actor-Network-Theory*. Oxford; New York: Oxford University Press, 2005.

Latour, Bruno. *The Making of Law: An Ethnography of the Conseil d'Etat.* London: Polity, 2010.

Lea, J. P. "Government Dispensation, Capitalist Imperative or Liberal Philanthropy? Responses to the Black Housing Crisis in South Africa." In *Living under Apartheid*, 198–216. London: Allen and Unwin, 1982.

Lee, Rebekah. "Hearth and Home in Cape Town." *Journal of Women's History* 18, no. 4 (2006): 55–78.

Legassick, Martin. "Legislation, Ideology and Economy in Post-1948 South Africa." *Journal of Southern African Studies* 1, no. 1 (1974): 5–35.

Legassick, Martin. "Race, Industrialization and Social Change in South Africa: The Case of R.F.A. Hoernle." *African Affairs* (1976): 224–39.

Lemke, Thomas. "'The Birth of Bio-Politics': Michel Foucault's Lecture at the Collège De France on Neo-Liberal Governmentality." *Economy and Society* 30, no. 2 (2001): 190–207.

Liebenberg, Sandra. "The Value of Human Dignity in Interpreting Socio-Economic Rights." *South African Journal of Human Rights* 21 (2005): 1.

Liebenberg, Sandra. "First Major Test Case on the Right to Water in South Africa." *Legal Brief Today*, May 12 2008.

Lipietz, Barbara. "'Muddling Through': Urban Regeneration in Johannesburg's Inner City." Paper presented at the N-Aerus Annual Conference, Barcelona, 2004.

Lipton, Merle. *Capitalism and Apartheid, South Africa, 1910–84.* Totowa, NJ: Rowman & Allanheld, 1986.

Loftus, Alex. "'Free Water as a Commodity': The Paradoxes of Durban's Water Service Transformation." In *The Age of the Commodity: Water Privatization in Southern Africa*, edited by David A. McDonald and Greg Ruiters, 189–203. London: Earthscan, 2005.

Loftus, Alex. "Reification and the Dictatorship of the Water Meter." *Antipode* 38, no. 5 (2006): 1023–45.

Lombard, J. A. *Freedom, Welfare and Order: Thoughts on the Principles of Political Co-Operation in the Economy of Southern Africa.* Pretoria: Benbo, 1978.

Lombard, J. A. *On Economic Liberalism in South Africa.* Bureau for Economic Policy and Analysis, University of Pretoria, Pretoria, 1979.

Lombard, J. A., and J. A. Du Pisanie. *Removal of Discrimination against Blacks in the Political Economy of the Republic of South Africa: A Memorandum for Assocom.* Pretoria: Bureau for Economic Policy and Analysis, University of Pretoria, 1985.

Louw, Leon. *South Africa: The Solution.* Bisho, Ciskei: Amagi Publications, 1986.

Lupton, Malcolm. "Collective Consumption and Urban Segregation in South Africa: The Case of Two Colored Suburbs in the Johannesburg Region." *Antipode* 25, no. 1 (1993): 32–50.

Mabin, Alan. "Dispossession, Exploitation and Struggle: An Historical Overview of South African Urbanization." In *The Apartheid City and Beyond: Urbanization and Social Change in South Africa*, 12–24, 1992.

Mabin, Alan. "'Forget Democracy, Build Houses': Negotiating the Shape of the City Tomorrow." Paper presented at the Wits History Workshop, 1–12. Johannesburg: University of the Witwatersrand, 1994.

MacIntyre, Alasdair C. *After Virtue: A Study in Moral Theory*. Notre Dame: University of Notre Dame Press, 1981.

Mahmood, Saba. *Politics of Piety: The Islamic Revival and the Feminist Subject*. Princeton: Princeton University Press, 2005.

Mains, Daniel. "Blackouts and Progress: Privatization, Infrastructure, and a Developmentalist State in Jimma, Ethiopia." *Cultural Anthropology* 27, no. 1 (2012): 3–27.

Makhulu, Anne-Maria. "The 'Dialectics of Toil': Reflections on the Politics of Space after Apartheid." *Anthropological Quarterly* 83, no. 3 (2010): 551–80.

Malkki, Liisa. "Speechless Emissaries: Refugees, Humanitarianism, and Dehistoricization." *Cultural Anthropology* 11, no. 3 (1996): 377–404.

Mamdani, Mahmood. *Citizen and Subject: Contemporary Africa and the Legacy of Late Colonialism*. Princeton: Princeton University Press, 1996.

Mandy, Nigel. *A City Divided: Johannesburg and Soweto*. New York: St. Martin's Press, 1984.

Mann, Michael. "The Giant Stirs: South African Business in the Age of Reform." In *State, Resistance and Change in South Africa*, edited by Philip Frankel, Noam Pines and Mark Swilling, 52–86. Johannesburg: Southern Book Publishers, 1988.

Mantena, Karuna. *Alibis of Empire: Henry Maine and the Ends of Liberal Imperialism*. Princeton: Princeton University Press, 2010.

Marais, Georg, and Robert Van der Kooy, eds. *South Africa's Urban Blacks: Problems and Challenges*. Pretoria: Centre for Management Studies, School of Business Leadership, UNISA, 1978.

Marais, Hein. *South Africa: Limits to Change: The Political Economy of Transition*. London: Palgrave Macmillan, 2001.

Marcuse, Herbert. *One Dimensional Man: The Ideology of Industrial Society*. Boston: Beacon Press, 1964.

Marres, Noortjie. *Material Participation: Technology, the Environment and Everyday Publics*. Basingstoke: Palgrave Macmillan UK, 2012.

Marshall, T. H. *Citizenship and Social Class: And Other Essays*. London: Pluto Press, 1992.

Marx, Karl. *Capital: A Critique of Political Economy*. vol. 1. Translated by Ben Fowkes and David Fernbach. London; New York: Penguin Books, 1990.

Mashabela, Harry. *A People on the Boil: Reflections on June 16, 1976 and Beyond*. Johannesburg: Jacana Media, 2006 [1987].

Maurer, Bill. "The Anthropology of Money." *Annual Review of Anthropology* 35 (2006): 15–36.

Maurer, Bill. "Incalculable Payments: Money, Scale, and the South African Offshore Grey Money Amnesty." *African Studies Review* 50, no. 2 (2007): 125–38.

Maurer, Bill. "Mobile Money: Communication, Consumption and Change in the Payments Space." *Journal of Development Studies* 48, no. 5 (2012): 589–604.

Mauss, Marcel. *The Gift: The Form and Reason for Exchange in Archaic Societies.* London: Routledge, 2002.

Mayekiso, Mzwanele. *Township Politics: Civic Struggles for a New South Africa.* New York: Monthly Review Press, 1996.

Mbembe, Achille. *On the Postcolony.* Berkeley: University of California Press, 2001.

Mbembe, Achille. "Necropolitics." *Public Culture* 15, no. 1 (2003): 11–40.

Mbembe, Achille. *Kritik der schwarzen Vernunft.* Frankfurt: Suhrkamp, 2014.

Mbembe, Achille, and Janet Roitman. "Figures of the Subject in Times of Crisis." *Public Culture* 7, no. 2 (1995): 323–53.

McCarthy, J. J., and Mark Swilling. "South Africa's Emerging Politics of Bus Transportation." *Political Geography Quarterly* 4, no. 3 (1985): 235–49.

McDonald, David. *Electric Capitalism: Recolonising Africa on the Power Grid.* Cape Town: HSRC Press, 2009.

McDonald, David A., and John Pape, eds. *Cost Recovery and the Crisis of Service Delivery in South Africa.* London; New York: Zed Books, 2002.

McFarlane, Colin. "Governing the Contaminated City: Infrastructure and Sanitation in Colonial and Post-Colonial Bombay." *International Journal of Urban and Regional Research* 32, no. 2 (2008): 415–35.

McKay, Ramah. "Afterlives: Humanitarian Histories and Critical Subjects in Mozambique." *Cultural Anthropology* 27, no. 2 (2012): 286–309.

McKinley, Dale T. *The ANC and the Liberation Struggle: A Critical Political Biography.* London: Pluto, 1997.

Mehta, Uday Singh. *Liberalism and Empire: A Study in Nineteenth-Century British Liberal Thought.* Chicago: University of Chicago Press, 1999.

Meintjes, Helen, and Caroline White. *Robbers and Freeloaders: Relations between Communities and Eskom in Gauteng Townships.* Johannesburg: Centre for Policy Studies, 1997.

Mirowski, Philip. "Realism and Neoliberalism: From Reactionary Modernism to Post-War Conservatism." In *The Invention of International Relations Theory: Realism, the Rockefeller Foundation, and the 1954 Conference on Theory*, edited by Nicolas Guilhot, 210–38. New York: Columbia University Press, 2011.

Mirowski, Philip, and Dieter Plehwe, eds. *The Road from Mont Pèlerin: The Making of the Neoliberal Thought Collective.* Cambridge: Harvard University Press, 2009.

Mitchell, Timothy. "State, Economy, and the State Effect." In *State/Culture: State-Formation after the Cultural Turn*, edited by George Steinmetz, 76–97. Ithaca, NY: Cornell University Press, 1999.

Mitchell, Timothy. *Rule of Experts: Egypt, Techno-Politics, Modernity.* Berkeley: University of California Press, 2002.

Mitchell, Timothy. "How Neoliberalism Makes Its World: The Urban Property Rights Project in Peru." In *The Road from Mont Pelerin: The Making of the*

Neoliberal Thought Collective, edited by Philip Mirowski and Dieter Plehwe, 386–416. Cambridge: Harvard University Press, 2009.

Mitchell, Timothy. *Carbon Democracy: Political Power in the Age of Oil*. London: Verso, 2011.

Miyazaki, Hirokazu. "The Materiality of Finance Theory." In *Materiality*, edited by Daniel Miller, 165–181. Durham, NC: Duke University Press, 2005.

Mol, Annemarie. "Ontological Politics: A Word and Some Questions." In *Actor Network Theory and After*, edited by John Law and John Hassard, 74–89. Oxford: Blackwell, 1999.

Mol, Annemarie. *The Body Multiple: Ontology in Medical Practice*. Durham, NC: Duke University Press, 2002.

Morris, Mike, and Vishnu Padayachee. "State Reform Policy in South Africa." *Transformation* 7 (1988): 1–26.

Morris, Rosalind C. "The Mute and the Unspeakable: Political Subjectivity, Violent Crime and "the Sexual Thing" in a South African Mining Community." In *Law and Disorder in the Postcolony*, edited by Jean Comaroff and John Comaroff, 57–101. Chicago: University of Chicago Press, 2006.

Morris, Rosalind C. "Rush/Panic/Rush: Speculations on the Value of Life and Death in South Africa's Age of AIDS." *Public Culture* 20, no. 2 (2008): 199–231.

Morris, Rosalind C. "Accidental Histories, Post-Historical Practice?: Re-Reading Body of Power, Spirit of Resistance in the Actuarial Age." *Anthropological Quarterly* 83, no. 3 (2010): 581–624.

Moyn, Samuel. *The Last Utopia: Human Rights in History*. Cambridge: Belknap Press, 2010.

Muehlebach, Andrea. "On Affective Labor in Post-Fordist Italy." *Cultural Anthropology* 26, no. 1 (2011): 59–82.

Muehlebach, Andrea. *The Moral Neoliberal: Welfare and Citizenship in Italy*. Chicago: University of Chicago Press, 2012.

Murray, Martin J. *South Africa: Time of Agony, Time of Destiny: The Upsurge of Popular Protest*. London: Verso, 1987.

Murray, Martin J. *Revolution Deferred: The Painful Birth of Post-Apartheid South Africa*. London: Verso Books, 1994.

Murray, Martin J. *City of Extremes: The Spatial Politics of Johannesburg*. Durham, NC: Duke University Press, 2011.

Naidoo, Prishani. "Struggles around the Commodification of Daily Life in South Africa." *Review of African Political Economy* 34, no. 111 (2007): 57–66.

Naidoo, Prishani. "Subaltern Sexiness: From a Politics of Representation to a Politics of Difference." *African Studies* 69, no. 3 (2010): 439–56.

Naidoo, Prishani, and Ahmed Veriava. "Re-Membering Movements: Trade Unions and New Social Movements in Neoliberal South Africa." *From Local Processes to Global Forces, Centre for Civil Society Research Reports* 1 (2005): 27–62.

Naidoo, Prishani, and Ahmed Veriava. "From Local to Global (and Back Again?): Anti-Commodification Struggles of the Soweto Electricity Crisis Committee." *Electric Capitalism. Recolonising Africa on the Power Grid* (2009): 321–37.

NEDLAC. "Report on the Masakhane Campaign: Activities and Assessments." Johannesburg: NEDLAC, 1996.

Nefale, Michael. "A Survey on Attitudes to Prepaid Electricity Meters in Soweto." Johannesburg: Centre for Applied Legal Studies, University of Witwatersrand, 2004.

Niehaus, Isak. "Witch-Hunting and Political Legitimacy: Continuity and Change in Green Valley, Lebowa, 1930–91." *Africa* (1993): 498–530.

Obarrio, Juan. *The Spirit of the Laws in Mozambique.* Chicago: University of Chicago Press, 2014.

O'Meara, Dan. *Volkskapitalisme: Class, Capital, and Ideology in the Development of Afrikaner Nationalism, 1934–1948.* Johannesburg: Ravan Press, 1983.

Osborne, Thomas. "Security and Vitality: Drains, Liberalism and Power in the Nineteenth Century." In *Foucault and Political Reason: Liberalism, Neo-Liberalism and Rationalities of Government*, edited by Andrew Barry, Thomas Osborne, and Nikolas Rose, 99–122. Chicago: University of Chicago Press, 1996.

Otter, Chris. "Making Liberal Objects: British Techno-Social Relations 1800–1900." *Cultural Studies* 21, no. 4–5 (2007): 570–90.

Otter, Chris. *The Victorian Eye: A Political History of Light and Vision in Britain, 1800–1910.* Chicago: University of Chicago Press, 2008.

Page, Ben. "Paying for Water and the Geography of Commodities." *Transactions of the Institute of British Geographers* 30, no. 3 (2005): 293–306.

Parnell, Susan, and Alan Mabin. "Rethinking Urban South Africa." *Journal of Southern African Studies* 21, no. 1 (1995): 39–61.

Peck, Jamie, Nik Theodore, and Neil Brenner. "Neoliberal Urbanism: Models, Moments, Mutations." *Sais Review* 29, no. 1 (2009): 49–66.

Peebles, Gustav. "The Anthropology of Credit and Debt." *Annual Review of Anthropology* 39, no. 1 (2010): 225–40.

Peebles, Gustav. *The Euro and Its Rivals: Currency and the Construction of a Transnational City.* Bloomington: Indiana University Press, 2011.

Peebles, Gustav. "Washing Away the Sins of Debt: The Nineteenth-Century Eradication of the Debtors' Prison." *Comparative Studies in Society and History* 55, no. 3 (2013): 701–24.

Pienaar, Gert. "Soweto Socio-Economic Study: Final Report." Johannesburg: EON Solutions Africa (Pty) Ltd, 2003.

Pillay, Suren. "Crime, Community and the Governance of Violence in Post-Apartheid South Africa." *Politikon* 35, no. 2 (2008): 141–58.

Pillay, Suren. "Translating 'South Africa': Race, Colonialism and Challenges of Critical Thought after Apartheid." In *Re-Imagining the Social in South Africa:*

Critique and Post-Apartheid Knowledge, edited by Heather Jacklin and Peter Vale, 235–67. Durban: University of KwaZulu Natal Press Scottsville, 2009.

Piot, Charles. *Nostalgia for the Future: West Africa after the Cold War*. Chicago: University of Chicago Press, 2010.

Pithouse, Richard. "A Politics of the Poor Shack Dwellers' Struggles in Durban." *Journal of Asian and African Studies* 43, no. 1 (2008): 63–94.

Planact. "The Soweto Rent Boycott." Johannesburg: Planact, 1989.

Plehwe, Dieter. "The Origins of the Neoliberal Economic Development Discourse." In *The Road from Mont Pelerin: The Making of the Neoliberal Thought Collective*, edited by Philip Mirowski and Dieter Plehwe, 238–79. Cambridge: Harvard University Press, 2009.

Plehwe, Dieter, Bernhard Walpen, and Gisela Neunhöffer, eds. *Neoliberal Hegemony: A Global Critique*. vol. 18. London; New York: Routledge, 2006.

Pocock, J.G.A. *Virtue, Commerce, and History: Essays on Political Thought and History, Chiefly in the Eighteenth Century*. Cambridge: Cambridge University Press, 1985.

Pointer, Rebecca. "Questioning the Representation of South Africa's 'New Social Movements': A Case Study of the Mandela Park Anti-Eviction Campaign." *Journal of Asian and African Studies* 39, no. 4 (2004): 271–94.

Polanyi, Michael. "The Logic of Tacit Inference." *Philosophy* 41, no. 155 (1966): 1–18.

Poovey, Mary. *Genres of the Credit Economy: Mediating Value in Eighteenth-and Nineteenth-Century Britain*. Chicago: University of Chicago Press, 2008.

Porter, Theodore M. *Trust in Numbers: The Pursuit of Objectivity in Science and Public Life*. Princeton: Princeton University Press, 1996.

Posel, Deborah. "Language, Legitimation and Control: The South African State after 1978." *Social Dynamics* 10, no. 1 (1984): 1–16.

Posel, Deborah. *The Making of Apartheid, 1948–1961: Conflict and Compromise*. Oxford, New York: Clarendon Press, 1991.

Posel, Deborah. "A Mania for Measurement: Statistics and Statecraft in Apartheid South Africa." In *Science and Society in Southern Africa*, edited by Saul Dubow, 116–142. Manchester: Manchester University Press, 2000.

Posel, Deborah. "Races to Consume: Revisiting South Africa's History of Race, Consumption and the Struggle for Freedom." *Ethnic and Racial Studies* 33, no. 2 (2010): 157–75.

Posel, Deborah. "Julius Malema and the Post-Apartheid Public Sphere." *Acta Academica*. Special issue, *Rethinking the publics* 46, no. 1 (2014): 32–54.

Pottage, Alain, and Martha Mundy, eds. *Law, Anthropology, and the Constitution of the Social: Making Persons and Things*. Cambridge; New York: Cambridge University Press, 2004.

Povinelli, Elizabeth A. *The Cunning of Recognition: Indigenous Alterities and the Making of Australian Multiculturalism*. Durham, NC: Duke University Press, 2002.

Povinelli, Elizabeth A. *The Empire of Love: Toward a Theory of Intimacy, Genealogy, and Carnality*. Durham, NC: Duke University Press, 2006.

Prakash, Gyan. *Another Reason: Science and the Imagination of Modern India*. Princeton: Princeton University Press, 1999.

Rabinow, Paul. *Reflections on Fieldwork in Morocco*. Berkeley: University of California Press, 2007.

Rancière, Jacques. *Disagreement: Politics and Philosophy*. Minneapolis: University of Minnesota Press, 1999.

Rancière, Jacques. "Who Is the Subject of the Rights of Man?" *South Atlantic Quarterly* 103, no. 2–3 (2004): 297–310.

Redding, Sean. *Sorcery and Sovereignty: Taxation, Power, and Rebellion in South Africa, 1880–1963*. Columbus: Ohio University Press, 2006.

Redfield, Peter. "The Half-Life of Empire in Outer Space." *Social Studies of Science* 32, no. 5–6 (2002): 791–825.

Redfield, Peter. "Bioexpectations: Life Technologies as Humanitarian Goods." *Public Culture* 24, no. 66 (2012): 157–84.

Redfield, Peter. *Life in Crisis: The Ethical Journey of Doctors Without Borders*. Berkeley: University of California Press, 2013.

Rich, Paul B. *White Power and the Liberal Conscience: Racial Segregation and South African Liberalism, 1921–60*. Manchester: Manchester University Press, 1984.

Riles, Annelise. "Anthropology, Human Rights, and Legal Knowledge: Culture in the Iron Cage." *American Anthropologist* 108, no. 1 (2006).

Riley, Stephen. "Observing the Breach: Dignity and the Limits of Political Theology." *Law and Critique* 19, no. 2 (2008): 115–38.

Robbins, David. *Learning the Hard Way*. Johannesburg: Auckland Park, 1997.

Robbins, Joel. "Rethinking Gifts and Commodities." In *Economics and Morality: Anthropological Approaches*, edited by Katherine Browne and B. Lynne Milgram, 43–58. New York: Rowman & Littlefield, 2009.

Robins, Steven. "Bodies out of Place: Crossroads and the Landscapes of Exclusion." In *Blank—: Architecture, Apartheid and After*. edited by Ivan Vladislavic and Hilton Judin, 458–69. Rotterdam: NAI Publishers, 1998.

Robins, Steven. "From 'Rights' to 'Ritual': AIDS Activism in South Africa." *American Anthropologist* 108, no. 2 (2006): 312–23.

Robins, Steven. "Humanitarian Aid Beyond 'Bare Survival': Social Movement Responses to Xenophobic Violence in South Africa." *American Ethnologist* 36, no. 4 (2009): 637–50.

Robins, Steven. *From Revolution to Rights in South Africa: Social Movements, NGOs & Popular Politics after Apartheid*. New York: James Currey, 2010.

Robins, Steven. "The 2011 Toilet Wars in South Africa: Justice and Transition between the Exceptional and the Everyday after Apartheid." *Development and Change* 45, no. 3 (2014): 479–501.

Robinson, Jennifer. *The Power of Apartheid: State, Power and Space in South African Cities*. Oxford: Butterworth-Heinemann, 1996.

Rogerson, Christian M. "Willingness to Pay for Water: The International Debates." *Water SA* 22 (1996): 373–80.

Roitman, Janet. *Fiscal Disobedience: An Anthropology of Economic Regulation in Central Africa*. Princeton: Princeton University Press, 2005.

Röpke, Wilhelm. *South Africa: An Attempt at a Positive Appraisal*. New York: Information Service of South Africa, 1964.

Rose, Nikolas S. *Powers of Freedom: Reframing Political Thought*. Cambridge; New York: Cambridge University Press, 1999.

Ross, Fiona C. *Bearing Witness: Women and the Truth and Reconciliation Commission in South Africa*. London: Pluto Press, 2003.

Rostow, Walt Whitman. *The Stages of Economic Growth, a Non-Communist Manifesto*. Cambridge: Cambridge University Press, 1960.

Rottenburg, Richard. *Far-Fetched Facts: A Parable of Development Aid*. Cambridge: MIT Press, 2009.

RSA. *Report of the Commission of Inquiry into Legislation Affecting the Utilisation of Manpower*. Pretoria: Government Printer, 1979.

RSA. *Commission of Inquiry into Labour Legislation*. 1st ed. Johannesburg: Lex Patria, 1977–1981.

RSA. *Report of the Department of Co-Operation and Development for the Period 1 April 1980 to 31 March 1981*. Pretoria: Government Printer, 1981.

RSA. *Measures Which Restrict the Functioning of a Free Market Oriented System in South Africa*. Cape Town: Government Printer, 1984.

RSA. *Report of the Committee for Economic Affairs on a Revised Urbanisation Strategy*. edited by President's Council. Cape Town: Government Printer, 1992.

Ruiters, Greg. "Contradictions in Municipal Services in Contemporary South Africa: Disciplinary Commodification and Self-Disconnections." *Critical Social Policy* 27, no. 4 (2007): 487–508.

Sachs, Albie. "The Judicial Enforcement of the Socio-Economic Rights: The Grootboom Case." *Democratising Development: The Politics of Socio-Economic Rights in South Africa* 64 (2005): 131–152.

Samson, Melanie. "Producing Privatization: Re-Articulating Race, Gender, Class and Space." *Antipode* 42, no. 2 (2010): 404–32.

Sarat, Austin, Lawrence Douglas, and Martha Merrill Umphrey, eds. *How Law Knows*. Stanford, CA: Stanford University Press, 2007.

Saul, John S. "Cry for the Beloved Country: The Post-Apartheid Denouement." *Review of African Political Economy* 28, no. 89 (2001): 429–60.

Saul, John S., and Stephen Gelb. *The Crisis in South Africa: Class Defense, Class Revolution*. New York: Monthly Review Press, 1981.

Schivelbusch, Wolfgang. *Disenchanted Night: The Industrialization of Light in the Nineteenth Century*. Berkeley: University of California Press, 1988.

Schwenkel, Christina.. "Spectacular Infrastructure and Its Breakdown in Socialist Vietnam." *American Ethnologist* 42, no. 3 (2015): 520–34.

Scott, David. *Refashioning Futures: Criticism after Postcoloniality*. Princeton: Princeton University Press, 1999.

Scott, David. *Conscripts of Modernity: The Tragedy of Colonial Enlightenment*. Durham, NC: Duke University Press, 2004.

Scott, David. *Omens of Adversity: Tragedy, Time, Memory, Justice*. Durham, NC: Duke University Press, 2014.

Scott, James C. *Weapons of the Weak: Everyday Forms of Peasant Resistance*. New Haven: Yale University Press, 1985.

Seekings, Jeremy. "Political Mobilization in the Black Townships of the Transvaal." In *State, Resistance and Change in South Africa.*, edited by Philip Frankel, Noam Pines and Mark Swilling, 197–228. Johannesburg: Southern Book Publishers, 1988a.

Seekings, Jeremy. *Why Was Soweto Different? Urban Development, Township Politics, and the Political Economy of Soweto, 1978–84*. University of the Witwatersrand, African Studies Institute, 1988b.

Seekings, Jeremy. "Powerlessness and Politics, Quiescence and Protest in Pretoria-Witwatersrand-Vaal Townships 1973–1985." Collected Seminar Papers. London: Institute of Commonwealth Studies, 1990.

Seekings, Jeremy. "Civic Organisations in South African Townships." *South African Review* 6 (1992): 216–38.

Seekings, Jeremy. "Civic Organisations During South Africa's Transition to Democracy, 1990–1996." In *The Post-Colonial Condition: Contemporary Politics in Africa*, edited by Pal Ahluwalia and Paul Nursey-Bray, 138–57. New York: Nova Science, 1997.

Seekings, Jeremy. *The UDF: A History of the United Democratic Front in South Africa, 1983–1991*. London: James Currey Publishers, 2000.

Seekings, Jeremy. "Facts, Myths and Controversies: The Measurement and Analysis of Poverty and Inequality after Apartheid." Paper presented at the After Apartheid Conference, 1–36. Cape Town, August 11–12, 2006.

Selfe, James. "South Africa's National Management System." In *War and Society: The Militarisation of South Africa: Cape Town*, edited by Jacklyn Cock and Laurie Nathan, 149–58. Cape Town: David Philip, 1989.

Shubane, Khehla. "The Soweto Rent Boycott." Honours Thesis, University of the Witwatersrand, 1987.

Silverstein, Michael. "Translation, Transduction, Transformation: Skating 'Glossando' on Thin Semiotic Ice." In *Cultures: Perspectives on Translation and Anthropology*, edited by Paula Rubel and Abraham Rosman, 75–105. Oxford: Berg, 2003.

Simone, AbdouMaliq. "People as Infrastructure: Intersecting Fragments in Johannesburg." *Public Culture* 16, no. 3 (2004): 407–29.

Slobodian, Quinn. "The World Economy and the Color Line: Wilhelm Röpke, Apartheid, and the White Atlantic." *German Historical Institute Bulletin Supplement* 10 (2014): 61–87.

Smith, David M., ed. *The Apartheid City and Beyond: Urbanization and Social Change in South Africa*. London: Routledge, 2003.

Smith, Laila. "Neither Public nor Private: Unpacking the Johannesburg Water Corporatization Model." Geneva: UNRISD, 2005.

South African Institute of Race Relations. *A Survey of Race Relations in South Africa*. Johannesburg: SAIRR, 1982.

Sparks, Stephen. "Dependence, Discipline and the Morality of Consumption: An Intellectual History of the Sasol Project." Paper presented at the Wits Interdisciplinary Seminar in the Humanities (WISH) series, 1–21. Johannesburg, 2013.

Spivak, Gayatri Chakravorty.."Can the Subaltern Speak?" *Marxism and the Interpretation of Culture, edited by Cary Nelson and Lawrence Grossberg*, 271–313. Basingstoke: Macmillan Education, 1988.

Star, Susan Leigh. "The Ethnography of Infrastructure." *American Behavioral Scientist* 43, no. 3 (1999): 377–91.

Stevenson, M. A. "Development of Prepayment Electricity Metering Systems for Use in First and Third World Environments," *Seventh International Conference on Metering Apparatus and Tariffs for Electricity Supply*. Glasgow: Power Division, Institution of Electrical Engineers, 1992.

Stokes, Eric. *The English Utilitarians and India*. Oxford: Clarendon Press, 1959.

Stoler, Ann Laura. "Imperial Debris: Reflections on Ruins and Ruination." *Cultural Anthropology* 23, no. 2 (2008): 191–219.

Stoler, Ann Laura. *Along the Archival Grain: Epistemic Anxieties and Colonial Common Sense*. Princeton: Princeton University Press, 2010.

Stoler, Ann Laura. *Imperial Debris: On Ruins and Ruination*. Durham, NC: Duke University Press, 2013.

Storey, Angela. "Making Experience Legible: Spaces of Participation and the Construction of Knowledge in Khayelitsha." *Politikon* 41, no. 3 (2014): 403–20.

Strathern, Marilyn. *Audit Cultures: Anthropological Studies in Accountability, Ethics, and the Academy*. London; New York: Routledge, 2000.

Sutcliffe, Michael O. "Regional Services Councils in Perspective: The Present Crisis, the Space Economy and the State's Response." South African History Archives, Mark Swilling Collection, AL 3067 A1, n.d.

Swanson, Maynard W. "Urban Origins of Separate Development." *Race* 10, no. 1 (1968): 31–40.

Swanson, Maynard W. "The Sanitation Syndrome: Bubonic Plague and Urban Native Policy in the Cape Colony, 1900–1909." *Journal of African History* (1977): 387–410.

Swilling, Mark, Richard Humphries, and Khehla Shubane. *Apartheid City in Transition*. Cape Town: Oxford University Press, 1991.

Swilling, Mark, and Mark Phillips. "State Power in the 1980s: From 'Total Strategy' to 'Counter-Revolutionary Warfare.'" In *War and Society: The Militarisation of South Africa*, edited by Jacklyn Cock and Laurie Nathan, 134–48. Cape Town: David Philip, 1989.

Swilling, Mark, and Mark Phillips. "The Powers of the Thunderbird: The Nature and Limits of the Emergency State." *South African Review* 5 (1990): 99–115.

Swilling, Mark, and Khehla Shubane. "Negotiating Urban Transition: The Soweto Experience." In *Transition to Democracy: Policy Perspectives*, edited by Robin Lee and Lawrence Schlemmer, 223–58. Cape Town: Oxford University Press, 1991.

Swyngedouw, Erik. *Social Power and the Urbanization of Water: Flows of Power*. Oxford; New York: Oxford University Press, 2004.

Tempelhoff, Johann W. N. *The Substance of Ubiquity Rand Water: 1903–2003*. Vanderbijlpark: Kleio Publishers, 2003.

Terreblanche, Sampie. *A History of Inequality in South Africa, 1652–2002*. Scottsville, South Africa: University of Natal Press, 2002.

Thompson, E. P. "Time, Work-Discipline and Industrial Capitalism." *Past & Present* 38, no. 1 (1967): 56–97.

Ticktin, Miriam. *Casualties of Care: Immigration and the Politics of Humanitarianism in France*. Berkeley: University of California Press, 2011.

Tilly, Charles. *Coercion, Capital, and European States, Ad 990–1990*. Cambridge: Blackwell, 1990.

Tomlinson, Richard. "International Best Practice, Enabling Frameworks and the Policy Process: A South African Case Study." *International Journal of Urban and Regional Research* 26, no. 2 (2002): 377–88.

University of South Africa. *Project Free Enterprise: An Analysis of the Comprehension of Business and Free Enterprise Concepts among Corporate Employees in South Africa*. Pretoria: School of Business Leadership, University of South Africa, 1984.

Valiani, Arafaat. *Militant Publics in India: Physical Culture and Violence in the Making of a Modern Polity*. London: Palgrave Macmillan, 2011.

Valverde, Mariana, and Ron Levi. "Studying Law by Association: Bruno Latour Goes to the Conseil d'état." *Law & Social Inquiry* 33, no. 3 (2008): 805–25.

van Heusden, Peter. "Discipline and the New 'Logic of Delivery': Prepaid Electricity in South Africa and Beyond." In *Electric Capitalism: Recolonising Africa on the Power Grid*, edited by David McDonald, 229–47. Cape Town: HSRC Press, 2009.

van Heusden, Peter, and Rebecca Pointer. "Subjectivity, Politics and Neoliberalism in Post-Apartheid Cape Town." *Journal of Asian and African Studies* 41, no. 1–2 (2006): 95–121.

Veck, Griffith. "The Politics of Power in an Economy of Transition: Eskom and the Electrification of South Africa, 1980–1995." PhD Thesis, Faculty of Commerce, University of the Witwatersrand, 2000.

Veriava, Ahmed. "Unlocking the Present? Two Theories of Primitive Accumulation." In *The Accumulation of Capital in Southern Africa: Rosa Luxemburg's Contemporary Relevance*, edited by Patrick Bond, Horman Chitonge, and Arndt Hopfmann, 46–62. Johannesburg: Rosa Luxemburg Foundation, 2007.

Veriava, Ahmed. "The South African Diagram: The Governmental Machine and the Struggles of the Poor." PhD Thesis, University of the Witwatersrand, 2014.

Verran, Helen. *Science and an African Logic*. Chicago: University of Chicago Press, 2001.

Verran, Helen. "Numbering Australia's Water Resources: Generalising, (Non)Equivalence, Accounting, and Calculating." Paper presented at the Number as Inventive Frontier Conference, Johns Hopkins University, 2008.

Verran, Helen. "Number as an Inventive Frontier in Knowing and Working Australia's Water Resources." *Anthropological Theory* 10, no. 1–2 (2010): 171–78.

Verwoerd, H. F. *Separate Development*. Pretoria: Information Service, Dept. of Native Affairs, 1958.

Vladislavic, Ivan. *Portrait with Keys: The City of Johannesburg Unlocked*. W. W. Norton & Company, 2009.

Von Holdt, Karl. "South Africa: The Transition to Violent Democracy." *Review of African Political Economy* 40, no. 138 (2013): 589–604.

Von Holdt, Karl, Malose Langa, Sepetla Molapo, Nomfundi Mogapi, Kindiza Ngubeni, Jacob Dlamini, and Adèle Kirsten. *The Smoke That Calls: Insurgent Citizenship, Collective Violence and the Struggle for a Place in the New South Africa: Eight Case Studies of Community Protest and Xenophobic Violence*. Johannesburg: Centre for the Study of Violence and Reconciliation, 2011.

von Mises, Ludwig. *Socialism: An Economic and Sociological Analysis*. Indianapolis, IN: Liberty Classics, 1981.

von Schnitzler, Antina. "Citizenship Prepaid: Water, Calculability, and Techno-Politics in South Africa." *Journal of Southern African Studies* 34, no. 4 (2008): 899–917.

von Schnitzler. "Traveling Technologies: Infrastructure, Ethical Regimes, and the Materiality of Politics in South Africa." *Cultural Anthropology* 28, no. 4 (2013): 670–93.

von Schnitzler. "Performing Dignity: Human Rights, Citizenship, and the Techno-Politics of Law in South Africa." *American Ethnologist* 41, no. 2 (2014): 336–50.

Wafer, Alex. "Scale and Identity in Post-Apartheid Soweto." *Transformation: Critical Perspectives on Southern Africa* 66, no. 1 (2008): 98–115.

Wages Commission. "Riekert: Don't Worry, Everything's Okay." Cape Town: UCT SRC, 1979.

Walpen, Bernhard. *Die offenen Feinde und ihre Gesellschaft: Eine hegemonietheoretische Studie zur Mont Pelerin Society*. Hamburg: VSA-Verlag, 2004.

Walsh, Shannon, Patrick Bond, Ashwin Desai, and Shannon Walsh. "'Uncomfortable Collaborations': Contesting Constructions of the 'Poor' in South Africa." *Review of African Political Economy* 35, no. 116 (2008): 255–79.

Warner, Michael. "Publics and Counterpublics." *Public Culture* 14, no. 1 (2002): 49–90.

Wassenaar, Andreas D. *Assault on Private Enterprise: The Freeway to Communism*. Cape Town: Tafelberg, 1977.

White, Hylton. "A Post-Fordist Ethnicity: Insecurity, Authority, and Identity in South Africa." *Anthropological Quarterly* 85, no. 2 (2012): 397–427.

Wilk, Richard. "Bottled Water: The Pure Commodity in the Age of Branding." *Journal of Consumer Culture* 6, no. 3 (2006): 303–25.

Wilson, Richard A. *The Politics of Truth and Reconciliation in South Africa: Legitimizing the Post-Apartheid State*. Cambridge: Cambridge University Press, 2001.

Wilson, Richard A. *Writing History in International Criminal Trials*. Cambridge: Cambridge University Press, 2011.

Wilson, Richard A., and Richard D. Brown, eds. *Humanitarianism and Suffering: The Mobilization of Empathy through Narrative*. Cambridge: Cambridge University Press, 2011.

Winner, Langdon. "Do Artefacts Have Politics." In *The Whale and the Reactor: A Search for Limits in an Age of High Technology*, edited by Langdon Winner, 19–39. Chicago: University of Chicago Press, 1980.

Wise, M. Norton, ed. *The Values of Precision*. Princeton: Princeton University Press, 1995.

Wolpe, Harold. "Capitalism and Cheap Labour-Power in South Africa: From Segregation to Apartheid 1." *Economy and Society* 1, no. 4 (1972): 425–56.

Woolgar, Stephen. "Configuring the User: The Case of Usability Trials." In *A Sociology of Monsters: Essays on Power, Technology and Domination*, edited by John Law, 58–99. London, New York: Routledge, 1991.

Work in Progress. "Rents: Paying for Incorporation." *Work in Progress* 12 (1980): 17–23

World Bank. "World Development Report: Infrastructure for Development." Washington, DC: World Bank, 1994.

Young, Katharine G. "The Minimum Core of Economic and Social Rights: A Concept in Search of Content." *Yale J. Int'l L.* 33 (2008): 113–75.

Zaloom, Caitlin. *Out of the Pits: Traders and Technology from Chicago to London*. Chicago: University of Chicago Press, 2006.

Zeiderman, Austin. "Living Dangerously: Biopolitics and Urban Citizenship in Bogotá, Colombia." *American Ethnologist* 40, no. 1 (2013): 71–87.

Zelizer, Viviana. *The Social Meaning of Money: Pin Money, Paychecks, Poor Relief, and Other Currencies*. Princeton: Princeton University Press, 1997.

Žižek, Slavoj. "Multitude, Surplus, and Envy." *Rethinking Marxism* 19, no. 1 (2007): 46–58.

Zuern, Elke. *The Politics of Necessity: Community Organizing and Democracy in South Africa*. Milwaukee: University of Wisconsin Press, 2011.

INDEX

accounting practices,132–33. *See also* metrology

activism, 17n26, 24–26, 32–33, 66–68, 84–87, 108, 172–75, 190, 195, 199; and numbers, 133–35, 137n10, 163–67, 182, 189, 191. *See also* human rights; social movements

administrative terrain, 4, 7–10, 12, 14, 17, 27, 29, 34–35, 51, 55, 61, 69, 77–78, 81–83, 86–87, 104, 200; boycotting of, 84, 89, 99, 120; politics via, 107, 125, 128

affective labor, 158, 161

African National Congress (ANC), 168–69, 197; legitimacy of, 92–93; neoliberal reforms and, 32–33, 67; protests and, 1–3, 15

African National Congress Youth League, 196

Afrikaners, 38–39, 47, 52–53, 79

Akrich, Madeleine, 106

Anti-Privatisation Forum (APF), 24, 65–66, 98, 162–63, 179, 183

antiapartheid struggle, 4–5, 7, 20–21, 23, 26–28, 55–56, 68–70, 82–83, 137; administrative terrain and, 6, 120; legacy of the, 71–72, 74, 86; neoliberalism and, 34, 53. *See also* boycotts

antiprogram, 128–29, 131

apartheid city, 89, 138

apartheid techno-politics, 11–17, 49–51, 55–56, 60–64, 78–81, 84–92, 107–8, 120–24

apartheid: administration during 60–61, 77–78; in crisis, 41, 44, 47–50, 53, 57, 59; infrastructure and, 13–15, 29–30, 68, 81, 197, 198; liberalism during, 35–38; the market during 40, 43; metrology and,

137–138, 143; political rationality during, 52, 54–55; protests of, 14–16, 29, 40–41, 48, 79, 79n23, 81–86; reforms during, 55, 61, 63, 80, 89; service provisioning and, 39, 78–80, 87, 91; urban, 12–14, 33–40, 48–64, 77–80, 83–89, 120–22

apartheid's debris, 17, 26, 29–30, 92

Arendt, Hannah, 116, 171, 171n6

Asad, Talal, 35, 170n5

Ashforth, Adam, 50, 74–75, 79n22, 99

Bantu Affairs Administration Boards (BAABs) 51, 60, 80–81, 84

Bantustans, 12, 39, 51, 53, 56, 58–60, 79, 120

Barchiesi, Franco, 6n9, 170n33

Barry, Andrew, 21n31, 134n3

Benjamin, Walter, 117

biopolitics, 101–2, 113–16, 171–73, 177–79, 188–93; apartheid and, 80–82, 92; colonialism and, 12, 76–77

Black Consciousness Movement, 48

Black Local Authorities (BLAs), 80–81, 89

Bond, Patrick, 23n35, 139

Botha, P. W., 49, 57

boycotts. *See* bus boycotts; rent boycotts

Breckenridge, Keith, 13n20, 137n8, 144n8

budgeting, 155–59, 165, 191

Burchell, David, 19, 93

bureaucracy, 87, 137–138, 143, 143fn16, 198, 200; apartheid, 13–14, 30, 41, 74–78, 82n29, 143; race and, 39, 136–39, 167

bus boycotts, 16, 27, 82, 85–86, 89, 122

calculability, 136, 143–45

calculation: capacities of, 136–37, 139, 144, 147, 149–50, 155–56, 158; forms of, 140–42, 146, 154; moral, 158–160;